Microsoft® SQL Server™ 2008

NEW FEATURES

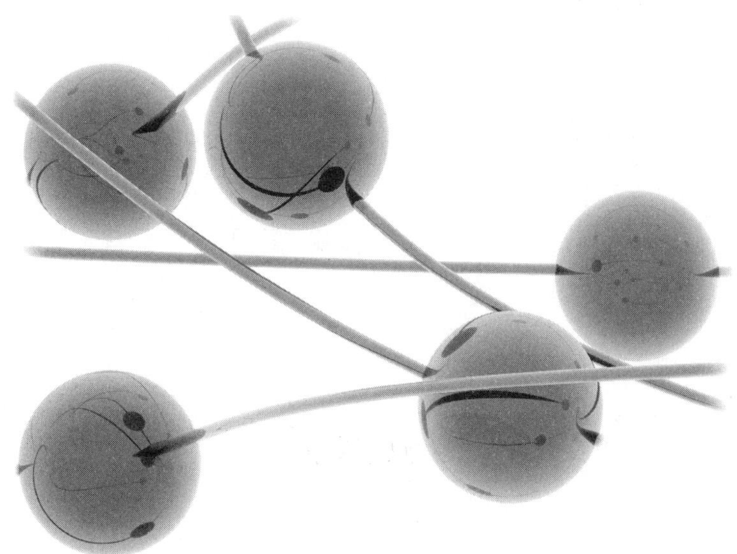

About the Author

Michael Otey is the technical director for both *Windows IT Pro* and *SQL Server Magazine*. He is the author of all editions of *SQL Server Developer's Guide* as well as the previous edition of this book.

About the Technical Editor

Since 2004 Dan Jones has been a member of the SQL Server product development team at Microsoft. Currently Mr. Jones is a Group Program Manager in the SQL Server Manageability Product Unit working on the next wave of innovation in manageability. He holds a Bachelor of Science degree from Cal Poly, San Luis Obispo and an MBA from Santa Clara University.

Microsoft® SQL Server™ 2008

NEW FEATURES

Michael Otey

New York Chicago San Francisco Lisbon
London Madrid Mexico City Milan
New Delhi San Juan Seoul Singapore
Sydney Toronto

The McGraw·Hill Companies

Cataloging-in-Publication Data is on file with the Library of Congress

McGraw-Hill books are available at special quantity discounts to use as premiums and sales promotions, or for use in corporate training programs. To contact a special sales representative, please visit the Contact Us page at www.mhprofessional.com.

Microsoft® SQL Server™ 2008 New Features

1 2 3 4 5 6 7 8 9 0 FGR FGR 0 1 9 8

ISBN 978-0-07-154640-9
MHID 0-07-154640-5

Sponsoring Editor
Wendy Rinaldi

Editorial Supervisor
Patty Mon

Project Manager
Harleen Chopra, International Typesetting and Composition

Acquisitions Coordinator
Mandy Canales

Technical Editor
Dan Jones

Copy Editor
Julie M. Smith

Proofreader
Bev Weiler

Indexer
Karin Arrigoni

Production Supervisor
Jim Kussow

Composition
International Typesetting and Composition

Illustration
International Typesetting and Composition

Art Director, Cover
Jeff Weeks

Cover Designer
Jeff Weeks

To my daughter, Sherry. Thank you for all your encouragement and love. You are the Star.

Contents at a Glance

Contents

Introduction

In February 2008, Microsoft launched Microsoft's SQL Server 2008, the latest version of their enterprise level relational database server system. SQL Server 2008 is a feature-rich release, providing a host of new functionality for both the database administrator as well as the database developer. This book is written to help the IT manager, database administrator, database developer, systems integrator, and consultant to quickly get up to speed on the most important new features found in the SQL Server 2008 release. This book will help you to understand how SQL Server 2008 is different from the previous releases and will provide you with information that you can use to evaluate the benefits of adopting the new release.

SQL Server 2008 is a feature-packed release. In order to keep the size of the book to a manageable level, I needed to make choices about which features to cover and the level of detail to give to each feature. This is both a good news and bad news story. The good news is that you'll get a concise yet in-depth look at what I considered to be the most important features in the new SQL Server 2008 release. The bad news is that there just isn't enough space in this book to provide comprehensive coverage of all these features. I had to make some hard choices about what features to cover and the depth of coverage to allocate to each of these features. When deciding between the features that I felt should be covered and those that might not be as important I opted to select the features that I felt would be the most significant for the enterprise and those features that embodied the biggest changes from the prior release. Hopefully, you'll agree that I made the right choices.

This book is intended mainly as a guide for introducing you to those new features. While I do provide numerous examples showing you how to make use of these features, the goal of those examples is to help you to better understand the purpose of the new features and get an idea of their implementation. This book is not intended to be a how-to guide, so a few small implementation differences should not affect the overall purpose of this book. Every effort has been made to make sure that the information presented here is as up-to-date as possible.

As an additional note I should stress that this book is not intended as a general tutorial on using Microsoft SQL Server 2008. It is written with the assumption that the reader has a basic familiarly with SQL Server. Instead, the focus of this book is on the new features found in SQL Server 2008 and the material here is intended as a guide and reference to get the reader quickly up to speed on the changes found in the new release. To achieve that aim I've split this book into three parts: reflecting the three general areas of Microsoft SQL Server 2005 itself.

Part I of this book covers the database administration features. Here you'll learn about the features that are most important to the database administrator. In this section you'll get an introduction to the new important security, architectural, high availability, and disaster recovery features the Microsoft has provided in SQL Server 2008. In addition, you'll also learn about the new policy-based Management enabling organizations to create and maintain standardized SQL Server implementations.

Part II covers the new features found in the database development area. One of the biggest changes found in SQL Server 2008 is the new Language Integrated Query (LINQ). LINQ fuses traditional database query development with the powerful and productive .NET development languages, enabling native query development in VB and C#. Additionally, the chapters in Part II will go on to cover the new T-SQL data types and language enhancements found in SQL Server 2008.

Part III hits the last big area of enhancements found in Microsoft SQL Server 2008. In Part III you'll learn about the new Business Intelligence (BI) features. The BI area for SQL Server 2008 has some of the richest new features found in the new release. With SQL Server 2008, Integration Services is now more scalable and powerful than any previous release. Analysis Services provides many new features, including an all new cube design tool, as well as MOLAP write-back capability. In addition Reporting Services in SQL Server 2008 provide new scale-out functionality and a new forms authentication feature. Part III will also introduce you to the new Microsoft Office integration capabilities.

SQL Server 2008 Design Goals

SQL Server 2008 is designed to be a full-featured enterprise level database capable of providing mission critical data access functionality to the largest organizations. To meet these requirements, Microsoft has designed SQL Server 2008 to be highly scalable, but beyond this to meet the needs to the enterprise it must also be secure, it must be a productive development platform, it must fulfill the most important information delivery needs for the organization, and it must provide good return on investment.

Enterprise Scalability

Scalability used to be an area where the early versions of Microsoft SQL Server were criticized. With its roots as a departmental system and the limitations found in the Microsoft SQL Server 6.5 and earlier releases, many businesses didn't view SQL Server as a legitimate player in the enterprise database market. However, all that changed. Beginning with the release of SQL Server 7 in 1998, Microsoft made great strides in the scalability of the SQL Server platform.

With its ability to use distributed partitioned views, SQL Server 7 jumped to the top of the TPC-C. In fact, its scores were so overwhelming it was a contributing factor to the Transaction Processing Council's (TPC) decision to break the transactional TPC-C test into clustered and non-clustered divisions. Although Microsoft and SQL Server 7 made impressive marks in the clustered TPC-C score, there was still some doubt about the SQL Server's ability to scale-up on a single platform. That too changed with the launch of Windows Server 2003 and the announcement of SQL Server 2000 Enterprise Edition 64-bit, where Microsoft announced for the first time that Microsoft SQL Server reached the top of the non-clustered TPC-C scores.

While these older scores have since been eclipsed by other platforms, SQL Server 2005 still ranks near the top of the non-cluster TPC-C score. The TPC-C benchmark is designed to reflect a real-world order entry system. The TPC-C measures scalability in transactions per minute (tpmC). The TPC-C is divided into two categories: Performance and Price/Performance. A database's ultimate scalability is measured in the Performance category, while its value is shown by the results of the Price/Performance category. At the time of this writing, SQL Server 2005 running on the 64-bit Itanium platform holds the fifth spot in the Performance category behind marks set by Oracle 11*g* and IBM DB2. In the Price/Performance category SQL Server holds eight of the top ten spots.

Another important TPC benchmark is the TPC-H. The TPC-H benchmark was developed as a means to measure the performance of decision support systems. The TPC-H benchmark is comprised of a set of ad-hoc queries. The TPC-H measures performance using a Queries-per-Hour (QphH) metric. The TPC-H results are also divided into Performance and Price/Performance. Additionally, the TPC-H results are separated according to database size. The TPC-H test queries over the following database sizes: 100GB, 300GB, 1,000GB, 3,000GB, 10,000GB, and 30,000GB. SQL Server 2005 running on the x64 platform holds the top nine rankings in the 100GB TPC-H Performance category. SQL Server 2005 is sixth in the 300GB results. It is first in the 1,000GB results and sixth in the 3,000GB results. In the TPC-H Price/Performance category, SQL Server has eight of the top ten 100GB results and is third in the 300GB results. In the 1,000GB results, SQL Server holds seven of the top ten price/performance marks and three of the top ten 3,000GB results.

The TPC-E is the newest of the TPC database benchmarks. Unlike the TPC-C benchmark, which was designed to represent an order processing system, the TPC-E is designed to represent a brokerage firm. Also, unlike the older TPC-C tests, which record results in transactions per hour, TPC-E results are measured according to the more modern transactions per second (tpcS) metric. Like the other TPC benchmarks, the results are divided by Performance and Price/Performance. Being a new benchmark there aren't many TCP-E scores. At the time of this writing, SQL Server 2008 holds all of the top entries in the TPC-E benchmarks.

SQL Server's TPC results clearly demonstrate that SQL Server can scale to meet the very highest of database requirements—even up to the mainframe level. And, SQL Server's self-tuning ability enables the database to quickly optimize its own resources to match usage requirements. You can view all the results of the different TPC benchmark results at www.tpc.org.

SQL Server 2008 takes off from this level set by the earlier releases of SQL Server by taking advantage of the latest in x64 and multicore technology; this is sure to push the scalability envelope higher than ever before.

Security

While scalability is the stepping stone that starts the path toward enterprise-level adoption, security is the door that must be opened to really gain enterprise wide adoption. In the past, SQL Server 2000 (and its close cousin MSDE) were hit by the infamous SQL Slammer worm, which cast some doubt on the security of SQL Server. While it's important, the SQL Slammer worm could have easily been avoided if businesses had followed the proper security measures, including patching and closing down unnecessary port access with their firewalls. Even so, Microsoft took this security call to heart and really put an emphasis on security in the SQL Server 2005 release, putting it through its Security Development Lifecycle (SDL). As attested by the National Vulnerability Database, in 2006 SQL Server 2005 had zero Critical Security Exposures (CSE) compared to 54 by Oracle and 14 from MySQL, four from IBM and two from Sybase. SQL Server 2005 has the most secure code base of any of the leading enterprise-oriented databases.

SQL Server 2008 starts off with the ultra secure code base inherited from SQL Server 2005 and extends the security to the users by adding a number of significant features, including transparent database encryption and key management, as well as backup encryption.

Improved Developer Productivity

Developer productivity is always one of Microsoft's primary design goals with each new release of SQL Server. SQL Server 2008 continues this evolutionary trend with the introduction of the new Language Integrated Query (LINQ) development capability along the new .NET Entity Framework.

LINQ addresses one of the biggest disconnects existing in the current database development model. In the current scenario, database developers use an object-oriented language like C# or VB to develop the client application and the business objects that exist in the data tier. This is because SQL Server applications are typically developed using a .NET framework and ADO.NET is the data access middleware that connects the application with the database. However, to create all the core database transactions, the developer needs to step out of the productivity Visual Studio object development environment and manually construct the T-SQL query that will actually interact with the SQL Server system. In this model, the development tools and compiler can't help the developer to insure that the query is syntactically correct or that it uses the right database tables or columns. The query isn't actually executed until the application is run, which would be the first time the developer would receive any error feedback. The new LINQ development model changes that paradigm completely. LINQ enables .NET programmers to access database and XML data sources using native query extension that Microsoft has added to the .NET C# and VB languages. LINQ enables the developer to use a single development language to both create the application as well as build the database access. In addition, the development environment can be connected to the database so you can get immediate feedback about the database objects in use as well as compile time checking for the database queries. While LINQ may be an entirely new paradigm, its tight binding to the development environment enables an all new level of developer productivity.

The new .NET Entity Framework is designed to facilitate the mapping of the relational database to the business objects used by a .NET object-oriented application. Based on the Entity Data Model, the .NET Entity Framework allows developers to design conceptual business entities like a customer object and then map those entities to the underlying database objects. The .NET Entity Framework essentially helps create a layer of abstraction that isolates the data access logic in an application enabling the developers to focus on the business application logic. The .NET Entity Framework includes an Entity Designer that enables you to generate an object model from a physical database. It also enables simple and complex entity mapping where you can map application objects to a single table or to multiple tables.

Enterprise Data Platform

Completing a trend that really begins back with SQL Server 2005, SQL Server 2008 has completed the transformation from a relational database system to an enterprise data platform. While relational queries and support for online transactional systems are clearly the core strengths of the product, SQL Server 2008 takes that core and extends the concept of data access into enterprise information access. SQL Server's built-in BI toolset provides a complete platform for importing and transforming data from multiple data sources using Integration Services, analyzing data and predicting data trends using Analysis Services and Data Mining, disseminating that data to end users using Reporting Services, and its end-user oriented reporting tool Report Builder.

Not only is SQL Server 2008 used as a standalone data platform, but Microsoft also uses SQL Server as the data store for many of its other server products like SharePoint and the System Center Family of products.

Return on Investment

One of the primary challenges for IT today is increasing return on investment and driving costs out of the business. That often means doing more with less. SQL Server 2008 provides the data platform capabilities that enable a business to do just that. SQL Server 2008 is far more than just a relational database. Its integrated BI suite includes the built-in Integration Services, Analysis Services, and Reporting Services and they bring more value to the table that any other database platform. All of the other enterprise level database platforms charge extra for this level of BI functionality. In addition, SQL Server 2008 provides many other features that provide value to the customer and lift SQL Server 2008 beyond just being a relational database and make it an enterprise data platform. The new LINQ-based application development functionality and SQL Server's SQLCLR integration enables a more productivity development experience than any previous version of SQL Server. Features like XML integration and built-in web services support enables better integration with other platforms and to customers. Reporting Services and the new Office integration features empower employees by turning data into useful information.

A Brief History of Microsoft SQL Server

Before jumping right into the new features in Server 2008, I thought it might be interesting to see some of the background leading up to the release of SQL Server 2008. In the next section, you can follow along with the steps that took SQL Server from its inception as a small departmental database system to the enterprise level relational database and Business Intelligence platform that it is today.

Microsoft SQL Server originated as Sybase SQL Server in 1987. In 1988, Microsoft joined in a partnership with Sybase and Aston-Tate to port the product to OS/2. Later, Aston-Tate dropped out of the SQL Server development picture and Microsoft and Sybase signed a co-development agreement to port SQL Server to Windows NT. The co-development effort culminated in the release of SQL Server 4.0 for Windows NT. After the 4.0 release, Microsoft and Sybase split on the development of SQL Server with Microsoft continuing forward with future releases targeted for the Windows NT platform. Sybase moved ahead with releases targeted for the UNIX platform which they still market today.

SQL Server 6.0 was the first release of SQL Server that was entirely developed by Microsoft. In 1996 Microsoft updated SQL Server with the 6.5 release. At this point SQL Server 6.5 was regarded as a departmental level database that had potential, but wasn't quite ready for the enterprise.

After an intensive two-year development cycle, Microsoft released the vastly updated SQL Server 7.0 release in 1998. Completely rearchitected, SQL Server 7.0 embodied many radical changes in the underlying storage and database engine technology used in SQL Server. SQL Server 7 had become an enterprise-capable database and was the first major relational database to include BI capabilities with the inclusion of its all new OLAP Services subsystem.

SQL Server 2000 was released in September of 2000. The accumulation of another two-year development effort, the move from SQL Server 7.0 to SQL Server 2000 is more of an evolutionary move, which doesn't entail the same type of massive changes that were made in the move from 6.5 to 7.0. Instead, SQL Server 2000 incrementally built on the new code base that was established in the 7.0 release. Starting with SQL Server 2000, Microsoft began releasing out-of-band updates to the basic release of SQL Server in the following year starting with XML for SQL Server Web Release 1, which added several XML features, including the ability to receive a result set as an XML document. The next year they renamed the web release to the more succinctly titled SQLXML 2.0, which among other things added the ability to update the SQL Server database using XML updategrams. This was quickly followed by the SQLXML 3.0 web release, which included the ability to expose stored procedures as web services.

Two years later in November of 2005, Microsoft released SQL Server 2005. SQL Server 2005 in many ways could be called the BI release. SQL Server 2005 uses the same basic architecture that was established with SQL Server 7 and that continued through SQL Server 2000. SQL Server 2005 extended the traditional capabilities of the SQL Server database platform in a number of ways. From the hardware standpoint, SQL Server 2005 included support for the emerging 64-bit x64 architecture. A couple of the major enhancements on the relational database engine include the integration of the .NET Common Language Runtime (CLR), which enables developers to write stored procedures, functions, triggers, aggregates, and user-defined types using one of the .NET languages like VB or C#. In addition, the new XML and varbinary (max) data types enhanced SQL Server's ability to incorporate XML and LOB data into SQL Server databases. However, the most important changes for SQL Server 2005 were found in the BI side. The old Data Transformation Services, a capable but limited data transfer engine, was replaced by the all new SQL Server Integration Services (SSIS). SSIS is an enterprise-level data transfer and transformation tool. In addition, Microsoft incorporated the new Reporting Services subsystem into the base SQL Server 2005 release. Reporting Services enables the development and deployment of database based reports throughout the enterprise.

For Microsoft, the SQL Server 2008 release marks the transition of SQL server from a relational database product to an enterprise data platform. Microsoft launched

SQL Server 2008, this latest release of the SQL Server product line, in February 2008. The details of all the major features in the new SQL Server 2008 release will be covered in the subsequent chapters in this book, but for the relational database engine, some of the main enhancements include the all new policy-based management, a new workload resource governor, as well as database encryption and compression. For the BI platform, SQL Server 2008 features include greater new cube design tools, scalability improvements for SSIS, and Reporting Services. In addition, there's an all new Office integration feature that enables Reporting Services reports to be consumed by Word and Excel.

The following timeline summarizes the development history of SQL Server:

1987 - Sybase releases SQL Server for UNIX.
1988 - Microsoft, Sybase, and Aston-Tate port SQL Server to OS/2.
1989 - Microsoft, Sybase, and Aston-Tate release SQL Server 1.0 for OS/2.
1990 - SQL Server 1.1 is released with support for Windows 3.0 clients. Aston-Tate drops out of SQL Server development.
1991 - Microsoft and IBM end joint development of OS/2.
1992 - Microsoft SQL Server 4.2 for 16-bit OS/2 1.3 is released.
1992 - Microsoft and Sybase port SQL Server to Windows NT.
1993 - Windows NT 3.1 is released.
1993 - Microsoft and Sybase release version 4.2 of SQL Server for Windows NT.
1994 - Microsoft and Sybase co-development of SQL Server officially ends. Microsoft continues to develop the Windows version of SQL Server. Sybase continues to develop the UNIX version of SQL Server
1995 - Microsoft releases version 6.0 of SQL Server.
1996 - Microsoft releases version 6.5 of SQL Server.
1998 - Microsoft releases version 7.0 of SQL Server.
2000 - Microsoft releases SQL Server 2000.
2001 - Microsoft releases XML for SQL Server Web Release 1 (download).
2002 - Microsoft releases SQLXML 2.0 (renamed from XML for SQL Server).
2002 - Microsoft releases SQLXML 3.0.
2005 - Microsoft releases SQL Server 2005 in November.
2008 - Microsoft launches SQL Server 2008 in February.
2008 – Microsoft releases SQL Server 2008 to manufacturing (RTM) in August

Part I

Database Administration Features

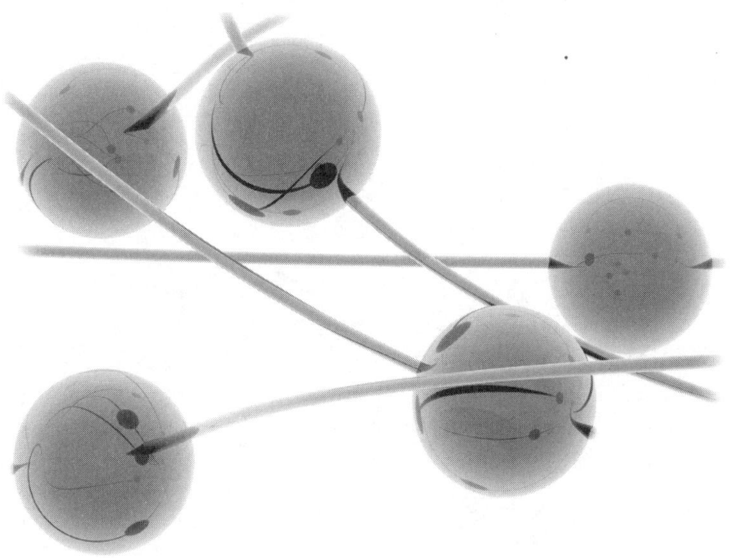

Chapter 1

Architecture

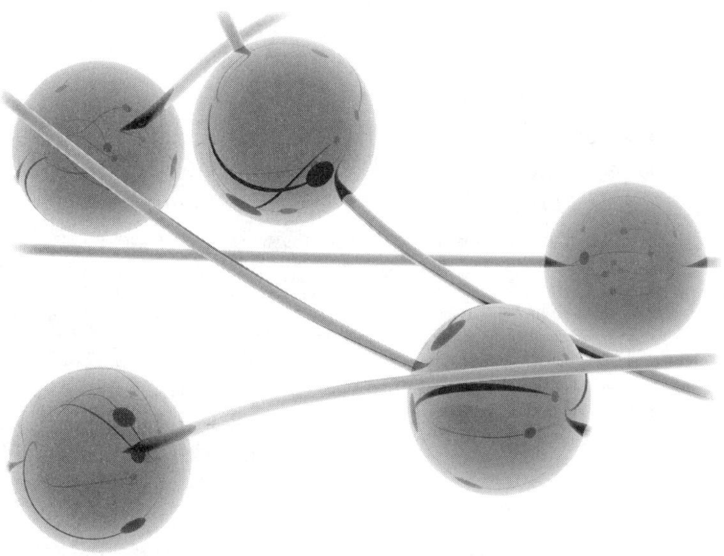

Each edition of SQL Server continues to evolve and SQL Server 2008 is no exception to that trend. SQL Server 2008 embodies a number of new architectural enhancements. In this chapter, you'll learn about the most important new architectural changes found in SQL Server 2008.

Enhanced Hardware Support

SQL Server has been designed from the ground up to be able to take advantage of multiple processors. It can also take full advantage of the vastly increased processing power that's supplied by the current crop of today's high powered multi-processor, multi-core systems.

32-bit, 64-bit x64, and 64-bit IA-64 Support

Unlike Exchange 2007 and some of the other recent Microsoft server products which are now 64-bit only, SQL Server 2008 will continue to be offered in both 32-bit and 64-bit versions. In addition, SQL Server is also unique in Microsoft's line-of-server products, in that Microsoft will deliver products for both the 64-bit x64 processor from Intel and AMD, as well as the 64-bit IA-64 Itanium processor from Intel.

32-bit x86 Editions of SQL Server 2008

SQL Server 2008 is designed for general purpose applications and small- and medium-sized business, and the 32-bit editions of SQL Server 2008 run on both Windows Server 2003 and Windows Server 2008. The following table lists the 32-bit editions of SQL Server 2008 and the Windows operating systems that support them:

SQL Server 2008 Edition	Windows Server Operating System Supported
SQL Server 2008 Express Edition	Windows Server 2008 Standard Edition x64 Windows Server 2008 Standard Edition x64 with Hyper-V Windows Server 2008 Enterprise Edition x64 Windows Server 2008 Enterprise Edition x64 with Hyper-V Windows Server 2008 Datacenter Edition x64 Windows Server 2008 Datacenter Edition x64 with Hyper-V Windows Server 2008 Web Edition Windows Server 2008 Standard Edition Windows Server 2008 Enterprise Edition

	Windows Server 2008 Datacenter Edition
	Windows Server 2003 Standard Edition SP2 x64
	Windows Server 2003 Enterprise Edition SP2 x64
	Windows Server 2003 Datacenter Edition SP2 x64
	Windows Server 2003 Standard Edition SP2
	Windows Server 2003 Enterprise Edition SP2
	Windows Server 2003 Datacenter Edition SP2
	Windows Vista Ultimate x64
	Windows Vista Enterprise x64
	Windows Vista Business x64
	Windows Vista Home Premium x64
	Wundiws Vista Home Basic x64
	Windows Vista Ultimate
	Windows Vista Enterprise
	Windows Vista Business
	Windows Vista Home Premium
	Wundiws Vista Home Basic
	Windows XP x64 Professional
	Windows XP Professional SP2
	Windows XP Media Center SP2
	Windows XP Tablet SP2
	Windows XP Home SP2
	Windows XP Embedded SP2
SQL Server 2008 Workgroup Edition	Windows Server 2008 Standard Edition x64
	Windows Server 2008 Standard Edition x64 with Hyper-V
	Windows Server 2008 Enterprise Edition x64
	Windows Server 2008 Enterprise Edition x64 with Hyper-V
	Windows Server 2008 Datacenter Edition x64
	Windows Server 2008 Datacenter Edition x64 with Hyper-V
	Windows Server 2008 Web Edition
	Windows Server 2008 Standard Edition
	Windows Server 2008 Enterprise Edition
	Windows Server 2008 Datacenter Edition
	Windows Server 2003 Standard Edition SP2 x64
	Windows Server 2003 Enterprise Edition SP2 x64
	Windows Server 2003 Datacenter Edition SP2 x64
	Windows Server 2003 Standard Edition SP2
	Windows Server 2003 Enterprise Edition SP2
	Windows Server 2003 Datacenter Edition SP2

	Windows Vista Ultimate x64 Windows Vista Enterprise x64 Windows Vista Business x64 Windows Vista Ultimate Windows Vista Enterprise Windows Vista Business Windows XP x64 Professional Windows XP Professional SP2 Windows XP Media Center SP2 Windows XP Tablet SP2
SQL Server 2008 Web Edition	Windows Server 2008 Standard Edition x64 Windows Server 2008 Standard Edition x64 with Hyper-V Windows Server 2008 Enterprise Edition x64 Windows Server 2008 Enterprise Edition x64 with Hyper-V Windows Server 2008 Datacenter Edition x64 Windows Server 2008 Datacenter Edition x64 with Hyper-V Windows Server 2008 Web Edition Windows Server 2008 Standard Edition Windows Server 2008 Enterprise Edition Windows Server 2008 Datacenter Edition Windows Server 2003 Standard Edition SP2 x64 Windows Server 2003 Enterprise Edition SP2 x64 Windows Server 2003 Datacenter Edition SP2 x64 Windows Server 2003 Standard Edition SP2 Windows Server 2003 Enterprise Edition SP2 Windows Server 2003 Datacenter Edition SP2 Windows Vista Ultimate x64 Windows Vista Enterprise x64 Windows Vista Business x64 Windows Vista Ultimate Windows Vista Enterprise Windows Vista Business Windows XP x64 Professional Windows XP Professional SP2 Windows XP Media Center SP2 Windows XP Tablet SP2

SQL Server 2008 Standard Edition	Windows Server 2008 Standard Edition x64 Windows Server 2008 Standard Edition x64 with Hyper-V Windows Server 2008 Enterprise Edition x64 Windows Server 2008 Enterprise Edition x64 with Hyper-V Windows Server 2008 Datacenter Edition x64 Windows Server 2008 Datacenter Edition x64 with Hyper-V Windows Server 2008 Web Edition Windows Server 2008 Standard Edition Windows Server 2008 Enterprise Edition Windows Server 2008 Datacenter Edition Windows Server 2003 Standard Edition SP2 x64 Windows Server 2003 Enterprise Edition SP2 x64 Windows Server 2003 Datacenter Edition SP2 x64 Windows Server 2003 Standard Edition SP2 Windows Server 2003 Enterprise Edition SP2 Windows Server 2003 Datacenter Edition SP2 Windows Vista Ultimate x64 Windows Vista Enterprise x64 Windows Vista Business x64 Windows Vista Ultimate Windows Vista Enterprise Windows Vista Business Windows XP x64 Professional Windows XP Professional SP Windows XP Media Center SP2 Windows XP Tablet SP2
SQL Server 2008 Enterprise Edition	Windows Server 2008 Standard Edition x64 Windows Server 2008 Standard Edition x64 with Hyper-V Windows Server 2008 Enterprise Edition x64 Windows Server 2008 Enterprise Edition x64 with Hyper-V Windows Server 2008 Datacenter Edition x64 Windows Server 2008 Datacenter Edition x64 with Hyper-V Windows Server 2008 Web Edition Windows Server 2008 Standard Edition

	Windows Server 2008 Enterprise Edition Windows Server 2008 Datacenter Edition Windows Server 2003 Standard Edition SP2 x64 Windows Server 2003 Enterprise Edition SP2 x64 Windows Server 2003 Datacenter Edition SP2 x64 Windows Server 2003 Standard Edition SP2 Windows Server 2003 Enterprise Edition SP2 Windows Server 2003 Datacenter Edition SP2

64-bit x64 Editions of SQL Server 2008

Designed for highly scalable mainstream computing, the SQL Server 2008 x64 editions provide the ability to access up to 1TB of memory. The x64 editions of SQL Server 2008 must run on the x64 editions of the Windows operating system.

SQL Server 2008 Edition	Windows Server Operating System Supported
SQL Server 2008 Express Edition	Windows Server 2008 Web Edition x64 Windows Server 2008 Standard Edition x64 Windows Server 2008 Standard Edition x64 with Hyper-V Windows Server 2008 Enterprise Edition x64 Windows Server 2008 Enterprise Edition x64 with Hyper-V Windows Server 2008 Datacenter Edition x64 Windows Server 2008 Datacenter Edition x64 with Hyper-V Windows Server 2003 Standard Edition SP2 x64 Windows Server 2003 Enterprise Edition SP2 x64 Windows Server 2003 Datacenter Edition SP2 x64 Windows Vista Ultimate x64 Windows Vista Enterprise x64 Windows Vista Business x64 Windows Vista Home Premium x64 Windows Vista Home Basic x64
SQL Server 2008 Workgroup Edition	Windows Server 2008 Web Edition x64 Windows Server 2008 Standard Edition x64 Windows Server 2008 Enterprise Edition x64 Windows Server 2008 Datacenter Edition x64 Windows Server 2003 Standard Edition SP2 x64 Windows Server 2003 Enterprise Edition SP2 x64

	Windows Server 2003 Datacenter Edition SP2 x64 Windows Vista Ultimate x64 Windows Vista Enterprise x64 Windows Vista Business x64 Windows Vista Home Premium x64 Windows Vista Home Basic x64 Windows XP Professional x64
SQL Server 2008 Web Edition	Windows Server 2008 Web Edition x64 Windows Server 2008 Standard Edition x64 Windows Server 2008 Enterprise Edition x64 Windows Server 2008 Datacenter Edition x64 Windows Server 2003 Standard Edition SP2 x64 Windows Server 2003 Enterprise Edition SP2 x64 Windows Server 2003 Datacenter Edition SP2 x64 Windows Vista Ultimate x64 Windows Vista Enterprise x64 Windows Vista Business x64 Windows XP Professional x64
SQL Server 2008 Standard Edition	Windows Server 2008 Web Edition x64 Windows Server 2008 Standard Edition x64 Windows Server 2008 Enterprise Edition x64 Windows Server 2008 Datacenter Edition x64 Windows Server 2003 Standard Edition SP2 x64 Windows Server 2003 Enterprise Edition SP2 x64 Windows Server 2003 Datacenter Edition SP2 x64 Windows Vista Ultimate x64 Windows Vista Enterprise x64 Windows Vista Business x64 Windows XP x64 Professional
SQL Server 2008 Enterprise Edition	Windows Server 2008 Standard Edition x64 Windows Server 2008 Standard Edition x64 with Hyper-V Windows Server 2008 Enterprise Edition x64 Windows Server 2008 Enterprise Edition x64 with Hyper-V Windows Server 2008 Datacenter Edition x64 Windows Server 2008 Datacenter Edition x64 with Hyper-V Windows Server 2003 Standard Edition SP2 x64 Windows Server 2003 Enterprise Edition SP2 x64 Windows Server 2003 Datacenter Edition SP2 x64

64-bit IA-64 Editions of SQL Server 2008

The Itanium-base IA-64 editions of SQL Server 2008 are designed to provide the absolute highest levels of performance and scalability.

SQL Server 2008 Edition	Windows Server Operating System Supported
SQL Server 2008 Enterprise Edition (64-bit) IA-64	Windows Server 2008 64-bit Itanium Windows Server 2003 SP2 64-bit Itanium Datacenter Edition Windows Server 2003 SP2 64-bit Itanium Enterprise Edition

Hot-add CPU Support

Another significant new architectural enhancement in SQL Server 2008 is hot-add CPU support. Hot-add CPU support enables SQL Server 2008 to recognize and utilize any new processors that are added to the system, without needing to reboot the server or stop and start the SQL Server service. For physical servers, the hardware must obviously support the ability to add CPUs while the system is running. However, the real value of this feature is when it is used for a SQL Server system running in a virtual machine (VM). When used in a VM, in conjunction with the hot-add memory support that Microsoft added to SQL Server 2008, this feature allows SQL Server 2008 to actively participate in Microsoft's dynamic IT vision. The ability to hot-add resources like CPU and memory allows the server to be dynamically reconfigured to adapt on-the-fly to varying workloads.

After hot-adding CPU or memory, you need to run the SQL Server RECONFIGURE command to enable SQL Server 2008 to recognize and utilize the new system resources.

The ability to hot add CPUs is only available in the SQL Server 2008 Enterprise Edition. It also requires either the x64 or IA-64 editions Windows Server 2008.

SQL Server Relational Engine Enhancements

SQL Server 2008 also provides a number of very significant enhancements to the relational database engine. Some of the most important of these new features include support for data compression, transparent data encryption, and a new extended events architecture.

Data Compression

Without a doubt, SQL Server 2008's most important new architectural enhancement is the ability to automatically compress the data stored in a database. SQL Server 2008's data compression is completely transparent to client applications and requires no application changes in order to take advantage of the compression. One of the big advantages of data compression is that along with being able to reduce the size of the data stored on disk, the fact that the data is compressed at the page level can also have a very significant effect on the backup and restore times required for a database. Backup and restore operations are typically I/O bound and, because data compression can radically reduce the amount of data that must be backed up or restored, compression can thereby drastically reduce backup and restore times. Data compression is only available in the SQL Server 2008 Enterprise, Developer, and Evaluation Editions.

If you're somewhat familiar with compression you probably know that there are two basic types of compression: lossy and lossless. Lossy data compression is used primarily with image formats like jpeg, and it is used for speed and to get better compression ratios. However, as its name implies, lossy data compression involves data loss that is not considered acceptable for a database application. On the other hand, lossless data compression doesn't provide the same degree of data compression, though a database application like SQL Server has the advantage of being able to completely reconstruct the original data from the compressed format. SQL Server 2008 uses a proprietary form of a dictionary-based algorithm to compress data. Essentially, dictionary-based data compression routines build a dictionary comprised of commonly recurring data patterns and then reference these patterns using a pointer that only allows the data pattern to be stored a single time. As you might surmise, the goal behind SQL Server 2008's data compression isn't to achieve the maximum possible data compression. Rather, it's to strike an optimum balance between the amount of compression and the performance cost of compressing and decompressing the data.

SQL Server 2008 actually provides two different types of compression: row-level compression and page-level compression.

NOTE

Many of the examples in this book are built in an example database that's called NewFeaturesDB. This database will be used in the following row-level and page-level database compression examples. You can see the code you'll need to create the NewFeaturesDB database in the following listing:

```
CREATE DATABASE NewFeaturesDB ON PRIMARY
( NAME = N'NewFeaturesDB', FILENAME = N'C:\Program Files\Microsoft SQL
Server\MSSQL10.MSSQLSERVER\MSSQL\DATA\NewFeaturesDB.mdf' , SIZE = 3072KB ,
MAXSIZE = UNLIMITED, FILEGROWTH = 1024KB )
 LOG ON
( NAME = N'NewFeaturesDB_log', FILENAME = N'C:\Program Files\Microsoft
SQL Server\MSSQL10.MSSQLSERVER\MSSQL\DATA\NewFeaturesDB_log.ldf' ,
SIZE = 1024KB , MAXSIZE = 2048GB , FILEGROWTH = 10%)
GO
```

Row-level Compression

SQL Server 2008's new row-level compression is essentially achieved using a variable length, data-type format for all data types. Row-level compression doesn't use a data compression algorithm; this is because the amount of repeating data on a row-by-row basis isn't very large. Instead, SQL Server 2008's row-level compression removes unneeded bytes from the column values by storing them in variable length format. For example, if you declare a CHAR(50) data type in a standard fixed format, it will always require 50 bytes of storage, even if you store a short string like the value "My Data." However, if you enable row-level compression, this data will be stored in variable length format, which only requires seven bytes of storage. In this case, that would be 86 percent space-saving.

Enabling Row-level Compression *Row-level compression* is enabled as a part of the CREATE TABLE or ALTER TABLES statements. You can see an example of the CREATE TABLE enabling row-level compression in the following example:

```
Use NewFeaturesDB
GO
CREATE TABLE MyTableRowCompression (MyCol1 int, MyCol2 char(100))
      WITH (DATA_COMPRESSION = ROW)
GO
```

Estimating Row-level Compression Savings To help you determine the effectiveness of using row-level compression you can run the sp_estimate_data_compression_savings stored procedure. The sp_estimate_data_compression_savings stored procedure can evaluate the effectiveness of compression for a standalone table or for a table and all of its related indexes. You can run the sp_estimate_data_compression_savings stored procedure to estimate the savings you'll receive from using row-level compression on the Product table by looking at the following AdventureWorks database example:

```
Use AdventureWorks
GO
EXEC sp_estimate_data_compression_savings  'Production', 'Product',
  NULL, NULL, 'ROW'
GO
```

Page-level Compression

SQL Server 2005's page-level compression is designed to save storage by minimizing data redundancy. SQL Server 2008's page-level compression uses both column prefix compression and a lossless dictionary-based data compression algorithm to store repeating values only once per page, and then replaces the data with a pointer from the respective columns within the page. With column prefix compression, SQL Server identifies a common byte pattern at the beginning of a column for all rows on the page. If two or more instances of the same columns have an identical byte pattern, SQL Server stores that byte pattern once and then replaces the byte pattern with a pointer to those respective columns. Dictionary compression is specific per page. In other words, there is a dictionary per page that stores just the repeating values for that page. The dictionary stores repeating values across all columns and rows on the page. Index values are inserted into each column, to point back to the dictionary for the stored common value. The entries in the dictionary are stored as an array with a 0-based index. If there are many occurrences of repeating values, you'll get compression savings that are proportional to the number of repetitive values.

Enabling Page-level Compression Page compression is enabled using either the CREATE TABLE or ALTER TABLE statements. The following example illustrates how to enable page-level compression for a table named MyTablePageCompression:

```
Use NewFeaturesDB
GO
CREATE TABLE MyTablePageCompression(MyCol1 int, MyCol2 nvarchar(100))
  WITH (DATA_COMPRESSION = PAGE);
GO
```

Estimating Page-level Compression Savings To help you determine the storage savings that might be gained by using row-level compression, you can run the sp_estimate_data_compression_savings stored procedure. The following example shows you how to estimate the storage savings of using page-level data compression on the Production.Product table in the AdventureWorks database:

```
Use AdventureWorks
GO
EXEC sp_estimate_data_compression_savings  'Production', 'Product',
  NULL, NULL, 'PAGE'
GO
```

NOTE

You can apply data compression to existing tables and indexes by using the ALTER TABLE and ALTER INDEX statements.

Transparent Data Encryption

Another important new architectural enhancement to the SQL Server 2008 relational database engine is support for transparent data encryption (TDE). TDE is only available in the SQL Server 2008 Enterprise, Developer, and Evaluation Editions. TDE addresses the issue of data security. SQL Server 2005 had the ability to encrypt data at the cell-level using encryption functions. However, managing the encryption keys was a manual process and accessing the encrypted data required code changes. SQL Server 2008's TDE encryption addressed both of these issues by adding the ability to encrypt an entire database and then allowing the encryption to be completely transparent to the applications accessing the database. TDE doesn't replace cell-level encryption, but adds another encryption option to SQL Server 2008. The older cell-level and the newer TDE are compatible and therefore can be used together.

SQL Server 2008's TDE encrypts the data stored in both the database's data file (.mdf) and log file (.ldf), using either AES or 3DES encryption. In addition, any backups for the database are also encrypted. This protects the data while it is at rest and provides protection against the loss of sensitive information from lost or stolen media.

Like the data compression feature, SQL Server 2008's database encryption is performed at the page level. Data is encrypted on the disk and is then decrypted as it is read into memory. Performing the encryption at the page level enables the encryption process to be completely transparent to the client applications. There are no limitations on your ability to search or query the data in the encrypted database. In addition, since most database applications are optimized to minimize I/O for performance reasons, tying the encryption process to database base I/O takes advantage of this existing application optimization and makes the encryption process very efficient. If the database is being used with either database mirroring or log shipping, the databases on all of the participating systems must be encrypted. The log transactions that are sent between the systems are unencrypted.

NOTE

While TDE encrypts the stored data in the database, it does not encrypt the communications link between the server and the client applications. Encrypting the client connections is accomplished using a Secure Sockets Layer (SSL) connection between the clients and the server.

Enabling Transparent Database Encryption

Using TDE is surprisingly simple. To encrypt a database using TDE, you first create a master key for the database. Then you create a certificate that is protected by the master key. Next, you create a special key that is used to protect the database, aptly called the database encryption key (DEK), and secure it using the certificate. Finally, you enable the encryption. The following code listing illustrates how to enable TDE on a sample database named NewFeaturesDB:

```
-- The master key must be in the master database
USE Master;
GO
-- Create the master key
CREATE MASTER KEY ENCRYPTION
BY PASSWORD='MyStrongPassword';
GO

-- Create a certificate
CREATE CERTIFICATE MySQLCert
WITH SUBJECT='NewFeaturesDB DEK';
GO

-- Go to NewFEaturesDB
USE NewFeaturesDB
GO

-- Associate the certificate to NewFeaturesDB
CREATE DATABASE ENCRYPTION KEY
WITH ALGORITHM = AES_128
ENCRYPTION BY SERVER CERTIFICATE MySQLCert;
GO

-- Encrypt the database
ALTER DATABASE NewFeaturesDB
SET ENCRYPTION ON;
GO
```

To use TDE you must first create a master key. It's important to note that the master key must be created in the master database. At the top of this listing you can see where the USE statement changes the current database to the master database. You can then see the CREATE MASTER KEY statement is used to create a master key and its associated password in the master database. Next, the CREATE CERTIFICATE statement is used to create a new certificate named MySQLCert. After the certificate is created, the USE statement switches the current database to the NewFeaturesDB database where the CREATE DATABASE ENCRYPTION KEY statement is used to create a new database encryption key using the AES encryption algorithm. TDE enables you to choose between the following encryption algorithms: AES_128, AES_192, AES_256, and TRIPLE_DES_3KEY. After the database encryption key is created you can enable TDE using the ALTER DATABASE command as is shown near the bottom of the listing. The encryption process runs as a background task and the database remains available while it is being encrypted, although there is a performance impact during this time.

NOTE

If any database on a server is encrypted using TDE the tempdb database will also be encrypted.

Restoring and Moving Encrypted Databases

Backing up the certificate is extremely important because the encrypted data can't be accessed or restored without the certificate. Likewise, if you need to move an encrypted database from one SQL Server 2008 server to another, you would need to move the certificate too. The following code shows you how to back up the certificate to a file in the file system. This file can then be backed up or moved to another system to allow the encrypted database to be restored:

```
-- Backup the certificate
USE Master
GO

BACKUP CERTIFICATE MySQLCert
TO FILE = 'c:\temp\MySQLCert'
WITH PRIVATE KEY (file='c:\temp\MySQLCertKey',
ENCRYPTION BY PASSWORD='MyStrongPassword2')
```

Since the master key is in the master database, the USE statement is used to switch to the master database. Then the BACKUP CERTIFICATE statement is used to copy the certificate to the c:\temp\MySQLCert file and the key to the file named c:\temp\MySQLCertKey.

To move or restore the database to another SQL Server 2008 instance you need to restore the certificate to the new server instance. The following listing illustrates how to move the backed up certificate to a new SQL Server instance:

```
USE Master
GO
-- Create a new Master Key
CREATE MASTER KEY ENCRYPTION
BY PASSWORD = 'MyNewStrongPassword'
```

```
-- Restore the certificate
CREATE CERTIFICATE MySQLCert
FROM FILE='c:\temp\MySQLCert'
WITH PRIVATE KEY (
FILE = 'c:\temp\MySQLCertKey',
DECRYPTION BY PASSWORD='MyStrongPassword2')
```

The USE statement switches the current database to the master database, which is where the new master key must be created. Next, the CREATE MASTER KEY ENCRYPTION statement is executed to create a new master key. The new master key has a strong password associated as well. Next, the CREATE CERTIFICATE STATEMENT is used to create a new certificate named MySQLCert. This statement is different from the earlier example as it uses the FROM FILE clause to point to the backup certificate file that was created earlier. The WITH PRIVATE KEY clause also points to the backup of the decryption key file. Finally, the password to decrypt the certificate is supplied using the DECRYPTION BY PASSWORD clause.

Disabling Transparent Database Encryption

To turn off TDE you can use the ALTER DATABASE statement with the SET ENCRYPTION OFF clause as is shown in the following listing. The database will be decrypted in the background and is available during the decryption process:

```
-- Disable TDE
ALTER DATABASE NewFeaturesDB
SET ENCRYPTION OFF;
GO
```

Transparent Database Encryption Dynamic Management Views

SQL Server 2008's new TDE can be managed and monitored using dynamic system views (DMVs). The following listing shows how to query the sys.certificates, and the sys.dm_data_encyption_keys DMVs to see the certificates that have been created and the databases that are encrypted using TDE:

```
/** TDE DMVs **/
USE master
GO

SELECT * FROM sys.certificates

-- encryption_state = 3 is encrypted
SELECT * FROM sys.dm_database_encryption_keys
  WHERE encryption_state = 3;
```

Extensible Key Management

SQL Server 2005 doesn't allow the use of third-party data encryption keys or key management. This prohibits third-party encryption software from working with SQL Server 2005. SQL Server 2008's new Extensible Key Management provides customers with a choice in cryptographic providers as well as encryption key management. Built using the Microsoft Cryptographic API (MSCAPI), SQL Server 2008's new extensible key management (EKM) feature enables encryption keys to be stored outside of SQL Server in special hardware devices called hardware security modules (HSMs). All encryption and decryption operations using these keys are performed by the third-party cryptographic provider. Only users who have access to the HSM keys can encrypt and decrypt the data. EKM and HSMs can stop even database administrators and other database users with high level permissions from accessing the encrypted data. EKM can be a more secure solution than TDE by itself because the HSMs enable the keys to be stored separately from the data that they protect. EKM is only available in the SQL Server 2008 Enterprise, Developer and Evaluation Editions.

EKM is supported for cell-level encryption using both symmetric and asymmetric keys. For TDE, EKM is only supported with asymmetric keys. Database certificates cannot be created using EKM.

Enabling EKM To use EKM, you first need to enable EKM on the server using the sp_configure stored procedure. Then you need to load the third-party cryptographic provider and enable the encryption for a given database. The following listing shows you how to make use of SQL Server 2008's EKM:

```
/** Extensibile Key Management **/
USE master;
GO
-- Enable EKM
EXEC sp_configure 'show advanced options', '1';
RECONFIGURE;
EXEC sp_configure 'EKM provider enabled', 1;
RECONFIGURE;

-- Load the Third Party cryptographic povider
CREATE CRYPTOGRAPHIC PROVIDER My_EKM_Provider
 FROM FILE = 'c:\windows\system32\My_EKM_Provider.dll'

CREATE CREDENTIAL MyEKMCredential
 WITH IDENTITY='My_EKM_Login', SECRET='MyStrongPassword!'
  FOR CRYPTOGRAPHIC_PROVIDER My_EKM_Provider
GO
```

```
/* Alter the login to use credential */
ALTER LOGIN Login1 ADD CREDENTIAL MyEKMCredential
GO
```

In the beginning of this listing you can see how the sp_configure system stored procedure is used to enable EKM support. First, you must enable advanced options using the sp_configure with the Show Advanced Options parameter. Then you need to run the sp_configure stored procedure again using the EKM Provider Enabled parameter to enable EKM support in the SQL Server instance. In each case, to make the change take effect, you must subsequently run the RECONFIGURE command.

After enabling EKM support in the SQL Server instance, you'll use the CREATE CRYPTOGRAPHIC PROVIDER statement to create a new EKM provider named My_EKM_Provider. The FROM FILE clause points to a third-party dynamic link library (DLL) that will perform the encryption. Next, the CREATE CREDENTIAL statement is used to create a new encryption credential named MyEKMCredential, which uses the My_EKM_Provider cryptographic provider that was registered with the prior statement. Then, the MyEKMcredential is connected to the account named Login1.

Disabling Extensible Key Management To disable EKM you can use the ALTER CRYPTOGRAPHIC PROVIDER statement in conjunction with the DISABLE keyword as is shown in the following listing:

```
ALTER CRYPTOGRAPHIC PROVIDER My_EKM_Provider
 DISABLE
```

Extensible Key Management Dynamic Management Views

You can query the status of SQL Server 2008's EKM configuration and usage using some of the dynamic management views (DMVs) that Microsoft has provided with SQL Server 2008. The following listing shows how to use the sys.cryptographic_providers, sys.configurations and the sys.dm_cryptograhic_provider_sessions DMVs to check for the EKM providers that are loaded on the system, any existing credentionals that use EKM providers, and any current cryptographic sessions that are active:

```
/** EKM DMVs **/
USE master
GO

SELECT * FROM sys.cryptographic_providers

SELECT * FROM sys.configurations
 WHERE name = 'EKM provider enabled'
```

```
SELECT * FROM sys.credentials
 WHERE target_type = 'CRYPTOGRAPHIC PROVIDER'

SELECT * FROM sys.dm_cryptographic_provider_sessions(1)
```

Filtered Indexes

Another important new enhancement to the SQL Server 2008 relational database engine is the addition of a new feature called *filtered indexes*. Filtered indexes are like a standard, non-clustered index. However, unlike a standard index they are capable of supporting a WHERE clause, which enables them to effectively select or filter the rows that the index covers. Filtered indexes can provide substantial performance benefits in certain situations. For instance, building a filtered index over a column that contains a high number of null values can allow you to get tremendous performance benefits by choosing to filter out all rows with null values. This action results in a smaller and much more efficient index. The following example shows how to create a filtered index on the Production.WorkOrder table in the AdventureWorks database:

```
USE AdventureWorks;
GO
IF EXISTS (SELECT name FROM sys.indexes
    WHERE name = N'FICompletedWorkOrders'
    AND object_id = OBJECT_ID(N'Production.WorkOrder'))
DROP INDEX FICompletedWorkOrders
    ON Production.WorkOrder;
GO
CREATE NONCLUSTERED INDEX FICompletedWorkOrders
    ON Production.WorkOrder (WorkOrderID, StartDate)
    WHERE EndDate IS NOT NULL;
GO
```

In this example, the T-SQL code first checks for the existence of an index named FICompletedWorkOrders in the sys.indexes table, which is a system table that tracks the entire created index. If the FICompletedWorkOrders index is found then the DROP INDEX statement is used to delete the index.

Next the CREATE NONCLUSTERED INDEX statement is used to create a new filtered index named FICompletedWorkOrders over the WorkOrderID and StartDate columns of the Production.WorkOrder table. So far, as you can see, it's like the creation of a normal nonclustered index. What makes a filtered index different is the WHERE clause. In this example, you can see that the WHERE clause is used to filter the index so that only those rows where the value of the EndDate column is not null will be included in the index. In this case, it means that the index covers just those work orders that have been completed.

Change Data Capture

The ability to capture database changes is another very significant new feature in SQL Server 2008. In scenarios where you want to populate a data warehouse or other heterogeneous database with ongoing changes, change data capture (CDC) alone can justify the upgrade to SQL Server 2008. In previous releases of SQL Server, in order to capture daily or other periodic changes to a database that needed to be propagated to some other external data source that was not well supported by replication, you typically needed to either buy some expensive third-party product or write involved custom code to capture the on-going changes. CDC eliminates that requirement by building in the capability to record the changes to a database's tables into separate change tables. CDC is only available in the Enterprise or Developer editions of SQL Server 2008. CDC works by periodically capturing the changes to one or more tables from the transaction log and then forwarding those changes to a copy of those tables. You can see an overview of the CDC process in Figure 1-1.

In Figure 1-1 you can see that CDC works by capturing changes from the transaction log. This has the benefit of allowing the source tables to remain unaffected so there is no performance overhead introduced by the CDC process. The changed data is then written to a set of CDC capture tables. The CDC capture tables have basically the same schema as the source tables. However, the CDC process adds five columns to the beginning of each table to help track the change process. All insert and delete operations appear as single rows in the CDC capture tables. For an insert, the CDC capture table will tack on

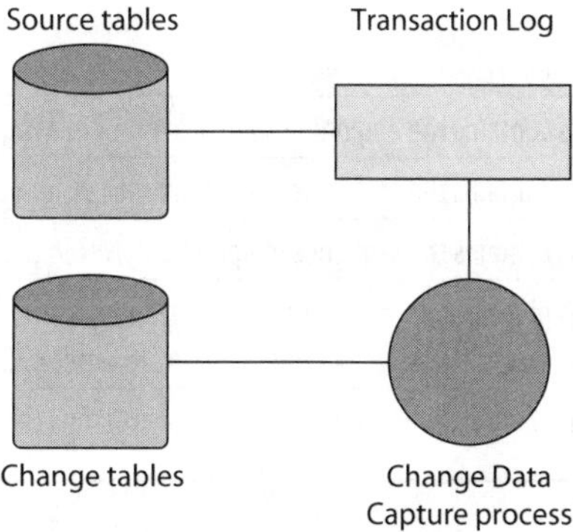

Figure 1-1 *An overview of the Change Data Capture process*

the row values after the insert operation. For deletes, the CDC capture tables will store the row values before the delete operation. The CDC process stores updates using two rows in the CDC capture table. The first row contains the values before the update operation, and the second row contains the values after the update operation.

Table 1-1 describes the columns that the CDC process adds to the capture tables.

If the table structure for the source tables changes, the CDC process continues to run. However, any column added after the CDC process is set up will not be captured. If a column is dropped from the source table, then the CDC capture table will record null values from the dropped column in the capture tables. To accommodate DDL changes, you can set up a maximum of two CDC process for a single table. Therefore, if a DDL change affects a table's structure, you can set up a second CDC process that captures the new data changes.

To prevent the change capture tables from growing without bounds, CDC has built-in the ability to periodically truncate the CDC target tables. By default, the CDC process prunes the target table every three days. However, the default CDC pruning value can be changed.

To enable CDC for a given database, you need to run the sp_cdc_enable system stored procedure as illustrated in the following listing:

```
USE NewFeaturesDB;
GO
EXEC sys.sp_cdc_enable_db;
```

After CDC has been enabled for a database you can use the sp_cdc_enable_table system stored procedure to specify the tables in the CDC-enabled database that you want to use as a capture source.

Column name	Description
__$start_lsn	This contains the beginning sequence number assigned to a transaction.
__$end_lsn	This contains the ending sequence number assigned to a transaction.
__$seqval	This contains the sequence of operations within the transaction.
__$operation	This identifies the operation associated with the source table change: 1=delete, 2=insert, 3=before update, 4=after update
__$update_mask	This contains a bit mask to identify the columns that have been changed.

Table 1-1 *CDC Capture Table Metadata*

NOTE

SQL Agent must be started before you enable CDC capture for a table.

You can see an example of using the cdc_enable_table stored procedure in the following listing:

```
-- Create a source table
CREATE TABLE DemoCDC
(
      colCDCID int PRIMARY KEY CLUSTERED,
      colCDCDATA char(100),
      colCDCDate datetime
)

-- Insert some base data
INSERT INTO DemoCDC VALUES(0, 'Data0', GETDATE());

-- Enable CDC for the table
USE NewFeaturesDB;
GO
EXEC sys.sp_cdc_enable_table
@source_schema = N'dbo'
,@source_name = N'DemoCDC'
,@role_name = N'cdc_admin'
,@capture_instance = N'CDC_dbo_DemoCDC'
,@supports_net_changes = 1
,@captured_column_list = NULL
,@filegroup_name = N'PRIMARY';

-- Insert some data
INSERT INTO DemoCDC VALUES(1, 'Data1', GETDATE());
INSERT INTO DemoCDC VALUES(2, 'Data2', GETDATE());
INSERT INTO DemoCDC VALUES(3, 'Data3', GETDATE());
INSERT INTO DemoCDC VALUES(4, 'Data4', GETDATE());
INSERT INTO DemoCDC VALUES(5, 'Data5', GETDATE());

-- Delete some date
DELETE FROM DemoCDC WHERE colCDCID = 3
```

```
-- Update some data
UPDATE DemoCDC SET colCDCDATA = 'DataFive'
  WHERE colCDCID = 5

-- Display the CDC capture table
SELECT __$operation AS [Change Code], colCDCID,colCDCDATA
 FROM cdc.CDC_dbo_DemoCDC_CT
```

At the top of this listing you can see where a table name DemoCDC is created in the NewFeaturesDB. This table has three columns: colCDCID, colCDCDATA, and colCDCDate. The colCDCID column is specified as the primary key. You can see that after the example table has been created some starting data has been inserted into the table.

The next section of code shows how to use the sp_cdc_enable_table stored procedure to begin capturing CDC data for the source table. The @source_schema parameter identifies the schema of the source table while the @source_name parameter specifies the name of the source table from which changes will be captured. The @role_name specifies the database role that is used to control access to the changed data tables. The @capture_instance parameter is used to name the CDC capture target table. The target name table is named using the value of instance name plus the suffix of _CT. The @supports_net_changes specifies if querying for net changes is allowed. To use this parameter, the source table must have a primary key. The @captured_column_list parameter can specify the columns to be captured. The value of NULL means that all columns in the source table will be captured. Finally, the @filegroup_name parameter specifies the FILEGROUP where the CDC capture table will be created.

After the CDC capture has been enabled for the DemoCDC table, some data update operations are performed on the table. First, five rows are inserted into the table. Then the third row is deleted from the table, and finally, the last row in the table is updated.

The next SELECT statement then queries the CDC_dbo_DemoCDC_CT capture table. You can see a selection of the CDC captured data in the following listing:

```
Change Code colCDCID    colCDCDATA
----------- ----------- ----------
2           1           Data1
2           2           Data2
2           3           Data3
2           4           Data4
2           5           Data5
1           3           Data3
3           5           Data5
4           5           DataFive
```

Here you can see that there is one row for each of the first five insert operations. The operations code for each of these rows has the value of 2, indicating that it is an insert operation. Next, there is one row with the value of 1 for the operations code. This is the deleted row. The two last rows have the operations codes of 3 and 4, showing the before and after values of the final update operation.

NOTE

You can disable CDC for a table by running the sp_cdc_disable table stored procedure.

More information about working with CDC data is presented in Chapter 8.

Managing Change Data Capture

You can track the database that has had CDC enabled by querying the is_cdc_enabled column from the sys.database table as shown in the following code:

```
SELECT is_cdc_enabled FROM sys.databases WHERE name = 'NewFeaturesDB'
```

Likewise, you can track the tables in the database where CDC has been enabled by querying the is_tracked_by_cdc column from the sys.tables table as is illustrated in the following listing:

```
USE NewFeaturesDB
GO
SELECT name from sys.tables WHERE is_tracked_by_cdc =1
```

Extended Events

Another important enhancement to SQL Server 2008's architecture is the introduction of extended events. SQL Server 2008's new extended event is an all-new, generic event-handling system. Extended events are designed to enable you to better monitor and troubleshoot SQL Server operations. For instance, you can use Extended Event to troubleshoot problems such as high CPU usage on the system. SQL Server 2008's new extended event allows you to create an event associated with a percentage of CPU utilization and then record the selected system state activity that was taking place at that time to a target like a database table or operating system file. For instance, you could record just the query plans of the currently executing query.

Before using SQL Server 2008's new extended events you need to have a basic understanding of the new extended event architecture. The core components of SQL

Extended Event Components	Description
SQL Server Extended Events Engine	The extended event engine is an event-processing engine that can filter and correlate SQL Server events with actions, and can record selected system data to a designated target.
Packages	Packages are containers for SQL Server extended events objects. A package can contain any or all of the following objects: events, targets, actions, types, predicates, and maps. Packages are identified by name, GUID, and the binary module that contains the package.
Event	Events are monitoring points of interest in SQL Server activities. An event fires when the point of interest is reached and it provides state information from the time the event was fired.
Targets	Targets process events.
Actions	Actions are preprogrammed responses to events
Predicates	Predicates are logical rules that are used to evaluate events when they are processed. Predicates enable filtering of events based on specific criteria.
Types	Types define the extended event objects.
Maps	Maps match an internal value to a string. Maps enable users to know what the internal value represents.

Table 1-2 *SQL Server 2008 Extended Event Objects*

Server 2008's new extended event architecture are the new extended event engine, package events, targets, actions, types, predicates, and maps. The usage of these objects is explained in the Table 1-2.

Adding Extended Event Sessions

Using SQL Server 2008's new extended events requires that you first create a new event session. You start by adding events which identify the SQL Server events that you want to monitor; next you add a target that specifies where you want to record the state information. The following example shows how you can make use of SQL Server 2008's extended events to track the locks acquired in the sample AdventureWorks database:

```
CREATE EVENT SESSION AdWLocks ON SERVER
 ADD EVENT sqlserver.lock_acquired (WHERE database_id =5)
 ADD TARGET package0.synchronous_bucketizer (
 SET FILTERING_EVENT_NAME='sqlserver.lock_acquired',
   SOURCE_TYPE=0, SOURCE='resource_0')
GO
```

```
ALTER EVENT SESSION AdWLocks ON SERVER
STATE=start
GO
```

At this point, the CREATE EVENT SESSION statement is used to create a new monitoring session named AdWLocks. The sqlserver.lock_acquired event is added for the AdventureWorks database, which has an ID of 5. Next, the package0.synchronous bucketizer target is added. In spite of its rather geeky-sounding name, the *bucketizer* simply records events and their data in an XML format in one or more slots (or buckets), where each slot contains data for separate events. The event tracing is activated using the ALTER EVENT SESSION statement to set the State property to a value of start.

Deleting Extended Event Sessions

You end extended event tracing by first using the ALTER EVENT SESSION statement to set the session's state to Stop. This halts the event tracing. Next you can delete the session using the DROP EVENT SESSION statement, as shown in the following listing:

```
ALTER EVENT SESSION AdWLocks ON SERVER state=stop
GO
DROP EVENT SESSION AdWLocks ON SERVER
GO
```

Extended Event Dynamic Management Views

SQL Server 2008's new extended events have a number of new DMVs. Some of the most important of these include sys.dm_xe_objects, dm_xe_object_columns, sys.dm_session_targets, and sys.server_event_sessions. The sys.dm_xe_objects view lists all of the extended event objects, while the dm_xe_object_columns view lists all the data columns available for each extended events package. The sys.dm_xe_session_targets DMV lists active monitoring sessions. To monitor active extended events the sys.dm_xe_session_targets and sys.server_event_sessions shows the open extended event target and active monitoring sessions, respectively. You can see these DMVs in the following listing:

```
SELECT * FROM sys.dm_xe_objects
GO
SELECT * FROM sys.dm_xe_object_columns
GO
SELECT * FROM sys.dm_xe_session_targets
GO
SELECT * FROM sys.server_event_sessions
GO
```

SQL Server Audit

Based on the new extended events architecture, the SQL Server Audit feature provides a new method for auditing SQL Server database activity. As you might guess, the SQL Server 2008 auditing feature enables you to track and log events that occur on the server. The Extended Event architecture is open and very granular, enabling a lot of flexibility in the events that you track and in the manner that they are recorded. SQL Server Audit builds on this base by using that architecture to group together collections of the most relevant SQL Server events that you want to monitor.

SQL Server Audit works at the SQL Server instance level and you can have multiple SQL Server Audit objects per SQL Server instance. Before using the SQL Server Audit capability, you need to create a Database Audit Specification object. The Database Audit Specification object collects database-level actions that are raised by SQL Server 2008's extended events.

The target for recording audited events can be a file, the Windows Security event log, or the Windows Application event log. Audits can be read using the Windows Event Viewer, the Log File Viewer, the fn_read_audit_file function, or a custom application.

Enabling SQL Server Audit You can see how to start SQL Server Auditing for failed logins in the following listing:

```
USE master;
GO
CREATE SERVER AUDIT MySQL2008Audit TO SECURITY_LOG ;
GO
CREATE SERVER AUDIT SPECIFICATION MyAuditSpec
 FOR SERVER AUDIT MySQL2008Audit
 ADD (FAILED_LOGIN_GROUP);
GO
ALTER SERVER AUDIT MySQL2008Audit WITH (STATE = ON);
GO
ALTER SERVER AUDIT SPECIFICATION MyAuditSpec WITH (STATE = ON);
GO
```

First the CREATE SERVER AUDIT statement creates a new SQL Server Audit object named MySQL2008Audit. The MySQL2008Audit object will be used to collect information about failed logins to the Windows Security log. Next, the CREATE SERVER AUDIT SPECIFICATION statement is used to create an audit specification that defines the event that will be monitored. In this example, the FAILED_LOGIN_GROUP indicates that SQL Server Audit will track failed logins. Finally, the ALTER SERVER AUDIT and ALTER SERVER AUDIT SPECFICATION statements turn on auditing by setting the state to ON.

Disabling SQL Server Audit You can turn SQL Server Auditing off by using the ALTER SERVER AUDIT statement as shown next. In this example, the ALTER SERVER AUDIT statement identifies the SQL Server Audit that will be disabled and sets its state to OFF. Then the DROP SERVER AUDIT SPECIFICATION and the DROP SERVER AUDIT statements delete the audit specifications and the SQL Server Audit object:

```
ALTER SERVER AUDIT MySQL2008Audit WITH (STATE = OFF);
GO
ALTER SERVER AUDIT SPECIFICATION MyAuditSpec WITH (STATE = OFF);
GO
DROP SERVER AUDIT SPECIFICATION MyAuditSpec
GO
DROP SERVER AUDIT MySQL2008Audit
GO
```

SQL Server Audit Dynamic Management Views SQL Server 2008 also provides a number of DMVs that can be used to manage SQL Server Audit. A few of the primary DMVs include sys.server_audits that show the audits that have been created, the sys.server_audit_specifications that show the audit specification, and the sys.server_audit_specification_details, which stores the details of each audit specification. You can see the usage of these SQL Server Audit DMVs in the following listing:

```
SELECT * FROM sys.server_audits
GO

SELECT * FROM sys.server_audit_specifications
GO

SELECT * FROM sys.server_audit_specification_details
GO
```

Summary

SQL Server 2008's newest architectural enhancements have given SQL Server 2008 several new capabilities, all of which add immediate value today and position it strategically for the future. The new, hot-pluggable CPUs feature will enable SQL Server 2008 to participate in Microsoft's view of the dynamic data center; this is done by enabling the server to dynamically scale up in a virtual environment to handle escalating workloads. Data compression is a technology that all organizations can put to use immediately. Data compression saves online storage and improves backup and restore times by reducing the amount of system I/O. For organizations that have greater security or compliance requirements, the new Transparent Data Encryption feature can encrypt one or more databases without requiring any changes to the client applications. For the enterprise, the new extended events capability and the new SQL Server auditing features address a couple of the problems that face larger organizations. Extended events can be used to attain fine-grained troubleshooting information, while SQL Server Auditing can assist the DBA in auditing SQL Server events and enable external auditors to audit SQL Server without granting them administrative rights.

Chapter 2

Administration

In each successive release of SQL Server, Microsoft has made significant improvements to the management tools that they ship with it. With the SQL Server 2005 they made a huge step forward with the introduction of the SQL Server Management Studio (SSMS) and the new .NET-based SQL Server Management Objects (SMO) Framework.

With SQL Server 2008, Microsoft has continued to build on this foundation by filling in some of the missing features in SSMS. They have also added a new Resource Governor that can help prevent run away queries and provide more consistent overall system response time, as well as a new policy-based management framework that is designed to make sure that all of the servers in the enterprise comply with the standards required by the organization. In this chapter you'll learn about these features and the other new management features that Microsoft has introduced in SQL Server 2008.

SQL Server Management Studio Enhancements

SQL Server Management Studio is both a management and a development tool. SSMS is built on the Visual Studio IDE and combines an Object Explorer that enables the administration of SQL Server systems with the Query Editor that enables you to write and run T-SQL queries. There is also a new reporting feature that enables you to run various server management reports. You can see the new SQL Server 2008 SSMS showing the new Server Dashboard report in Figure 2-1.

The Object Explorer allows you to manage all of the different SQL Server subsystems including the SQL Server Database Engine, Analysis Services, Reporting Services, SQL Server Compact Edition, and Integration Servers. Both the Object Explorer and the Query Editor can run on local or remote SQL Server instances.

SSMS for SQL Server 2008 is quite similar to the version that Microsoft provided in SQL Server 2005. For the Object Explorer, the main difference is that it is capable of working with the new SQL Server 2008 features like the new Policy Management and the Resource Governor (which you can see listed in the Object Explorer window shown in Figure 2-1). There is also the new capability of starting PowerShell, Microsoft's new scripting shell and language. SQL Server 2008 includes a new PowerShell provider that enables you to work with SQL Server databases. I'll present more information about PowerShell, Policy-Based Management, and the Resource Governor later in this chapter.

SSMS also features an expanded set of server reports. You can run the new reports by right clicking the server instance in Object Explorer and then selecting the Reports menu. Some of the reports, like the Server Dashboard shown in Figure 2-1, display overall system health and performance metrics, while other reports show application usage such as All Cursors, Top Sessions and Transactions by Locks Count.

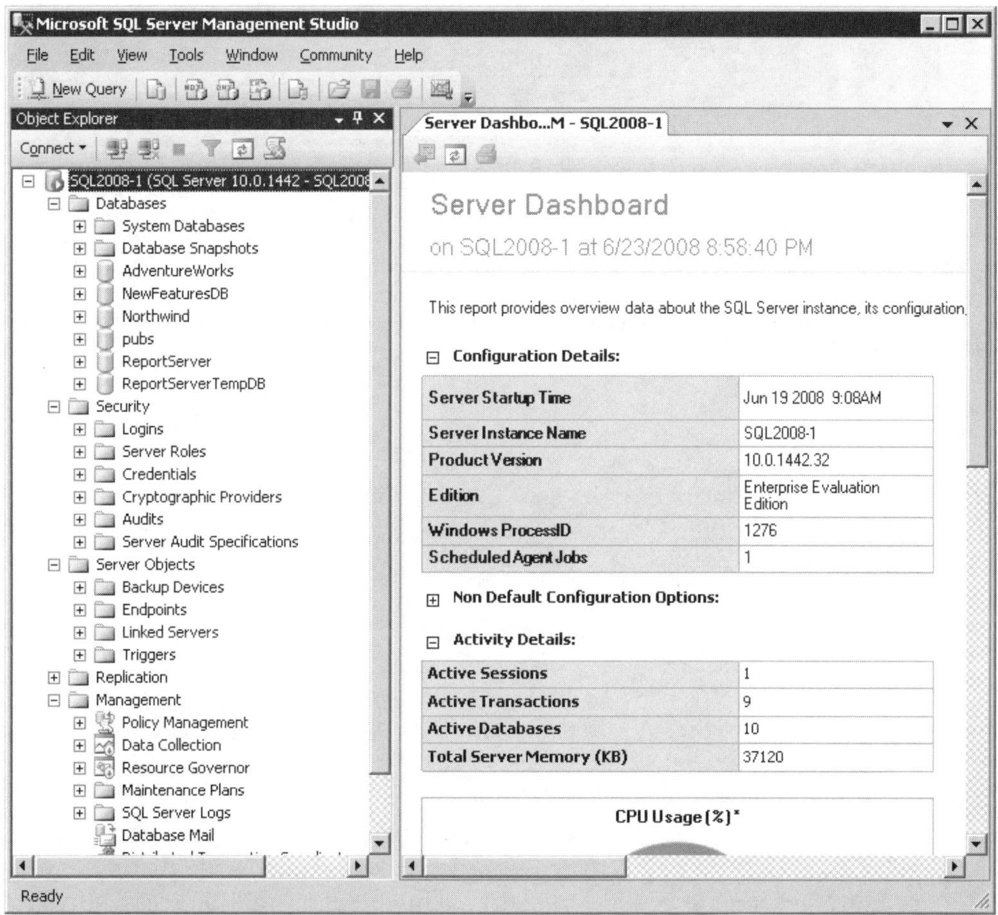

Figure 2-1 *SQL Server Management Studio*

Central Management Servers

The addition of Central Management Servers is another new feature in SSMS for SQL Server 2008. A Central Management Server contains information about server groups. As the name implies, server groups are groups of one or more registered SQL Server instances. Configuration Servers are used in applying policies, a practice covered later in this chapter. Configuration Servers can also be used to run T-SQL statements on all of the servers in a server group. Because Configuration Servers can run queries against multiple SQL Server systems, you must connect to a Configuration Server using Windows authentication in order to preserve the security context.

Figure 2-2 *Configuration Servers*

To add a Configuration Server you can either select the View | Registered Servers option from the SSMS menu or right-click the server instance in Object Explorer and then select Register from the Context menu. This will display the Registered Server menu shown in Figure 2-2.

IntelliSense

In the SQL Server 2008 release, the main enhancement to Query Editor is the inclusion of IntelliSense. While the move to the Visual Studio-based SSMS in SQL Server 2005 was well accepted, one of the biggest missing features was the lack of T-SQL IntelliSense. IntelliSense is one of the primary features in the Visual Studio development environment, and its absence in SQL Server 2005 was a notable omission. With SQL Server 2008, Microsoft rectified this situation so that the Query Editor in SQL Server 2008 provides support for IntelliSense. You can see SQL Server 2008's IntelliSense in action in Figure 2-3.

The new IntelliSense support provides T-SQL syntax checking, automatic prompting for database tables, and View names. Incomplete T-SQL syntax is displayed with a red squiggly marker at the end of each T-SQL statement.

However, SQL Server 2008's IntelliSense is still not completely full featured because it doesn't perform T-SQL statement completion or display column names. The new T-SQL IntelliSense will prompt for stored procedure names, but you need to first supply the correct schema. One nice feature of the new IntelliSense is the fact that it will display the stored procedure's return values and all parameters in a tool tip format if you move your mouse over the stored procedure name.

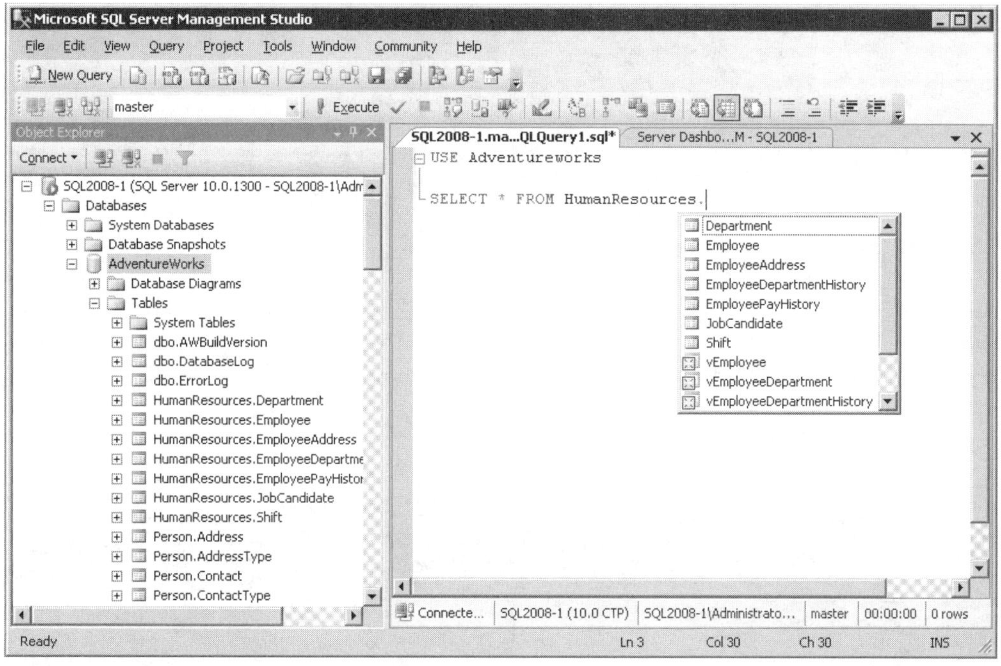

Figure 2-3 *IntelliSense in action*

T-SQL Debugging

Another extremely important enhancement to Query Editor in SQL Server 2008 is the ability to perform T-SQL debugging. T-SQL debugging was one of the biggest missing features from SQL Server 2005. Just as with Visual Studio's debugging capabilities, you can set breakpoints by clicking in the left margin of the editor. You can start a debugging session by either clicking on the green arrow icon or by selecting the Debug | Start Debugging option from the Query Editor menu.

After the debugging session has started, a yellow arrow indicates the currently executing line. In addition, a Locals window displays the value of all the variables in the current batch or procedure, while a Call Stack window displays the current call stack. A Debug Toolbar is also displayed in the Query Editor menu that enables you to Run, Pause, Stop, Show Next Statement, Step Into, Step Over, and Step Out. You can see SQL Server 2008's new T-SQL debugging capability illustrated in Figure 2-4.

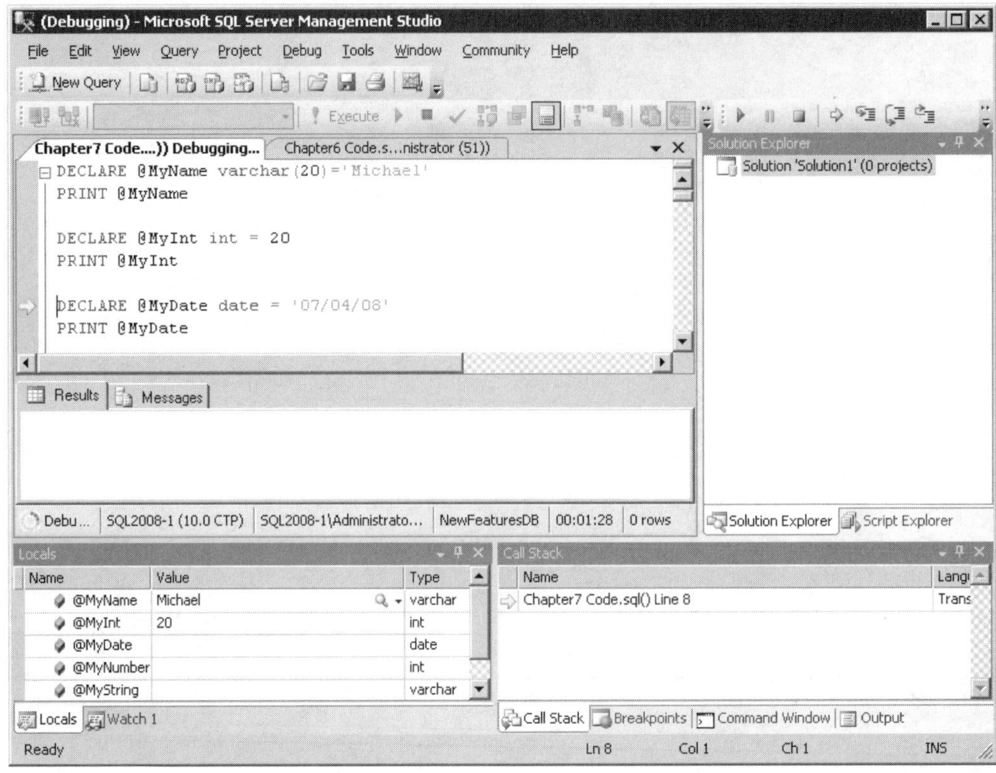

Figure 2-4 *Integrated T-SQL debugging*

Code Outlining

Code outlining is a new feature that can make your code more readable. It's especially useful for longer stored procedures and T-SQL batches. The new code outlining feature adds a + sign to the beginning of a block of code, enabling you to click on that + sign to either expand or collapse the code within that block. You can see an example of the new code outlining feature shown in Figure 2-5.

The new code outline feature works with the following T-SQL code groups:

- **Batches** T-SQL batches end with the GO keyword. The code from the start of the file to either the first GO statement or the end of the file is considered a batch. If there is no GO keyword, then the entire script is considered a batch. Code starting from a GO statement to either the next GO statement or until the end of the script is also considered one batch.

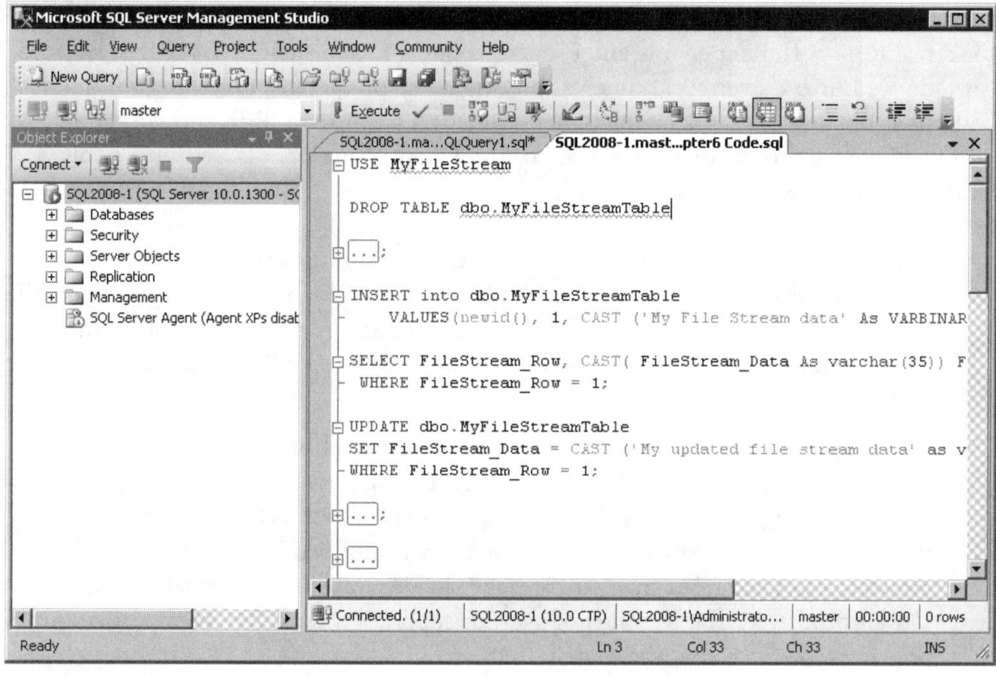

Figure 2-5 *Query Editor code outlining*

- **Blocks** T-SQL blocks are delimited by the following keywords: BEGIN – END, BEGIN TRY - END TRY, BEGIN CATCH - END CATCH. The code outlining feature collapses the entire block.
- **Multiline statements** *Multiline statements* are T-SQL statements that continue on to two or more lines in the Query Editor window. The outlining feature enables them to be collapsed back to the first line.

Code outlining is also available for Analysis Services MDX queries.

Resource Governor

One of the most important new management features in the SQL Server 2008 release is the new Resource Governor. The new Resource Governor allows you to control the amount of system resources that SQL Server will allocate to a given workload. The principle benefit of the Resource Governor is its ability to prevent poorly constructed end-user ad-hoc queries from adversely impacting the overall performance of the system.

This is particularly important, as tools like Reporting Services and end user reporting tools like Report Builder enable end users to create and run their own reports. Beyond this, the Resource Governor also helps to bring more predictable execution for queries and other jobs running on a system where there is a mixture of different workloads.

The Resource Governor is composed of three main components: resource pools, workload groups, and a classifier.

- **Resource Pools** By default, the Resource Governor uses two pools: the Internal Pool and the Default Pool. The Internal Pool is used by SQL Server itself and all user activity takes place in the Default Pool. The Internal Pool cannot be altered. The Default Pool cannot be dropped but it can be altered. You can make your own custom user-created resource pools.
- **Workload Groups** Workloads represent the connections running on the system. By default, SQL Server 2008 comes configured using two workload groups: Internal Workgroup and the Default Group. All internal system activity is grouped into the Internal Workgroup, while all user activity is grouped into the Default Group. You can also make your own custom workload groups. The internal Workgroup cannot be altered. The Resource Governor supports three different workload group priorities: low, medium, and high.
- **Classifier** The Classifier is a function that evaluates incoming job requests and categorizes them into the appropriate workload group. Only one user-defined classifier can be active at a time.

Each workload group is associated with a resource pool. As you might expect, the Internal Group is associated with the Internal Pool, while the Default Group is associated with the Default Pool. To take the best advantage of the Resource Governor, you can create your own custom workload groups and pools. One or more workload groups can use each pool. A user defined classifier function running on the system identifies running jobs and puts them into the appropriate workload group.

Using the Resource Governor

To take advantage of the new Resource Governor you need to create your own resource pools, workload groups, and classifier function. You can see an example of how to setup the Resource Governor in the following listing:

```
USE master;
GO
-- Resource pools
CREATE RESOURCE POOL MyLOBAppPool
```

```
WITH(
 MIN_CPU_PERCENT=50,
 MIN_MEMORY_PERCENT=50);
GO
CREATE RESOURCE POOL MyDBAPool
WITH(
 MAX_CPU_PERCENT=20,
 MAX_MEMORY_PERCENT=20);
GO
CREATE RESOURCE POOL MyReportingPool
WITH(
 MAX_CPU_PERCENT=30,
 MAX_MEMORY_PERCENT=30);
GO

-- Workload groups
CREATE WORKLOAD GROUP MyLOBAppGroup USING MyLOBAppPool
GO
CREATE WORKLOAD GROUP MyDBAGroup USING MyDBAPool
GO
CREATE WORKLOAD GROUP MyReportingGroup
WITH (IMPORTANCE=Low) USING MyReportingPool;
GO

-- Classifier
CREATE FUNCTION dbo.MyClassifier()
RETURNS SYSNAME WITH SCHEMABINDING
BEGIN
 DECLARE @WorkGroup AS SYSNAME = 'default';
 IF ISNULL(IS_SRVROLEMEMBER('sysadmin'),0)=1
    SET @Workgroup = 'MyDBAGroup';
ELSE IF (APP_NAME() = 'MyLOBApp')
 SET @Workgroup =  'MYLOBAppGroup';
ELSE IF 'ReportingUser' = SUSER_SNAME()
 SET @Workgroup = 'MyReportingGroup';
 RETURN @Workgroup;
END;
GO
-- Add Classifier
ALTER RESOURCE GOVERNOR WITH (CLASSIFIER_FUNCTION=dbo.MyClassifier)
GO
```

At the top of the listing you can see where the database is set to Master, which you'll need to use to create your resource pools and workload groups. Three resource pools are now created: MyLOBAppPool, MyDBAPool, and the MyReportingPool. The resource pools represent portions of the physical resources available on the SQL Server system. As you can see in the previous listing, you have the ability to specify MIN or MAX for both CPU and memory. Min represents the guaranteed minimum level of resources that will be available for the workload group. Max represents the maximum amount of system resources that will be allocated to a given workload. In this example, the MyLOBAppPool is guaranteed to have at least 50 percent of the available CPU and memory, whereas the MyDBAPool is limited to using a maximum of 20 percent of the system's CPU and memory. Likewise, the MyReportingPool is limited to 30 percent of the system's CPU and memory utilization. The values used for your pools cannot exceed 100 percent.

Next, three Workload Groups are created: MyLOBAppGroup, MyDBAGroup, and MyReportingGroup. In this case, for simplicity, each Workload Group will use a different Resource Pool. However, it is possible to set workload groups to share resource pools. The MyLOBAppGroup and MyDBAGroup both use the default priority. The MyReportingGroup uses a lower priority to minimize the impact that work in this group has on the other two groups.

After the Resource Pools and Workgroups have been created, your next step in utilizing the Resource Governor is to create a classifier function. In the previous listing the custom classification function is named MyClassifier. The MyClassifier function identifies SQL Server jobs and then categorizes them into Workload Groups and Resource Pools. In this example, the MyClassifier function first loads the value of default into the variable named @Workgroup. Then the function checks to see whether the job's user is a member of the sysadmin role and, if so, assigns the workload group name of MyDBAGroup to the @Workload variable. Otherwise, the next test checks that the application name is equal to the value of MyLOBApp. (In a real world case this would be the name of your application's executable program.) If the application name matches MyLOBApp, then the value of the @Workgroup variable is set to MyLOBAppGroup, which matches the name of the workload group for the line of business application that was created earlier. If neither of those values matches, the user name is checked to determine whether they are reporting users. If so, then the value of @Workgroup is set to MyReportingGroup. The value of the @Workgroup value is then returned at the end of the function.

Next, the ALTER RESOURCE GOVERNOR statement is used to activate the new MyClassifier function. User-defined classifier functions are not used until after you run the ALTER RESOURCE GOVERNOR RECONFIGURE statement.

You can view the Resource Governor's properties using SQL Server Management Studio (SSMS). Open SSMS, expand the Management node, right-click on the Resource

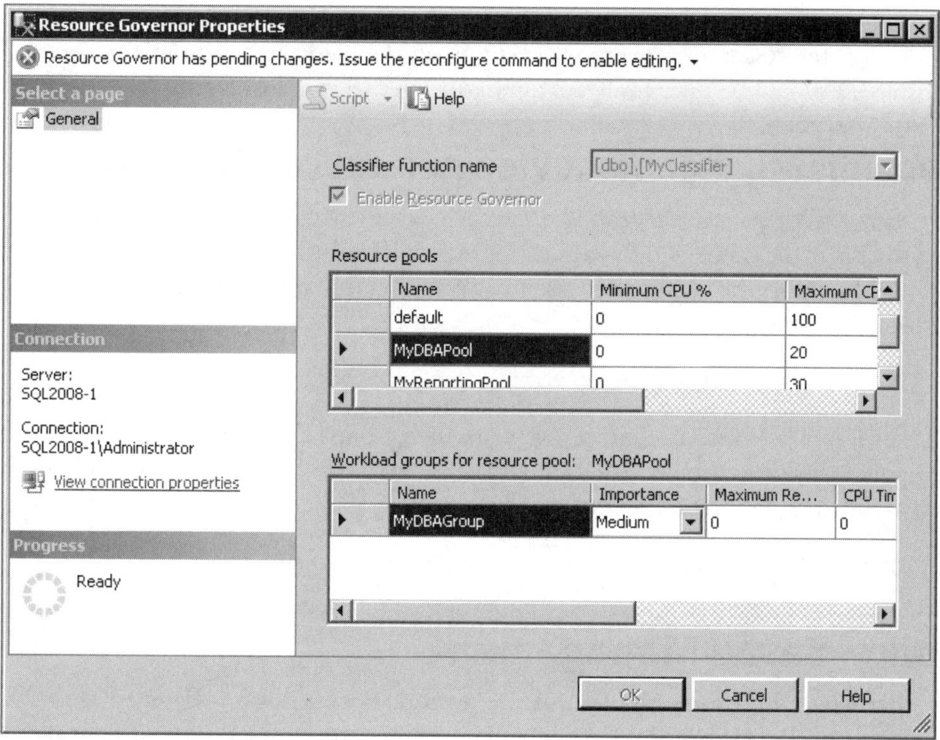

Figure 2-6 *Resource Governor Properties*

Governor, and then select Properties from the pop-up menu. This will display the Resource Governor Properties dialog shown in Figure 2-6.

Limitations

With the SQL Server 2008 release, the Resource Governor only works with memory and CPU usage. It doesn't take into account other system resources such as disk I/O or network bandwidth utilization. In addition, Resource Governor only works for the SQL Server relational database engine, and doesn't work with the other SQL Server 2008 subsystems such as Analysis Services, Integration Services, or Reporting Services. In addition, the Resource Governor is limited to working with the current SQL Server Instance.

If multiple instances are installed, each instance must use its own Resource Governor. In addition, the Resource Governor doesn't affect the Dedicated Administrators Console (DAC). DAC queries always run in the internal workload group.

Dynamic Management Views: Resource Governor

SQL Server 2008 provides several Dynamic Management Views (DMVs) which can be used to display the status of the Resource Governor. The sys.resources_governor_resource_pools DMV shows the configured Resource Pools; you can use that DMV as shown in the following listing:

```
SELECT * FROM sys.resource_governor_resource_pools
```

Likewise, the sys.resource_governor_workload_groups DMV enables you to view the configured workload groups. You can use the sys.resource_governor_workload_groups view as illustrated in the following listing:

```
SELECT * FROM sys.resource_governor_workload_groups
```

Policy-Based Management

Another new, enterprise-oriented feature in SQL Server 2008 is Policy-Based Management. Policy-Based Management simplifies the management of multiple SQL Server 2008 systems throughout the enterprise. While policies can't be stored on SQL Server 2005 or previous releases of SQL Server they can be evaluated either on-demand or using PowerShell.

Policy-Based Management enables the database administrator to check and enforce standards such as object naming conventions and database settings across multiple servers. This is an especially useful feature for a geographically dispersed organization that needs the capability to centrally control all of its database servers deployed throughout the company. Using Policy-Based Management, the administrator in a central enterprise office can set policies that control SQL Server 2008 server and database settings for systems that are local, as well as systems located in other parts of the world, even in other continents. Policy-Based Management utilizes Microsoft's Service Modeling Language (SML) as a standard for managing distributed systems, making it compatible with Microsoft System Center family of management products.

With Policy-Based Management, the administrator creates a set of policies that will be applied throughout the enterprise. The administrator then selects one or more target servers where the policies will be applied and also determines how the policies will be applied. Policies have four different execution modes, including On Demand, On Change: Prevent, On Change: Log Only, and On Schedule.

- **On Demand** The On Demand mode specifies that the policy is evaluated when the user initiates the action.
- **On Change: Prevent** The On Change: Prevent execution mode utilizes Data Definition Language (DDL) triggers to prohibit policy violations. This execution mode is automated and an event will be written to the event log.
- **On Change: Log Only** The On Change: Log Only execution mode uses event notifications to evaluate system changes and writes policy violations to a log. This execution mode is automated and an event will be written to the event log.
- **On Schedule** The On Schedule mode uses the SQL Server Agent to run a job that periodically evaluates policies and logs violations. This execution mode is automated and an event will be written to the event log.

Creating a Policy

In this section, you'll learn how to create a policy that enforces a standard naming convention. Using standardized database object names is a common practice. However, each different organization tends to use their own individual set of standards. Here you'll see how you can create a policy that requires all stored procedures in the NewFeaturesDB database to begin with the prefix usp_. The prefix usp_ is commonly used to designate user-created stored procedures; as opposed to sp_, which is used by SQL Server's built-in stored procedures. Policies are created using SQL Server Management Studio (SSMS).

1. Create a policy by opening SSMS. Expand the Management node and then select the Policies node as shown in Figure 2-7.
2. Next, right-click the Policies node and then select New Policy from the Context menu to display the Create New Policy dialog.

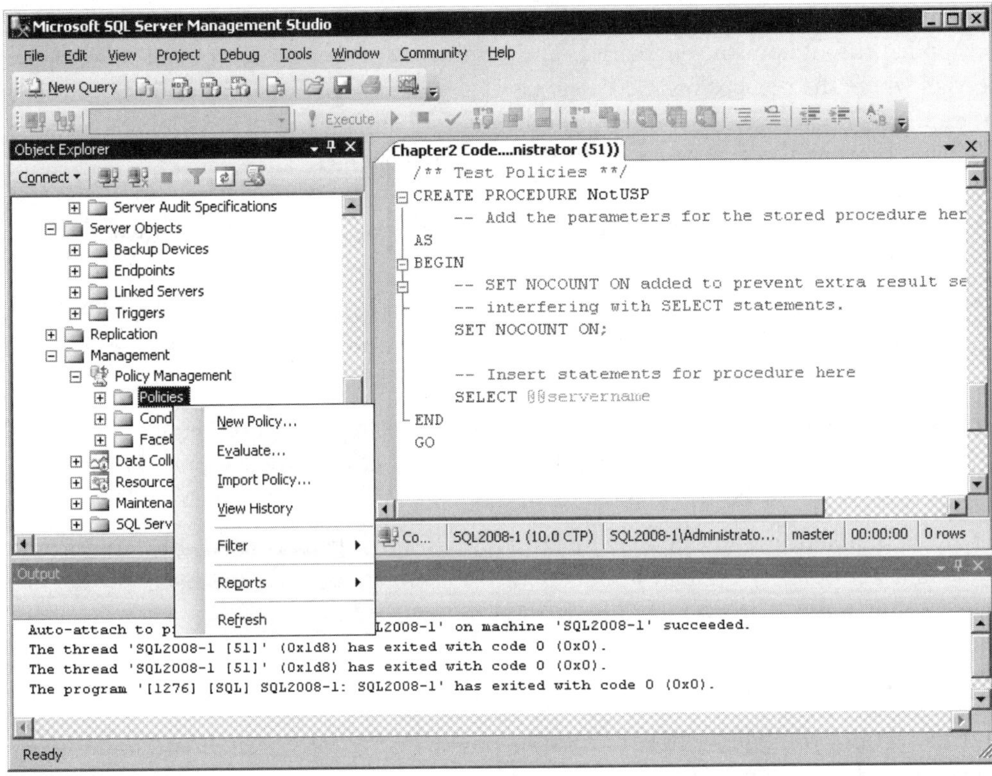

Figure 2-7 *Creating a new policy using SQL Server Management Studio*

3. Give the policy a name (in this example, I'll use the name MyNamingConvention) and then check the Enable checkbox.
4. Next, use the Check condition drop-down list and select New Condition to display the Create New Condition dialog shown in Figure 2-8.

In the Create New Condition dialog box, you can see that the condition is named SPName and that it will be applied to the stored procedure Facet. A Facet is a set of logical properties that model the behavior of a target object. In this case, the Facet

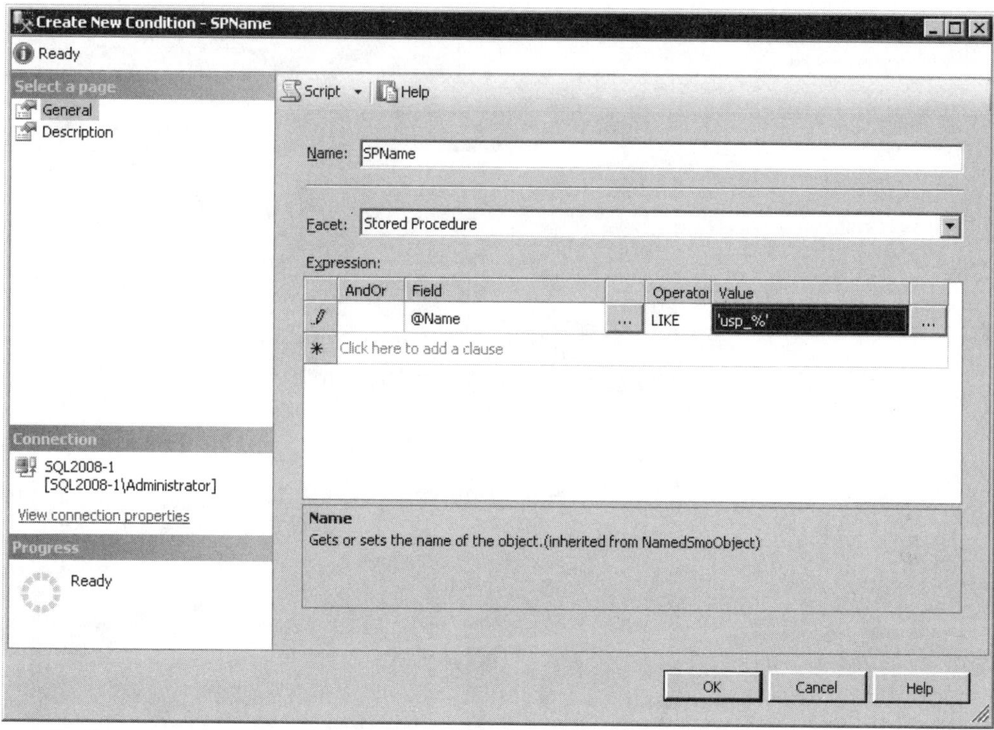

Figure 2-8 *Creating a new condition*

represents a stored procedure. Clicking OK creates the condition and then returns to the Create New Policy dialog that you can see in Figure 2-9.

First, you'll need to name the policy. In Figure 2-9 you can see that the policy has been named MyNamingConvention. Next, the Enabled box is checked, which requires the use of one of the automated execution modes. In this example the On Change: Prevent mode has been selected, which will prevent stored procedures from being created that don't comply with the stored procedure naming condition you created earlier. By default, the Against Targets specifies Every Stored Procedure in Every Database. To restrict the use of this condition to just the NewFeaturesDB database, you'll need to create a new condition where the database name is equal to the name of the NewFeaturesDB database. To create the condition, click the Every link and then select

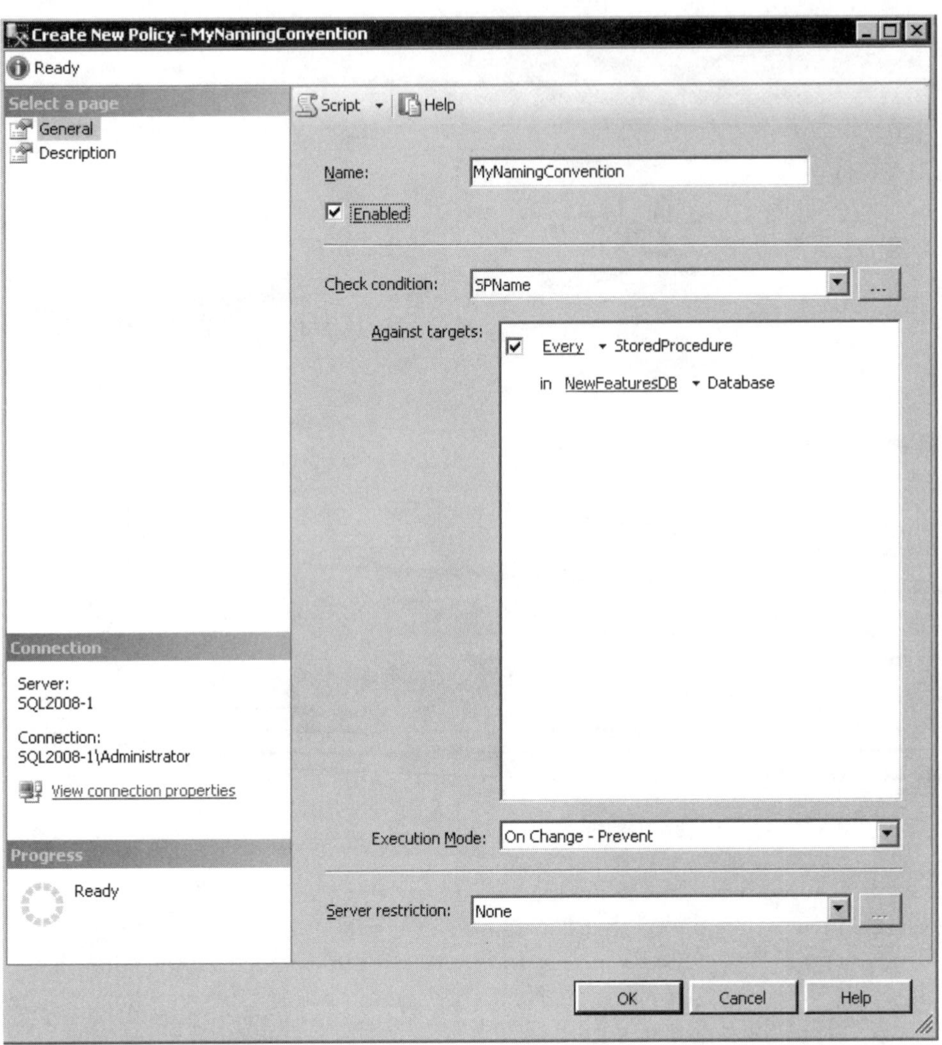

Figure 2-9 *Creating a new policy*

New Condition from the list. The Create New Condition dialog that you saw in Figure 2-7 will be displayed. This time, name the condition NewFeaturesDB and then set the expression to @Name = 'NewFeaturesDB.' Next, click OK to return to the Create New Policy dialog box, where the condition will be displayed as shown in Figure 2-8.

After the policy has been created, any attempt to create stored procedure that violates the policy will end in the following error:

```
Policy 'MyNamingConvention' has been violated by '/Server/(local)/Database/
NewFeaturesDB/StoredProcedure/dbo.NotUSP'.
This transaction will be rolled back.
Policy description: ''
Additional help: '' : ''.
Msg 3609, Level 16, State 1, Procedure sp_syspolicy_dispatch_event, Line 50
The transaction ended in the trigger. The batch has been aborted.
```

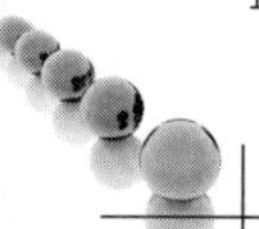

NOTE

Policies are stored in SQL Server's msdb database. Administrators using Policy-Based Management need to be sure to backup the msdb database in order to save the created conditions and policies.

PowerShell Integration

PowerShell is Microsoft's newest scripting environment and command shell. Unlike the older Windows command shell, PowerShell is completely object-oriented and it features an all-new syntax built around the use of single function cmdlets. You can find more information about Windows PowerShell at: http://www.microsoft.com/windowsserver2003/technologies/management/powershell/default.mspx.

It's clear that Microsoft's future direction is to build the management consoles of their server products on top of PowerShell, thereby integrating scripting at a very deep level. Microsoft has done this with the latest version of Exchange 2007, as well as with the System Center Virtual Machine Manager 2007 and 2008. SQL Server 2008 does not have a level of integration with PowerShell as deep as this because SQL Server Management Studio continues to be built on top of the Visual Studio IDE. However, the SQL Server 2008 setup does install PowerShell 1.0 if it is not already installed on the system. In addition, it installs SQL Server PowerShell Providers, a set of SQL Server cmdlets, and adds PowerShell as an option to SQL Server Management Studio and SQL Server Agent.

The sqlps Utility

The first place that you'll probably notice SQL Server 2008's PowerShell integration is the new sqlps utility included in SQL Server Management Studio. You launch the sqlps utility by first opening Object Explorer, right-clicking on the SQL Server 2008

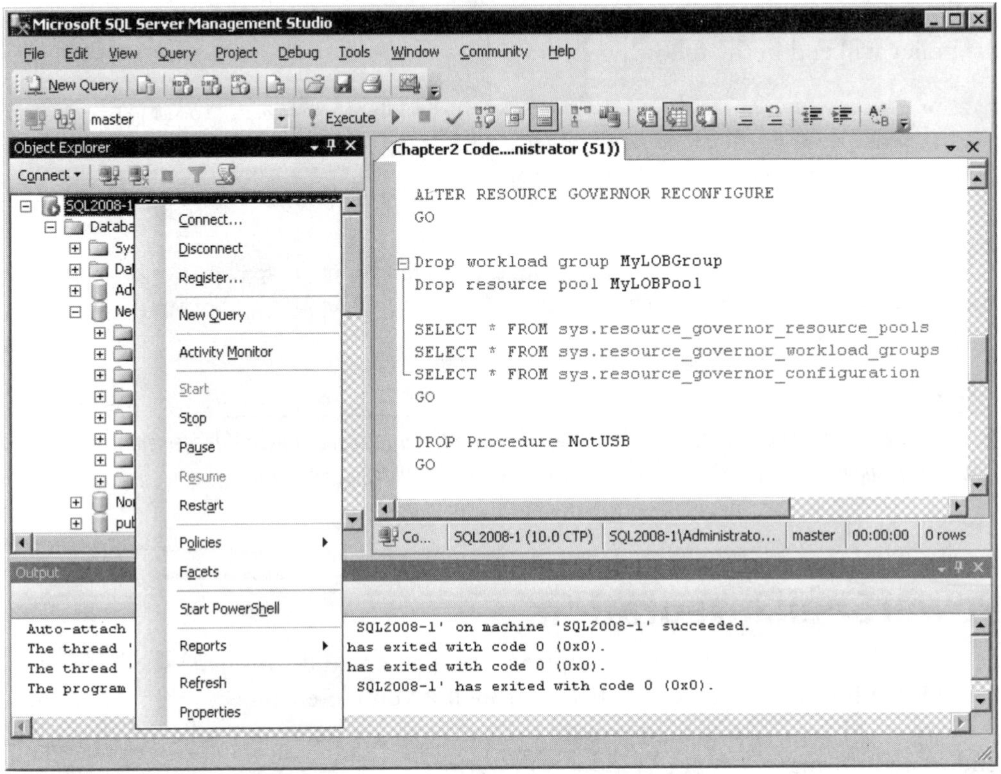

Figure 2-10 *Launching the sqlps utility from SQL Server Management Studio*

instance that you want to connect to, and then selecting Start PowerShell from the Context menu as is shown in Figure 2-10.

Selecting the Start PowerShell option starts the sqlps utility. Sqlps is different from the standard PowerShell prompt because it uses the SQL Server Provider in conjunction with your SSMS authentication information to make a connection to SQL Server. Unlike the standard PowerShell command prompt (which displays your Windows file system directory), the sqlps utility uses the SQL Server Provider to display the SQL: drive connection prompt consisting of PS SQLSERVER:\SQL\<ComputerName>\<InstanceName>. More information about using the SQL Server Provider is presented later in this section. You can see the sqlps utility in Figure 2-11.

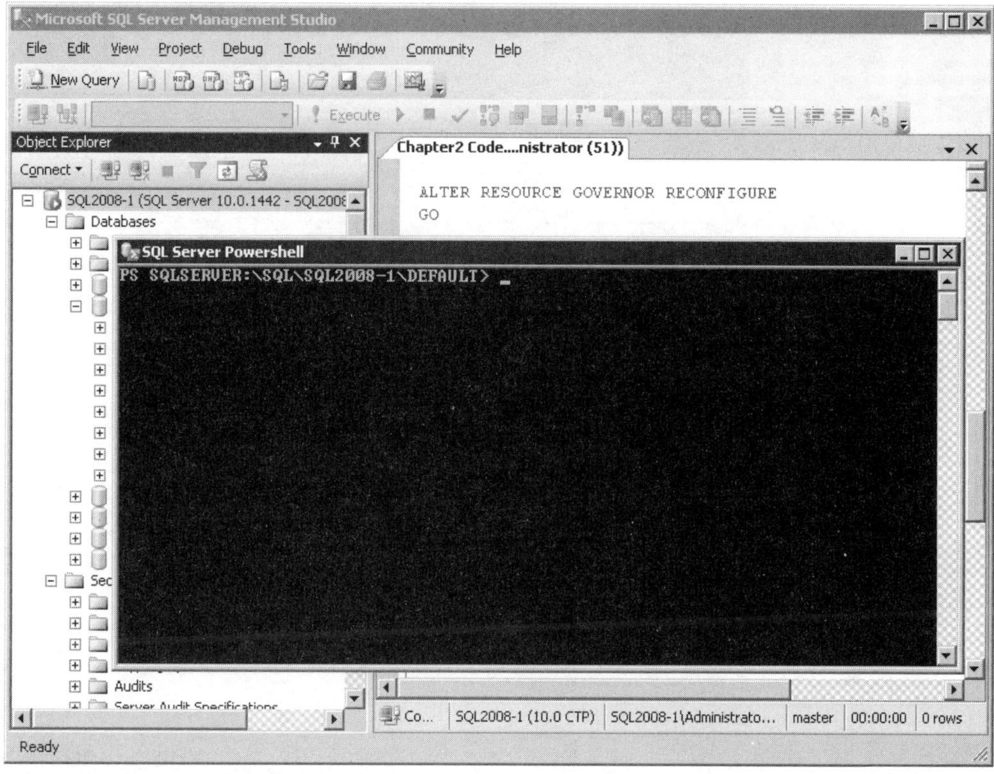

Figure 2-11 *The sqlps command shell*

PowerShell SQL Agent Integration

In addition to being integrated into the SQL Server Management Studio, PowerShell has also been integrated with the SQL Server Agent. SQL Server Agent jobs contain one or more job steps which can perform a number of different tasks, such as running T-SQL commands and executing operating system commands using the CmdExec command shell. With SQL Server 2008, PowerShell has been added to the types of actions that can be performed by a SQL Server Agent job step. You can see the new SQL Server Agent PowerShell option shown in Figure 2-12.

Selecting PowerShell as the type of task enables you to run PowerShell scripts from your SQL Server Agent job.

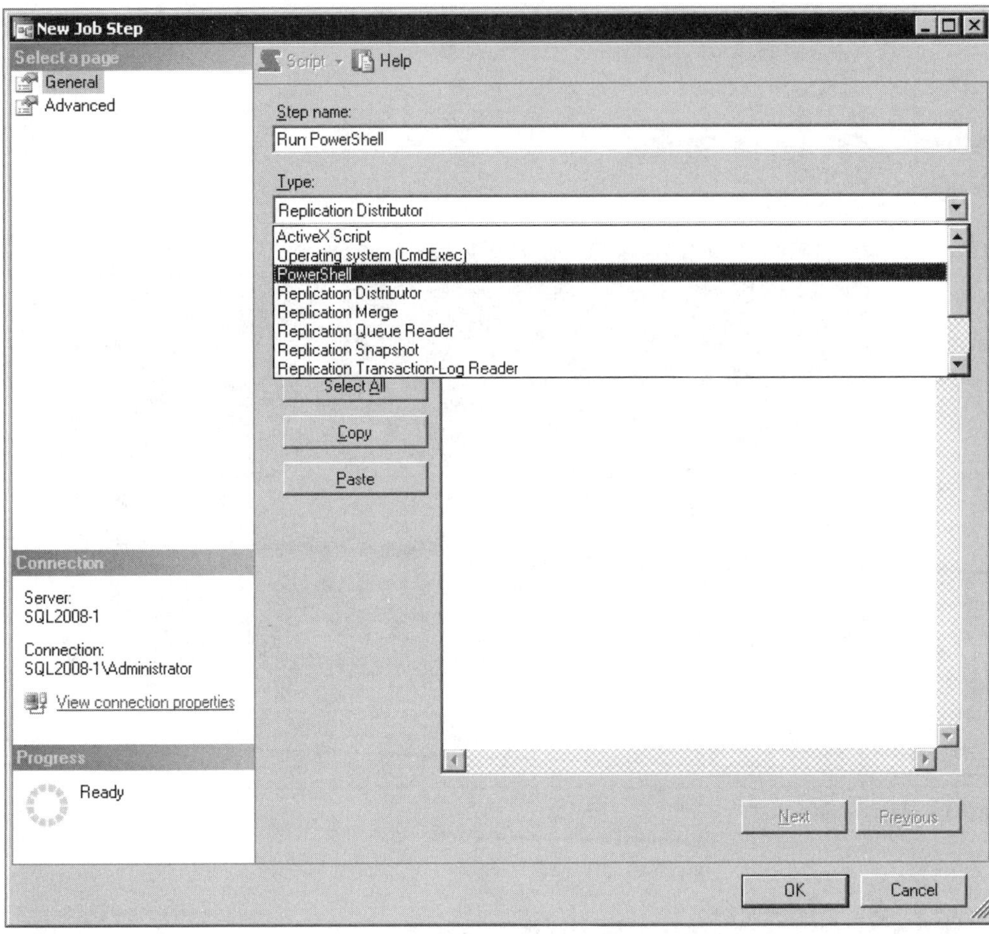

Figure 2-12 *SQL Server Agents PowerShell option*

PowerShell SQL Server Provider

PowerShell itself is both a command console and a scripting language. In order to connect to servers and other services, PowerShell utilizes specific providers. SQL Server 2008 comes with a PowerShell provider that enables you access to relational database objects, SQL Server policy objects, the Data Collector, and Registered Servers.

The PowerShell SQL Server Provider is built on top of SQL Server Management Objects (SMO) and enables you to navigate through SQL Server instances and database objects using the same hierarchy as the SMO framework. You can also utilize the methods and properties of the Microsoft.SqlServer.Managment.Smo class from PowerShell to manage SQL Server instances and databases. The SQL Server Provider begins with a drive designated as either SQLSERVER:\SQL, SQLSERVER:\SQLPolicy, SQLSERVER:\SQLRegistration, or SQLSERVER:\DataCollection, which all map to the SMO namespaces shown in the following table.

Provider Drive	SMO Namespaces Used
SQL:	Microsoft.SqlServer.Management.Smo Microsoft.SqlServer.Managment.Smo.Agent Microsoft.SqlServer.Management.Smo.Broker Microsoft.SqlServer.Managment.Smo.Mail
SQLPolicy	Microsoft.SqlServer.Management.Dmf Microsoft.SqlServer.Managment.Facets
SQLRegistration:	Microsoft.SqlServer.Management.RegisteredServers
DataCollection:	Microsoft.SqlServer.Management.Collector Microsoft.SqlServer.Management.CollectorEnum

The path structure that the provider uses is similar to the Windows file system. The SQL Server Relational Engine Provider begins with a path named SQL\SERVER: and works with a path as follows:

```
SQLSERVER:\SQL\ComputerName\InstanceName
```

When using the sqlps utility and the SQL Server Relational Database Provider, PowerShell will connect to the specified database instance and display the command prompt. At this point you can enter PowerShell commands or execute PowerShell scripts. In the following listing you can see the results of connecting the sqlps utility to the default instance on the SQL Server 2008 system named SQL2008-1.

```
PS SQLSQLSERVER:\SQL\SQL2008-1\DEFAULT> dir
Audits
BackupDevices
Credentials
CryptographicProviders
Databases
Endpoints
FullTextService
JobServer
Languages
LinkedServers
Logins
```

```
Mail
ProxyAccount
Roles
ServerAuditSpecifications
SystemDataTypes
SystemMessages
Triggers
UserDefinedMessages
PS SQLSERVER:\SQL\SQL2008-1\DEFAULT>
```

Here you can see that the Powershell Provider is connected using a path of SQL:\SQL2008-1\DEFAULT. Running the dir command (which is an alias for the native PowerShell get-children command) returns a top-level list of SQL Server management objects. You can drill down into any of these nodes using the cd command (an alias for the native PowerShell set-location command). Just as with the Windows command shell, wildcards work as well. For example, the following listing shows you how to get a listing of all of the tables in the AdventureWorks database using the Production schema.

```
PS SQLSERVER:\SQL\SQL2008-1\DEFAULT> cd Databases\AdventureWorks\Tables
PS SQLSERVER:\SQL\SQL2008-1\DEFAULT\Databases\AdventureWorks\Tables> dir
Production.*

Schema                   Name                          Created
------                   ----                          -------
Production               WorkOrderRouting              7/6/2007 9:44 PM
Production               WorkOrder                     7/6/2007 9:44 PM
Production               UnitMeasure                   7/6/2007 9:44 PM
Production               TransactionHistoryArchive     7/6/2007 9:44 PM
Production               TransactionHistory            7/6/2007 9:44 PM
Production               ScrapReason                   7/6/2007 9:44 PM
Production               ProductSubcategory            7/6/2007 9:44 PM
Production               ProductReview                 7/6/2007 9:44 PM
Production               ProductProductPhoto           7/6/2007 9:44 PM
Production               ProductPhoto                  7/6/2007 9:44 PM
Production               ProductModelProductDescription 7/6/2007 9:44 PM
                         Culture
Production               ProductModelIllustration      7/6/2007 9:44 PM
Production               ProductModel                  7/6/2007 9:44 PM
Production               ProductListPriceHistory       7/6/2007 9:44 PM
Production               ProductInventory              7/6/2007 9:44 PM
Production               ProductDocument               7/6/2007 9:44 PM
Production               ProductDescription            7/6/2007 9:44 PM
Production               ProductCostHistory            7/6/2007 9:44 PM
Production               ProductCategory               7/6/2007 9:44 PM
Production               Product                       7/6/2007 9:44 PM
```

```
Production                     Location                          7/6/2007 9:44 PM
Production                     Illustration                      7/6/2007 9:44 PM
Production                     Document                          7/6/2007 9:44 PM
Production                     Culture                           7/6/2007 9:44 PM
Production                     BillOfMaterials                   7/6/2007 9:44 PM

PS SQLSERVER:\SQL\SQL2008-1\DEFAULT\Databases\AdventureWorks\Tables>
```

At the top of this listing, you can see where the cd command is used to change directories into the Tables hierarchy of the AdventureWorks database. The dir command is then used with a wildcard symbol (*) to get a listing of all of the tables that use the Production schema.

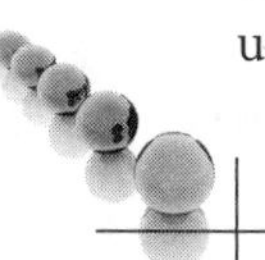

NOTE

Depending on your OS and database configuration, the PowerShell SQL Server Provider may be case sensitive. If your commands don't seem to work, you may need to use the exact database object capitalization.

The Invoke-Sqlcmd Cmdlet

Another PowerShell addition that's found in the SQL Server 2008 release is the new PowerShell cmdlets. There are actually a few different cmdlets, but the most important cmdlet is the Invoke-Sqlcmd cmdlet. The Invoke-Sqlcmd cmdlet executes a T-SQL statement or query on the SQL Server system. You can see an example of using the Invoke-Sqlcmd cmdlet in the following listing.

```
PS SQLSERVER:\SQL\SQL2008-1\DEFAULT> Invoke-Sqlcmd -Query "SELECT @@servername"

Column1
-------
SQL2008-1

PS SQLSERVER:\SQL\SQL2008-1\DEFAULT>
```

Here the Invoke-Sqlcmd cmdlet uses the –Query parameter to execute a query on the connected SQL Server instances. The query is enclosed in double quotes. In this example, the query returns using the @@servername system variable to return the SQL Server instance name.

The Invoke-Sqlcmd cmdlet can be run from the sqlps command shell as shown above, or it can be run from the standard external PowerShell command prompt. Invoke-Sqlcmd can perform many of the functions that you can do using the Sqlcmd and osql utilities.

Summary

SQL Server 2008 has a number of enhancements that make the DBA more productive and effective than ever before. SQL Server Management Studio now offers a set of dashboard performance reports that can give you a quick look at the overall health and performance of your servers. Plus, the new debugging, code outlining, and IntelliSense enhancements to Query Editor make writing T-SQL batches and stored procedures faster and less error prone. However, the most important new management feature in SQL Server 2008 is probably the new Resource Governor. The Resource Governor enables you to provide a more predictable execution environment and prevents poorly written queries from impacting the system's performance by limiting the system resources that are assigned to specific workloads. In addition, the new Policy-Based Management feature enables you to ensure that your organization's standards and required server and database configurations are consistent across all of the SQL Server 2008 servers in the enterprise. Finally, the new PowerShell integration enables you to write PowerShell scripts that manage SQL Server database objects and policies, as well as performing tasks from within SQL Server Agent jobs.

Chapter 3

Availability

New improvements in SQL Server 2008 have continued to enhance SQL Server's availability by increasing its failover clustering capabilities and providing new database options that facilitate both continuous availability as well as improved database recovery capabilities.

Achieving high availability is relatively easy on a small scale, but it gets exponentially more difficult as the size of the system increases. SQL Server 2008 provides a number of new features that enhance database availability and recoverability by addressing the primary obstacles that hinder enterprise level database availability. In this chapter, we'll take a look at the new availability and recovery options found in SQL Server 2008 so that you can understand how these features can be used to enhance SQL Server 2008's availability and speed your recovery in the event of unplanned downtime.

Protection Against Server Failure

A server failure is a disruption of server availability that's caused by either a hardware failure or a software issue that renders the server inoperable for a period of time. Server level outages can result from either planned events like routine system maintenance and upgrades, or they can be unplanned events like a hardware breakdown. Database server failure can also be caused by operator error or environmental factors like a natural disaster. In this section you'll learn about some of the most important new features that SQL Server 2008 provides for addressing database server failures.

Improved Failover Clustering Support

One significant, high-availability benefit that SQL Server 2008 derives in part from enhancements to Windows Server 2008 is improved support for failover clustering. In this section you'll get an overview of Windows Server 2008 failover clustering support and the SQL Server 2008 failover clustering enhancements.

Windows Failover Clustering Overview

Failover Clustering is Microsoft's primary high availability technology. With Windows Failover Clustering, multiple servers act together to provide a set of services. Each server in the cluster is called a *node*. All of the nodes in a cluster are in a state of constant communication. If one of the nodes in a cluster becomes unavailable, another node will take over running the services that were running on the failed node. This process is called *failover*. Users who are accessing the cluster are switched automatically to the new node. When the failed node is repaired, services can be restored to the node. This process is usually referred to as a *failback*.

Clustering can be set up in a couple of basic ways: active-active clustering, where all of the nodes are performing work, or active-passive clustering, where one or more of the nodes is dormant until an active node fails. For example, with a 16-node cluster you can have 15 of the 16 nodes set up to provide different services while the 16th node is a passive node that can assume the services of any of the 15 active nodes. While multi-node clusters like 16-node configurations are suitable for larger organizations, many smaller- and medium-sized businesses use two-node failover clustering configurations. In a two node configuration, both nodes can be active or one can be passive. If both nodes are active, the key point is to ensure that the nodes have adequate system resources to run both their primary workload as well as the workload from the failed node. Figure 3-1 illustrates an example two-node cluster, where a second node assumes the services run by the first node in the event of a server failure in the first node.

Failover Clustering Enhancements in Windows Server 2008

Some of the main enhancements to Failover Clustering that Windows Server 2008 provides are

- Support for up to 16 nodes in a failover cluster
- Broader hardware support
- A new cluster validation tool
- Simplified cluster configuration
- A new cluster configuration wizard
- A new Majority Quorum Model
- Support for geographically dispersed clusters across different subnets
- Support for IPv6

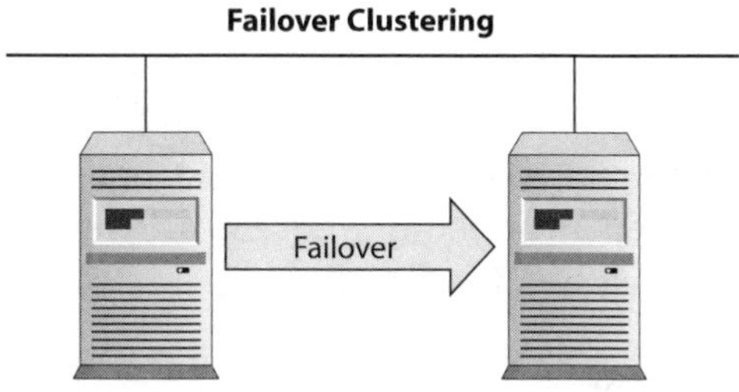

Figure 3-1 *Failover clustering*

For more detailed information about Windows Server 2008 Failover Clustering you can refer to http://www.microsoft.com/Windowsserver2008/en/us/clustering-home.aspx.

SQL Server 2008 Failover Clustering Enhancements

Taking advantage of the enhanced clustering support found in Windows Server 2008, SQL Server 2008 can now be implemented on up to 16 node clusters in Windows Server 2008 Datacenter Edition and Windows Server 2008 Enterprise Edition. SQL Server 2008 Standard Edition supports a maximum of two nodes. In addition, SQL Server 2008 supports eight-node clustering on Windows Server 2003 Enterprise Edition and Windows 2000 Datacenter Server. A maximum of two-node clustering is supported in Windows 2000 Advanced Server. A summary of Windows Server and SQL Server 2008 Failover Clustering maximum node support is shown in the following table:

Windows Server Edition	SQL Server 2008 Enterprise Edition	SQL Server 2008 Standard Edition	SQL Server 2008 Web Edition	SQL Server 2008 Workgroup Edition	SQL Server 2008 Express Edition
Windows Server 2008 Datacenter Edition	16	2	0	0	0
Windows Server 2008 Enterprise Edition	16	2	0	0	0
Windows Server 2008 Standard Edition	0	0	0	0	0
Windows Server 2008 Web Edition	0	0	0	0	0
Windows Server 2003 Datacenter Edition	8	8	0	0	0
Windows Server 2003 Enterprise Edition	8	8	0	0	0
Windows Server 2003 Standard Edition	0	0	0	0	0

Some of the clustering-specific improvements in SQL Server 2008 include support for an unattended cluster setup. In addition, all of the different services within SQL Server 2008 are fully cluster-aware including the

- Relational database engine
- Analysis Services
- Integration Services

- Reporting Services
- SQL Server Agent
- Full-Text Search
- Service Broker

Improved Support for Rolling Upgrades

Another important clustering enhancement in SQL Server 2008 is its improved support for rolling upgrades. With SQL Server 2008, you no longer need to take your cluster offline in order to apply patches and upgrades. Instead, you upgrade your passive nodes and then do a rolling upgrade. This makes upgrading your cluster easier, as you would essentially have just one failover required.

Hot-add CPU Support

SQL Server 2008's new hot-add CPU support can also help increase availability by eliminating one of the factors that can cause planned downtime. SQL Server 2008's hot-add CPU support enables it to recognize and utilize any new processors that are added to the system without affecting SQL Server 2008 uptime. With hot-add CPU support there's no need to reboot the server or to stop and start the SQL Server service in order to add new system processors. For physical servers the hardware must obviously support the ability to add CPUs while the system is running. When used in a VM, this facilitates dynamic reconfiguration, which allows SQL Server 2008 to adapt to changing workloads. More information about SQL Server 2008's hot-add CPU support is available in Chapter 1.

Database Availability Enhancements

While Failover Clustering protects against server-level failure, not all downtime is the result of a server-level failure. SQL Server 2008 also includes new features that can provide increased database-level availability. Three of the most important new availability features that provide increased database availability in SQL Server 2008 are database mirroring, peer-to-peer replication, and database backup.

Database Mirroring Enhancements

Database mirroring was first added to SQL Server with the SQL Server 2005 release; it protects against database or server failure by mirroring all of the changes in a database to a backup database and providing database level failover. In the event that the primary database fails, database mirroring enables a second standby database to be available in seconds. Database mirroring can be set up with a single database or it can be set up for multiple databases. It provides zero data loss, and the mirrored database will always be up-to-date with the most recent transactions from the principal database server. Database mirroring can be set up for user databases but not system databases. The impact of running database mirroring to transaction throughput is minimal. Database mirroring works with all of the standard hardware that supports SQL Server, so there is no need for special systems, and the primary server and the mirrored servers do not need to be identical to the principal servers. You can see an overview of how the database mirroring feature works in Figure 3-2.

Database mirroring works by sending transaction logs from the principal server to the mirroring server. So in essence, the database mirroring feature is a real-time, log shipping application. When a client system writes a request to the primary server, the request actually gets written to the primary server's log file before being written into the data file because SQL Server uses a write-ahead log. Next, the transaction record gets sent to the mirroring server where it is written to the data mirroring server's transaction log. In order to keep the data files up-to-date on the mirroring server, it is essentially in a state of continuous recovery: taking the data from the log and updating the data file.

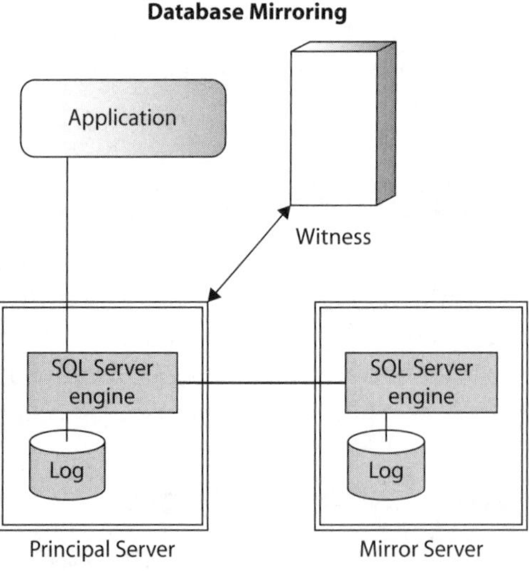

Figure 3-2 *Database mirroring*

Database Mirroring Performance Enhancements

SQL Server 2008's database mirroring has had a number of performance enhancements that improve availability as you'll see in the following sections.

Compression of the Mirroring Data Stream With SQL Server 2008, the performance of data mirroring has been significantly enhanced by compressing the data stream sent between the principal server and the mirror server. Compressing the data stream improves the performance of database mirroring by reducing the data that's sent over the network from the principal server to the mirror server. The new SQL Server 2008 data stream compression ratios very based on the data but achieve a minimum of 12.5 percent compression.

Write-ahead Log Data The ability to perform write-ahead for the incoming log data on the mirror server is another important performance enhancement in SQL Server 2008's database mirroring. Write-ahead allows the mirror to asynchronously write incoming log data to disk. This enables the processing of the data written to the transaction log to occur at the same time that log data is received at the mirror server.

More Efficient Use of Log Send Buffers Another performance enhancement in SQL Server 2008 is the improved use of log send buffers. SQL Server 2005 always used the entire log send buffers for every log flush action initiated by the principal server. For SQL Server 2008, the system checks if there is adequate space in the log send buffer for the data flushed from the log. If adequate space is available, the data will be appended to the current log buffer, which allows database mirroring to make more efficient use of the network bandwidth.

Read-ahead During Undo Database mirroring in SQL Server 2008 also features the ability to perform read-ahead processing during the undo phase of recovering the transaction log. SQL Server 2008's new read-ahead capability allows the mirror server to tell the principal server which pages it needs to perform and undo for the transaction log early in the undo process. This enables the principal server to read ahead and retrieve the required pages. This makes the undo process faster for the mirror server.

Automatic Recovery of Corrupted Pages

Another new enhancement to database mirroring in SQL Server 2008 is automated recovery from corrupted pages. If the mirroring partner is unable to read a data page, then that page will be reread from the other system. Automated recovery of data pages makes database mirroring more resilient and more resistant to data corruption.

Peer-to-Peer Replication

Peer-to-peer replication enables SQL Server 2008 to maintain copies of a database on multiple SQL Server instances. It was first introduced in SQL Server 2005 and was built on SQL Server's transactional replication technology. Peer-to-peer replication enables SQL Server to propagate database changes for identical databases across multiple systems in near real time. It can be used as a scale-out technology to increase query performance by spreading queries across multiple SQL Server instances. It can also act as an availability technology. Unlike failover clustering or database mirroring, applications must be coded to connect to an available node if the primary database is unavailable.

Hot-add New Replication Nodes

With SQL Server 2008, peer-to-peer replication has been enhanced to enable the addition of new replication nodes to an existing peer-to-peer replication configuration without requiring the replication process to be stopped and restarted. This provides improved business continuity for all systems participating in the peer-to-peer replication setup.

Graphical Configure Peer-to-Peer Topology Wizard

Another new enhancement to SQL Server 2008 peer-to-peer replication is the new graphical Configure Peer-to-Peer Topology wizard. The new Configure Peer-to-Peer wizard enables you to visually configure peer-to-peer replication. The Configure Peer-to-Peer Topology enables you to add nodes, delete nodes, and create links between SQL Server systems participating in peer-to-peer replication.

To use the new Configure Peer-to-Peer Topology Wizard you first need to create a new publication. Next, you need to enable peer-to-peer subscriptions by right-clicking on the publication and then selecting the Properties option to display the publication properties. Finally, use the Subscription Options properties and change the Allow Peer-to-Peer Subscriptions property to True as shown in Figure 3-3.

After you've set the Allow Peer-to-Peer Subscription property to True, right-clicking on the subscription in SQL Server Management Studio displays a new Configure Peer-to-Peer Topology option. Selecting that option starts the Configure Peer-to-Peer

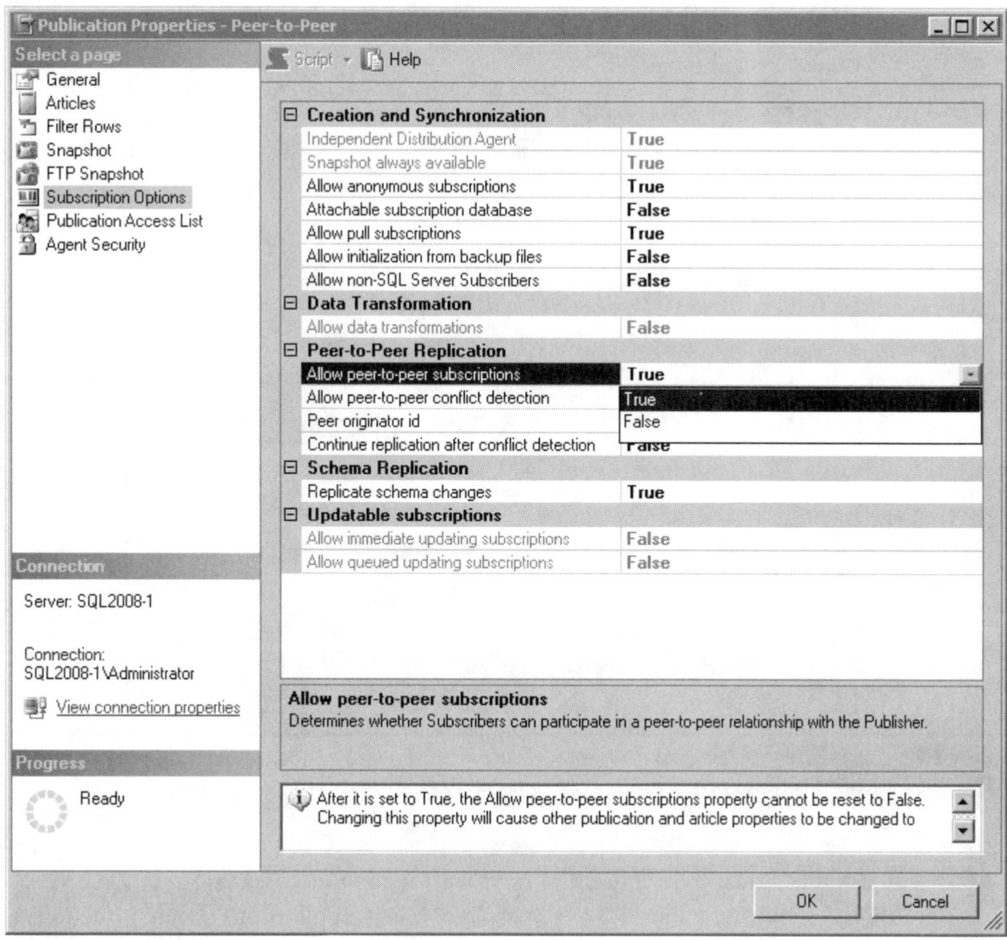

Figure 3-3 *Enabling peer-to-peer subscriptions*

Topology wizard. You can see an example of the graphical design surface of the Configure Peer-to-Peer Topology wizard in Figure 3-4.

Conflict Detection

SQL Server 2008's peer-to-peer replication has also been enhanced with the ability to detect conflicts. *Conflicts* can be caused when an application inserts the same row on multiple nodes with potentially different data. If SQL Server 2008's peer-to-peer replication detects a conflict in the databases that are participating in peer-to-peer replication,

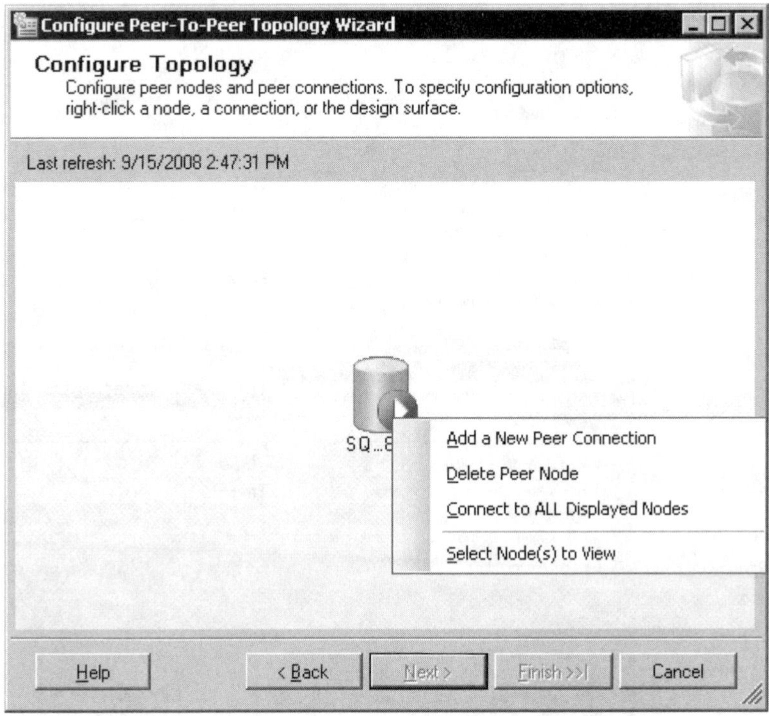

Figure 3-4 *Configure Peer-to-Peer Topology Wizard*

SQL Server 2008 will treat the conflict as a critical error and the distribution service will be stopped until the conflict is resolved. To help avoid conflicts, applications should be coded to ensure that they only update data on a single node in the peer-to-peer replication topology.

Backup Compression

SQL Server 2008 database compression capability extends into the area of database backups as well as online storage. Database backup compression can result in compression ratios of up upwards of 50 percent, which can significantly reduce the I/O required to backup your databases. Reducing the I/O required for SQL Server 2008's backup operations results in faster backup times, which simultaneously reduce the required database backup window and increase the availability of the database to the end users.

NOTE

You can't use database backup compression with TDE because encrypted data can't be compressed.

Data Availability

In addition to server and database availability, another level of availability is at the data level. Factors such as locking and concurrency can reduce end user access to data. One new feature in SQL Server 2008 that improves data availability is SQL Server 2008's new table-level lock escalation capability.

Table Level Lock Escalation

Table-level lock escalation increases data availability by enabling you to have more control over how the SQL Server relational engine places locks on partitioned tables. With SQL Server 2005, any table-level locks that were acquired by the database engine would lock the entire table, including all of the partitions for partitioned tables. SQL Server 2008 provides the ability to control the way locks are placed on partitioned tables. You can see how to use SQL Server 2008's table lock escalation feature in the following listing:

```
USE NewFeaturesDB
GO

CREATE TABLE MyPartitionedTable (ID INT, Data VARCHAR(50))
GO

ALTER TABLE MyPartitionedTable SET (LOCK_ESCALATION = AUTO)
GO
```

In the previous listing you can see where the current database is set to the NewFeaturesDB database (which is used for many of the samples in this book). Next, the CREATE TABLE is used to create a new table named MyPartitionedTable. Finally, the ALTER TABLE statement is used to set the table's lock escalation to AUTO.

NOTE

Table lock escalation can only be set using the ALTER TABLE statement

You can see the available values for the ALTER TABLE's LOCK_ESCALTION option in the following table.

LOCK_ESCALTION Value	Description
TABLE	Lock escalation will always be at the table level. This is the default value
AUTO	Lock escalation will be at the partition level if the table is partitioned. For unpartitioned tables the lock escalation will at the table level.
DISABLE	Lock escalation will be disabled. However, this does not prevent table locks. SQL Server 2008 will still acquire table locks when it needs to.

Lock Escalation Dynamic Management Views

You can use SQL Server 2008's Dynamic Management Views (DMV) to determine a table lock's escalation status. The following query shows you how to retrieve the lock_escalation_desc column from the sys.tables DMV:

```
SELECT lock_escalation_desc FROM sys.tables
  WHERE name = 'MyPartitionedTable'
```

You can see the results in the following listing.

```
lock_escalation_desc
------------------------------------------------------------
AUTO

(1 row(s) affected)
```

Summary

In this chapter you've seen a number of enhancements that have improved SQL Server's availability at the server level, the database level, and the data level. At the server level, SQL Server is able to take full advantage of Windows Server 2008's increased nodes capacity to make it more resistant to server failures. At the database level, enhancements to database mirroring, such as the automatic recovery of corrupted database pages, improve the resiliency of the database mirroring process. At the data level, enhancements to the SQL Server table-lock escalation can improve the availability of data in partitioned tables.

In the next chapter, you'll get an introduction to the new ADO.NET Entity Framework.

Part II

Database Development Features

Chapter 4

ADO.NET Entity Framework

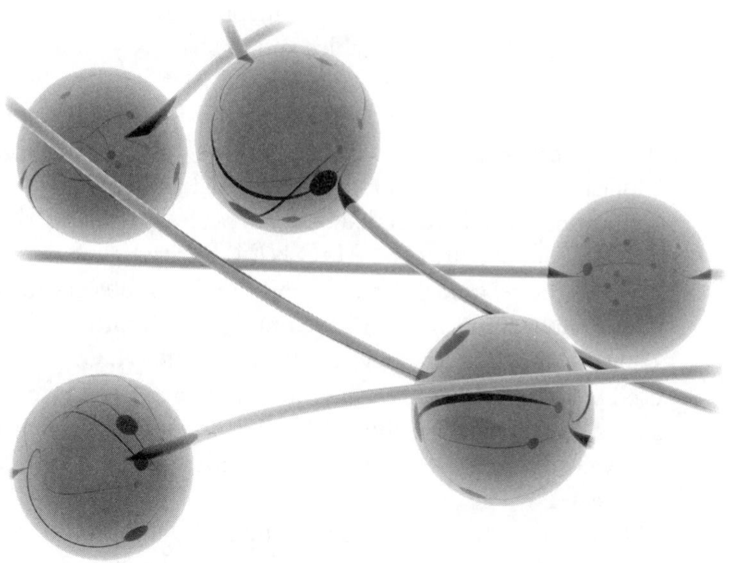

While it's not technically a part of SQL Server 2008, the ADO.NET Entity Framework embodies a new development tool and methodology for SQL Server database developers. The ADO.NET Entity Framework is a set of technologies built on the Microsoft ADO.NET middleware, which enables you to abstract an underlying database into a set of .NET based objects. This enables your application developers to focus more on the business level and on solving business problems, and less on the details of the underlying relational database implementation. In the first part of this chapter, you'll get an overview of the ADO.NET Entity Framework and see how it relates to ADO.NET and the .NET Framework. You'll also learn about the object-relational mapping performed by the ADO.NET Entity Framework. In the second part of this chapter, you'll learn about how the ADO.NET Entity Framework can be used to generate .NET code from relational database data sources and how you can make use of that code in your .NET applications.

An Overview the ADO.NET Entity Framework

The ADO.NET Entity Framework is included with the .NET Framework 3.5 as well as with Visual Studio 2008. It provides relational-to-object mapping for relational databases. The primary benefit of mapping your relational database objects to .NET objects is the fact that it enables you to abstract your application's database access layer from your application's business objects. This enables the application developer to focus on the logic and details of the business application without needing to be aware of the details of the raw underlying database schema and objects. This enables applications to work in a more conceptual and application-centric model, freeing the application from hard-coded dependencies on the underlying database. To enable this development scenario, the ADO.NET Entity Framework creates a set of mappings between the relational database and the .NET objects and classes that are consumed by the application. You can have multiple conceptual object models mapped to the same schema. Plus, the objects created by the ADO.Net Entity Framework can be used by the new Language Integrated Query (LINQ) features of the .NET Framework 3.5. More information about LINQ is presented in the next chapter. You can see an overview of the basic functionally provided by the ADO.NET Entity Framework in Figure 4-1.

In Figure 4-1, you can see that the ADO.NET Entity Framework works by first taking relational database objects from the database source and then using them to create a conceptual .NET object representation of those database objects. The .NET objects will have properties that map to the relational database objects and as code that enables the .NET objects to retrieve data from the relational data source, as well as

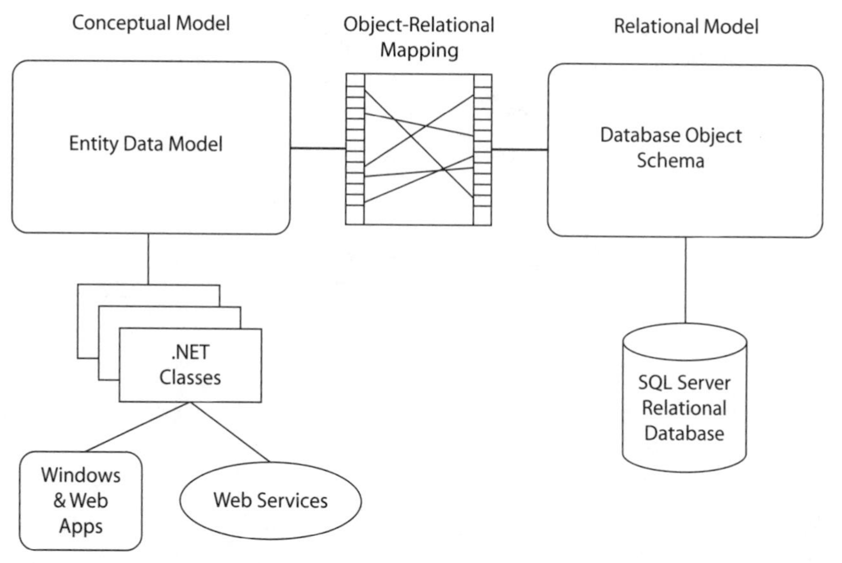

Figure 4-1 *An overview of the ADO.NET Entity Framework*

code that posts inserts and updates to the data source. For example, a Customers table in the database might be mapped to a Customers class. The Customers class would contain properties that represent columns and methods that perform data access operations. A .NET application, like a Windows, Web, or Web Services application, then incorporates the .NET-based classes generated by the ADO.NET Entity Framework and uses them for database access.

The ADO.NET Entity Framework and the .NET Framework

The .NET Entity Framework was first introduced with Visual Studio 2008 in conjunction with SQL Server 2008, but technically because it is built on ADO.NET it can connect to any data source that has a .NET data provider. You can see an overview of the relationship of the ADO.NET Entity Framework and the.NET Framework stack in Figure 4-2.

Working your way up from the bottom of the diagram shown in Figure 4-2, you can see that the relational data source is the core of the data that's used by the ADO .NET Entity Framework. The ADO.NET Entity Framework can build Entity Data

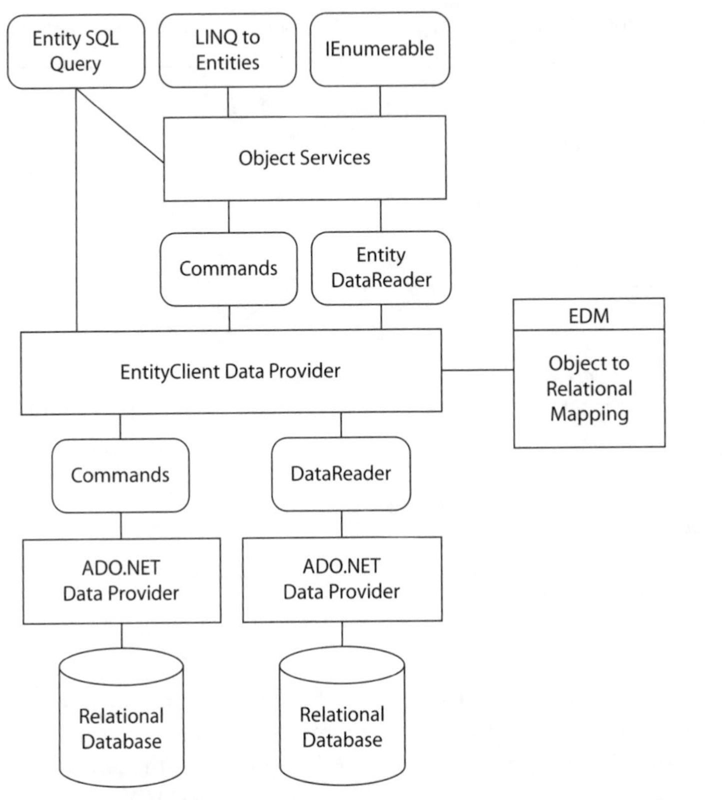

Figure 4-2 *The ADO.NET Entity Framework and the .NET Framework*

Models (EDM) using one or more relational databases. ADO.NET is the data access middleware used by the ADO.NET Entity Framework to connect to relational databases. The ADO.NET Entity Framework can connect to any data source that has an ADO.NET Data Provider. Just as one or more data sources can be used in an EDM, one or more EDMs can be built over the same data source. The ADO.NET Entity Framework's EntityClient Data Provider is an object layer on top of the ADO .NET Data Provider. The EntityClient Data Provider uses the ADO.Net DataReader to read data from the ADO.NET Data Provider, and the ADO.NET Command object to execute commands using the ADO.NET Data Provider. The EntityClient Data

Provider manages the connection to the ADO.NET Data Providers and transforms entity queries into relational SQL queries. Object Services uses the EDM to translate object queries into data provider-specific queries. Object Services also translates query results into objects. The ADO.NET Entity Framework responds to three types of queries: Entity SQL queries, LINQ queries, and IEnumerables requests. IEnumerable requests simply return lists of data. LINQ queries return objects to applications. You can learn more about LINQ in Chapter 5. Entity SQL is a SQL-like language that is supported by the ADO.NET Entity Framework and can be used to send queries through object services or directly to the EntityClient Data Provider. For more information about the basic concepts of the ADO.NET Entity Framework you can refer to: http://msdn.microsoft.com/en-us/library/aa697427(VS.80).aspx.

Using the ADO.NET Entity Framework with SQL Server 2008

The basis for using the ADO.NET Entity Framework with SQL Server 2008 is the creation of a new Entity Data Model (EDM). There are several different ways to create the EDM. SQL Server 2008 ships with the command-line SqlMetal tool as well as with the O/R Designer. You can learn more about those tools in Chapter 5, but in this chapter you'll see how you can use Visual Studio 2008 to create the EDM.

Creating a New Entity Data Model with Visual Studio 2008

To create a new EDM using Visual Studio 2008, first start Visual Studio 2008 Professional and then open a new project.

NOTE

Creating entity data models is not supported in the Express Editions of Visual Studio 2008.

In this example, you'll see how to create a new ADO.NET Entity Framework project using a Visual Basic Windows Forms application. From the Visual Studio 2008 menu select the File | New Project option to display the New Project dialog, as shown in Figure 4-3.

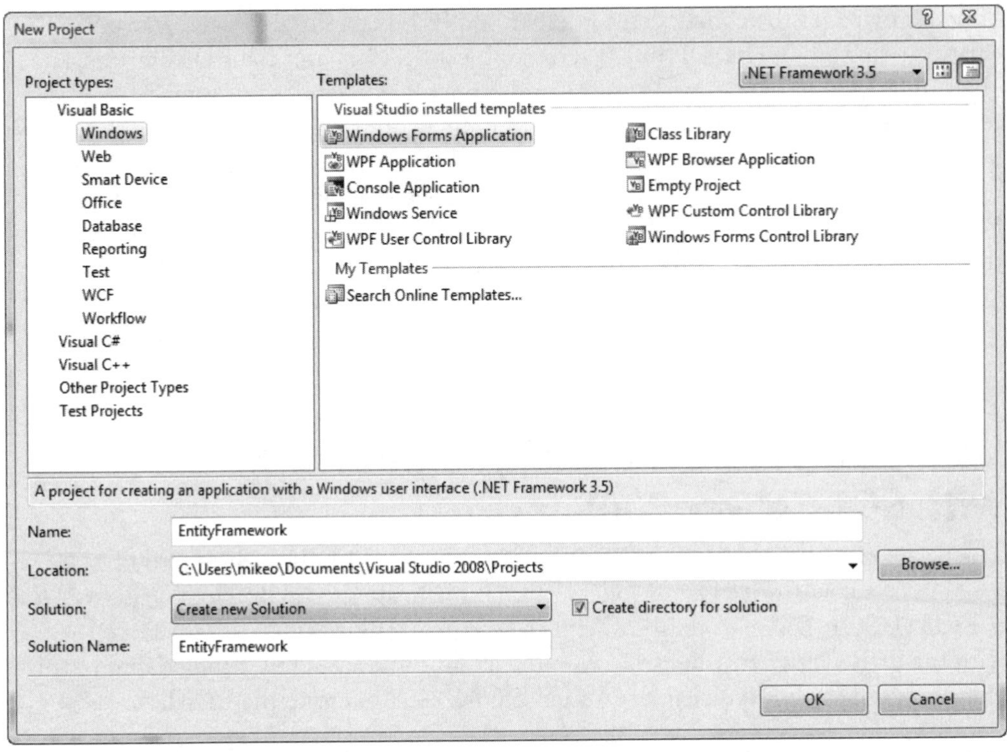

Figure 4-3 *Building a new ADO.NET Entity Framework project*

In Figure 4-3, you can see that I've selected a Windows Forms Application and have named the applications Entity Framework. Clicking on the OK button will cause Visual Studio to create a new Windows Forms application. To create a new EDM for the Windows Forms application, right click on the project name in the Solution Explorer window and then select the Add | New Item option from the context menu to open the Add New Item dialog that you can see in Figure 4-4.

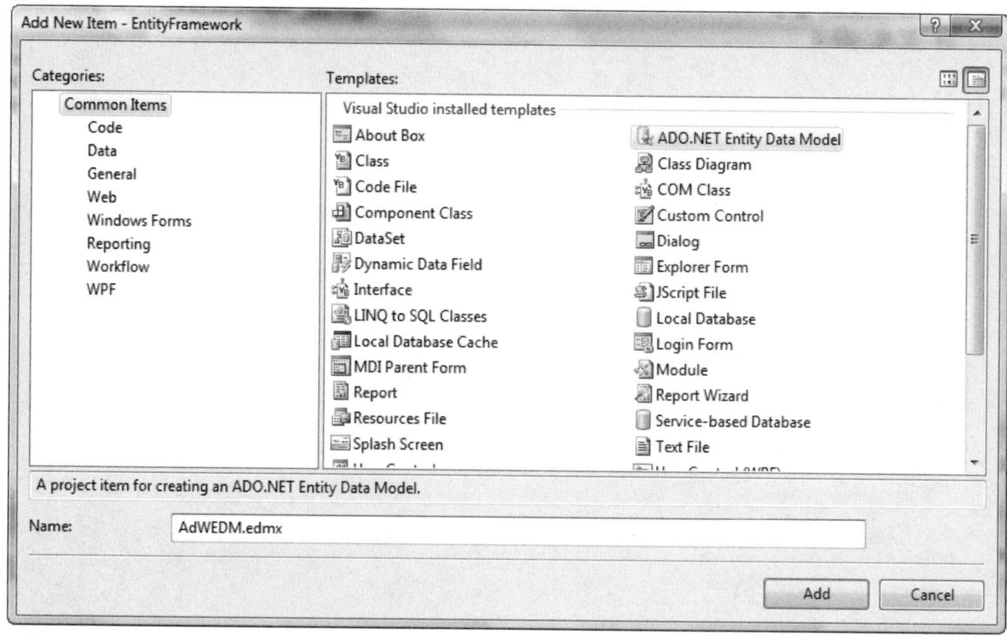

Figure 4-4 *Adding an ADO.NET Entity Framework item*

From the Add New Item dialog, scroll in the Templates list until you see the ADO .NET Entity Data Model option. Select that option from the list and then click Add to start the Entity Data Model Wizard shown in Figure 4-5.

The first screen in the Entity Data Model Wizard asks you how you want to create the EDM. You can choose to create the EDM from an existing database, or you can choose to create the EDM from scratch by visually designing the EDM. Building the EDM from the database is certainly the quickest method and can automate much of the process for you. However, it essentially generates a relatively simple one-class-per-table EDM. If you want to build more complex object-to-relational maps, then you would want to use the visual designer. For this example, choose the Generate from Database

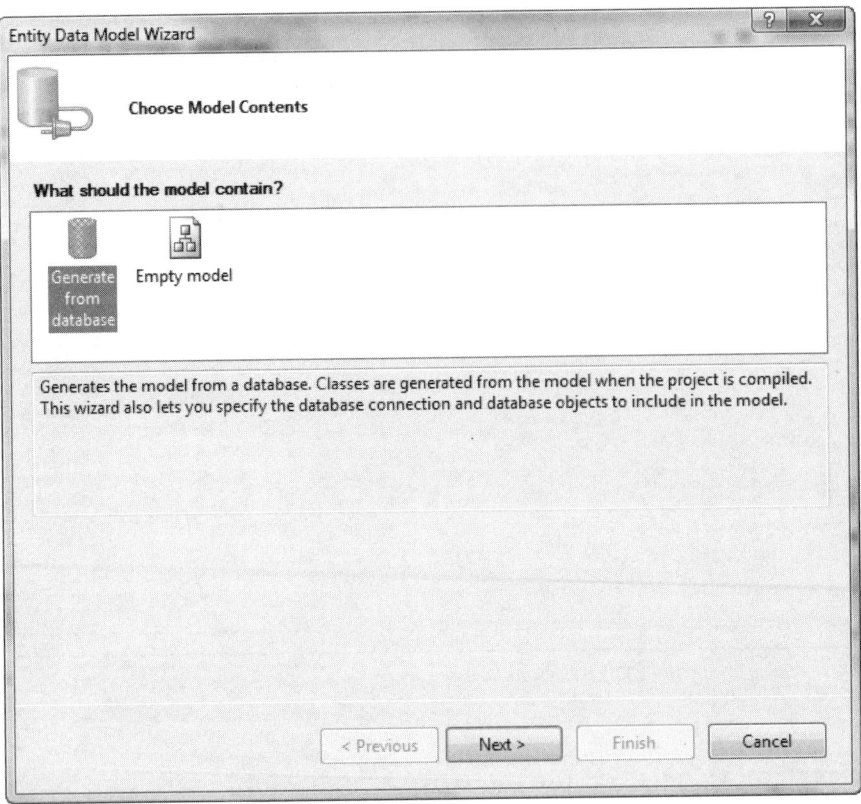

Figure 4-5 *Entity Data Model Wizard – Choose Model Contents*

option and then click Next. This will display the Choose Your Data Connection dialog that is shown in Figure 4-6.

The Entity Data Model Wizard's Choose Your Data Connection screen enables you to choose the Visual Studio Data Connection that you want to use. Visual Studio 2008 Data Connections are created by opening the Server Explorer and then right clicking and selecting the New | Data Connection option. This will present a dialog that allows you to select the desired database server, authentication method, and database. Alternatively, if you haven't previously created a Data Connection, you can click the New Connection button on the wizard dialog and create the Data Connection at this point. In this example you can see that the existing Data Connection name, sql2008-1.AdventureWorks.dbo, has been selected. The other prompts on the dialog allow you to specify if you will be saving potentially sensitive information and if you

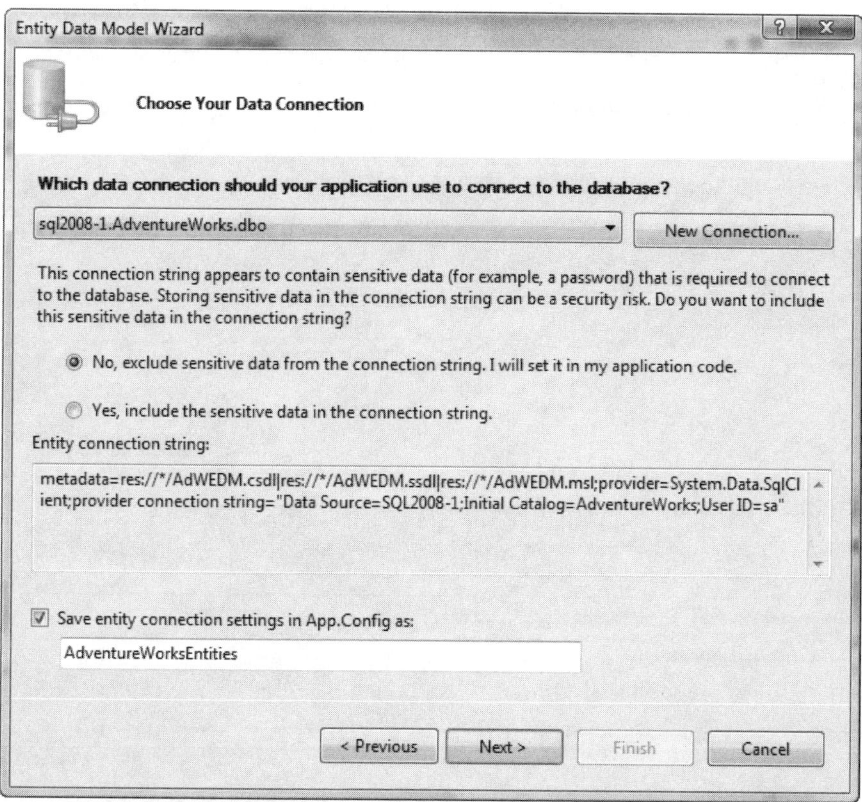

Figure 4-6 *Entity Data Model Wizard – Choose Your Data Connection*

want to create an App.Config file. Sensitive information essentially refers to your authentication information and including it is typically not recommended. The App .Config file contains database connection information. In most cases you will want to use an App.Config file. Clicking Next displays the Choose Your Database Objects dialog shown in Figure 4-7.

You can use the Entity Data Model Wizard's Choose Your Database Objects screen to select the database objects that the wizard will map into .NET classes. In Figure 4-7 you can see that all of the Tables, Views, and Stored Procedures in the AdventureWorks database will be mapped. However, you could also selectively map individual objects by clicking on the plus sign in front of each node and then drilling into and checking just the desired database objects. After choosing the desired database, clicking Finish generates the EDM.

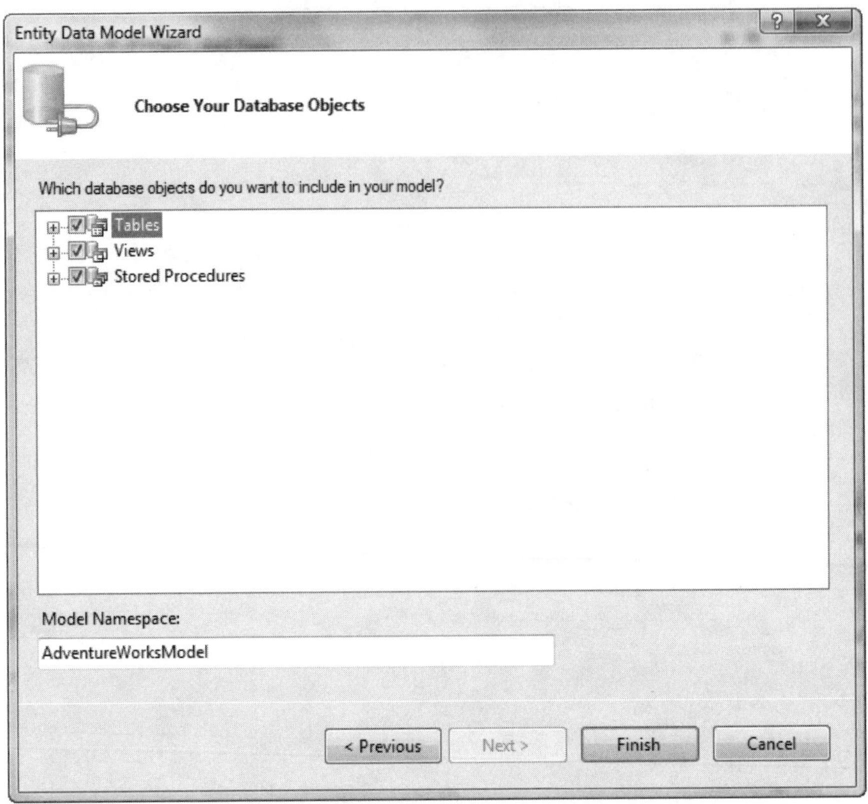

Figure 4-7 *Entity Data Model Wizard – Choose Your Database Objects*

The ADO.NET Entity Frameworks EDM is stored in an XML file ending in .edmx. In the previous example, you saw that the name of AdWEDM was used for the EDM. This directed the wizard to generate the EDM, as shown in the file named AdWEDM.edmx. You can see the partial output of the Entity Data Model Wizard in Figure 4-8.

The ADO.NET Entity Model Designer, shown in the upper left of Figure 4-8, provides a graphical representation of the EDM. Clicking on any of the different objects shown in the Object Browser will populate the Mapping Details pane shown in the lower left portion of Figure 4-8. The Mapping Details pane shows the .NET object properties names and data types and how each property is mapped to the SQL Server database objects and data types. The Model Browser shown in the upper right portion of the screen lists all of the generated classes and their foreign key associations.

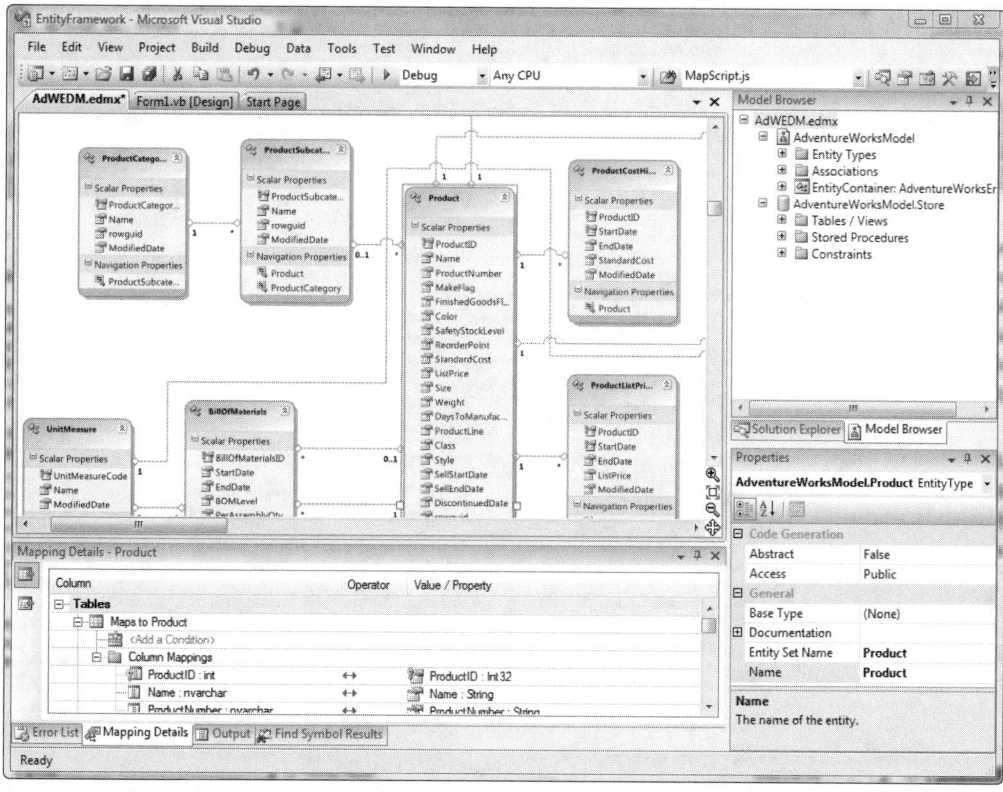

Figure 4-8 *The completed Entity Data Model*

The generated .edmx file is an XML file; opening the AdWEDM.edx file with Visual Studio 2008's XML Editor will show you the XML contents shown in Figure 4-9.

All of the selected database objects are represented by different XML elements; in Figure 4-9 you can see how the Purchasing.vVendor view from the AdventureWorks databases is mapped to the EntityType named "vVendor."

With ADO.NET Entity Framework you need to add import statements for the System.Data.Objects and System.Data.Objects.DataClasses assemblies and then instantiate the EDM in your applications. Example Visual Basic code using the AdWEDM entity model created in the previous section is shown in the next section of this chapter.

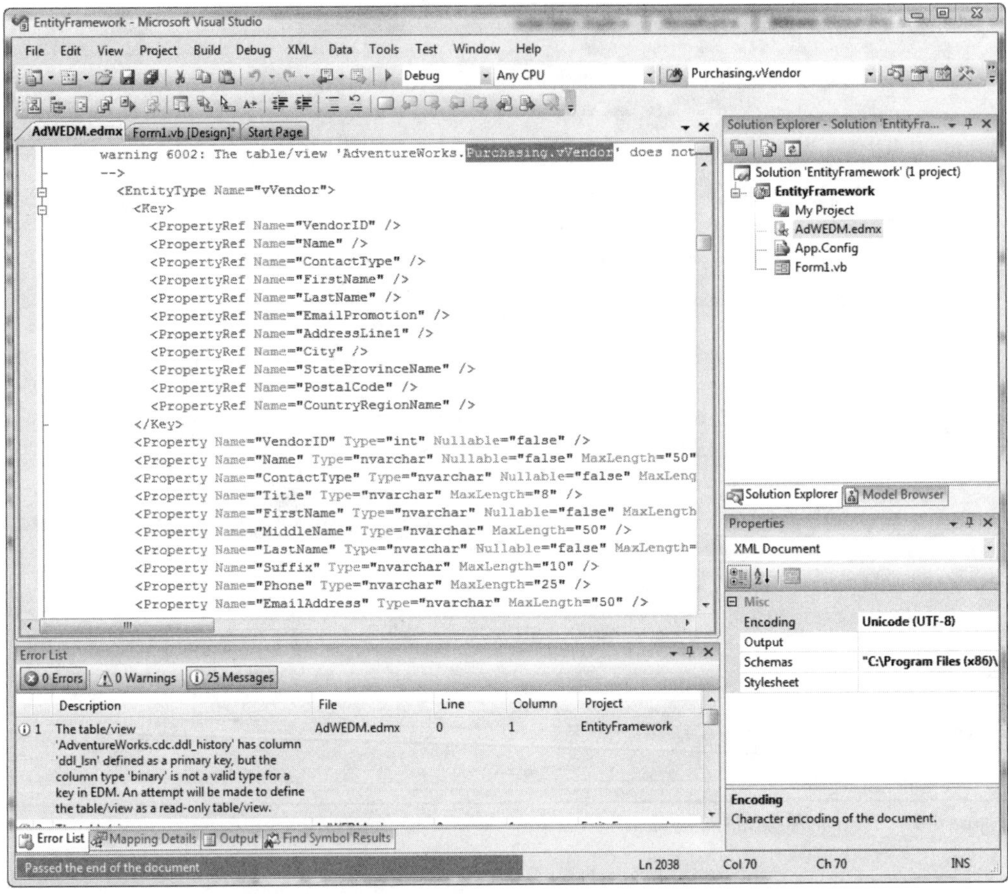

Figure 4-9 *The Entity Data Model's XML representation*

Using the Entity Data Model in Your Applications

The Entity Data Model Wizard generates the .edmx file that is added to your Visual Studio 2008 project. It also adds references to the System.Data.Entity, System .Runtime.Serialization, and System.Security assemblies to your project. At this point, you can add the .NET code to use the new entity data model in your applications.

To use the ADO.NET Entity Framework in your application, double click on the form you created when you first created the new Windows Forms project. This will open the form in the Visual Studio Designer. Then open the toolbox and scroll down until you see the DataGridView. Click on the DataGridView and then drag it onto the Form in the Designer. This will cause the DataGridViewTasks dialog to automatically open up, as you can see in Figure 4-10.

Click the Choose Data Source drop-down list and then choose the Add Project data source option from the bottom of the dialog box. This will display the Data Source Configuration Wizard that you can see in Figure 4-11.

The first screen in the Data Source Configuration Wizard prompts you to choose the type of data source that you want to connect the new DataGridView to. One of the benefits of the ADO.NET Entity Framework is that you can use it as a data binding source, just as you can use relational database tables and views as data sources. To use the ADO.NET Entity Framework as the data source, select the Object icon and

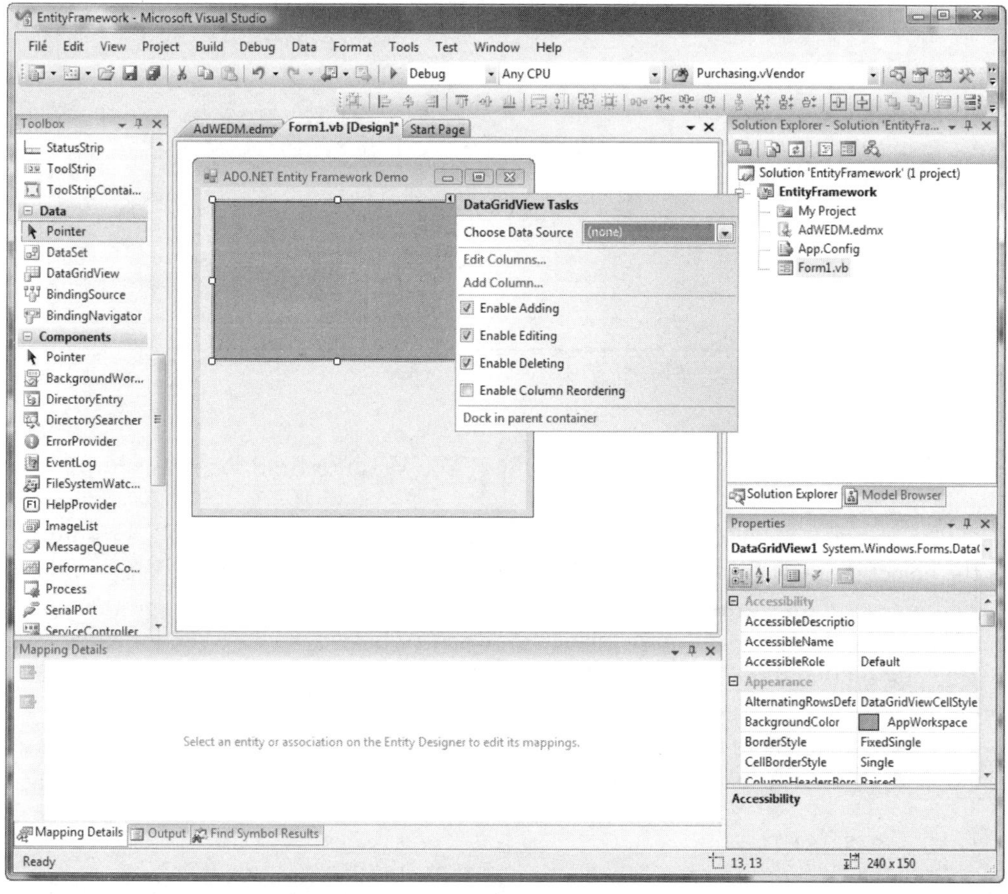

Figure 4-10 *Connecting the DataGridView to the Entity Data Model*

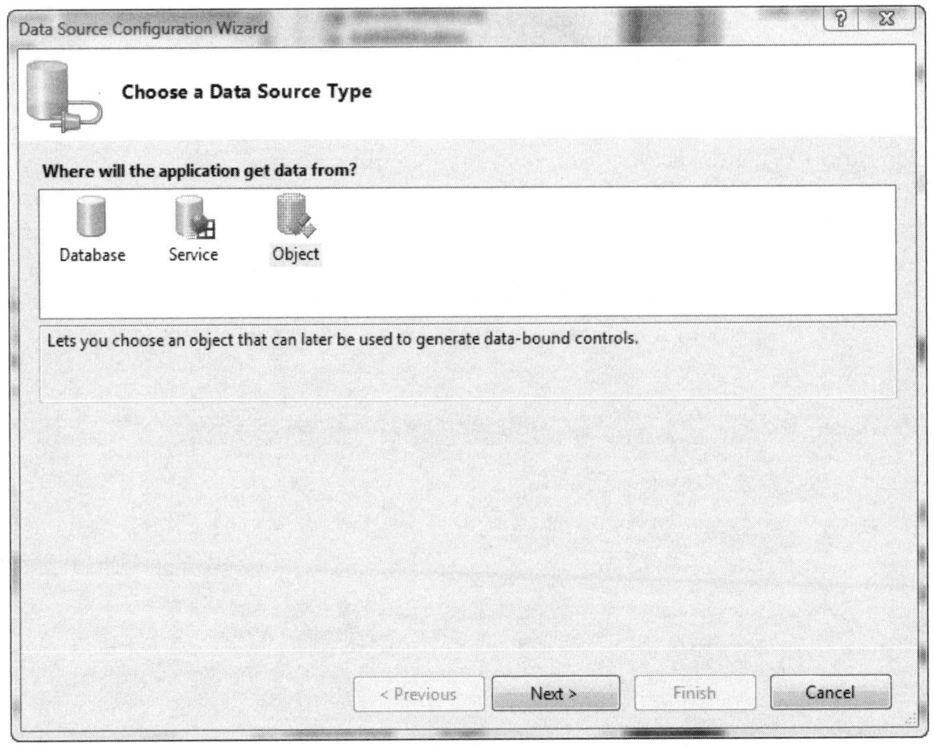

Figure 4-11 *Data Source Configuration Wizard – Choose a Data Source Type*

then click Next to display the Select the Object You Wish to Bind to screen shown in Figure 4-12.

The EntityFramework will be shown at the top of the list entitled In what assembly is the object located? In this example, you'll see how to bind the DataGridView to the vVendor class. Expand the EntityFramework by clicking on the plus sign and then scroll through the list until you see the vVendor entry. Select the the vVendor entry by clicking on it and then click Finish. This will add a vVendorBindingSource to your project.

Next, add the code to your project to set the DataGridViews DataSource property to the vVendor object. You can see the required data binding code in the following listing:

```
Public Class Form1
    Private AdWContext As AdventureWorksEntities

    Private Sub Form1_Load(ByVal sender As Object, _
```

```
        ByVal e As System.EventArgs) Handles Me.Load
        AdWContext = New AdventureWorksEntities()

        Try
            ' Query all data from the vVendor object
            Dim vendors = AdWContext.vVendor
            ' Bind the vendors object to the DataGridView
            DataGridView1.DataSource = vendors
        Catch ex As Exception
            MessageBox.Show(ex.Message)
        End Try

    End Sub
End Class
```

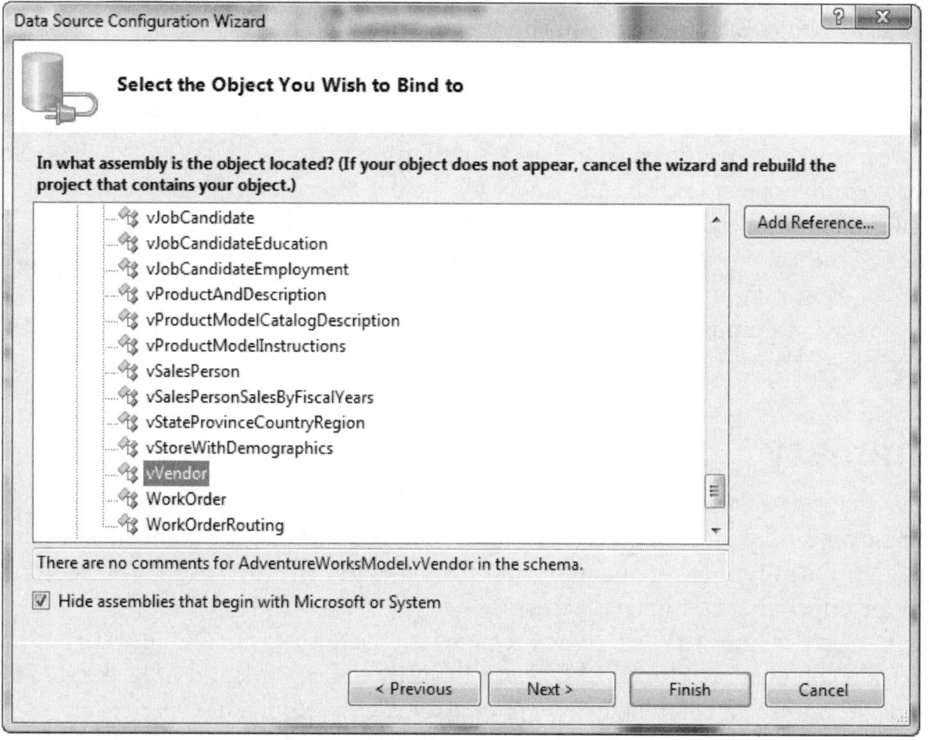

Figure 4-12 *Data Source Configuration Wizard – Select the Object You Wish to Bind to*

ADO.NET Entity Framework Demo

VendorID	Name	ContactType	Title
1	International	Assistant Sales A...	Ms.
2	Electronic Bike R...	Assistant Sales A...	Mr.
9	A. Datum Corpor...	Assistant Sales A...	Mr.
16	Image Makers Bi...	Assistant Sales A...	Ms.
26	First National Spo...	Assistant Sales A...	Ms.
28	Wide World Impo...	Assistant Sales A...	Ms.
29	Integrated Sport ...	Assistant Sales A...	Mr.
31	Federal Sport	Assistant Sales A...	Ms.
34	Indiana Bicycle C...	Assistant Sales A...	
37	Inner City Bikes	Assistant Sales A...	Ms.
39	Hill's Bicycle Serv...	Assistant Sales A...	Mr.
59	Electronic Bike Co.	Assistant Sales A...	Mr.

Figure 4-13 *Using the ADO.NET Entity Framework in your applications*

At the top of this listing, a new Object Context object named AdWContext is declared using the AventureWorksEntities definition from the AdWEDM class. Next, a new Vendors object is created to query all the data from the vVendors object. The DataGridView1 object's DataSource property is assigned the Vendors object.

Resize the Form and DataViewGrid to fit your screen requirements and then click the green Run icon in the Visual Studio 2008 toolbar to execute the VB application. You can see the example application using the ADO.NET Entity Framework shown in Figure 4-13.

Summary

In this chapter you've seen how the ADO.NET Entity Framework can abstract your database objects by providing a .NET object layer for SQL Server 2008 databases. The ADO.NET Entity Framework automates the generation of the business object model from the underlying relational database.

In the next chapter you'll see how the new Language Integrated Query (LINQ) can be used in conjunction with the ADO.NET Entity Framework and SQL Server 2008 to provide a new and completely integrated database development experience.

Chapter 5

Language Integrated Query (LINQ)

One of the most important new features in SQL Server 2008 for database developers is the introduction of Language Integrated Query (LINQ). LINQ is an evolutionary step forward for application developers because it simplifies the development process by enabling developers to work in a single, familiar language for both application development and database access. In this chapter, you'll learn about Microsoft's new LINQ technology and see some examples illustrating ways you can use LINQ with Visual Studio 2008 to access SQL Server 2008.

LINQ Concepts

LINQ addresses the problem of needing to master the multiple development modes that exist in the current database development model. Traditionally, Microsoft database application developers use an object-oriented language like C# or VB.NET to develop their business applications. The application uses ADO.NET as the object-oriented, data access, middleware that connects the application to the database. Although the language and the data access technology are all object oriented, the actual code that is sent to the database is still written in procedural T-SQL. While ADO.NET provides an object-oriented wrapper around the T-SQL code, it is still T-SQL that's actually being written to retrieve and manipulate the data. This means that the developer must know the object-oriented .NET language, such as VB or C#, and the ADO.NET data access framework, as well as T-SQL.

In addition to requiring more knowledge on your part (as the developer), the traditional application development model also has a disconnect that can hinder your productivity. Visual Studio 2008, with its IntelliSense and code completion features, type checking, and compile-time error-checking can help you quickly write correct .NET code by providing you with error feedback as you writes code. However, Visual Studio provides no design-time help with the T-SQL portion of the development. Visual Studio's IntelliSense doesn't help with the T-SQL code because that code is typically embedded in the application as a string. In addition, the only time you'll know if the query has a syntax or logic error is at runtime, when SQL Server will raise an exception.

LINQ addresses these problems by implementing a set of extensions to the .NET VB or C# languages that enable database developers to write database access routines using their native .NET development language without the need to drop down into T-SQL code. Integrating the data access capabilities into the development language enables developers to benefit from the rich metadata, compile-time syntax checking, type checking, and IntelliSense available for the native .NET code.

NOTE

LINQ queries are expressed in the programming language itself and not as string literals embedded in the application code.

Architecture

You can see an overview of the LINQ architecture shown in Figure 5-1.

As you can see in Figure 5-1, the LINQ architecture extends the VB and C# languages. It does so by adding query operators (listed later in this chapter) to the languages. The current version of LINQ uses four different data sources: LINQ to Objects, LINQ to DataSet, LINQ to SQL, and LINQ to XML. Both LINQ to DataSet and LINQ to SQL are implemented on top of ADO.NET and can be used to access SQL Server 2008, as well as other ADO.NET-compatible data sources like SQL Server 2005, Oracle, and IBM DB2. All of the different LINQ implementations use the same sets of operators. Different providers are used to connect to the different data sources.

LINQ to Objects

LINQ to Objects is used to traverse in memory data sources. Any IEnumerable or IEnumerable(T) collection can be accessed and navigated using LINQ to Objects. No specialized LINQ# providers are required to access the .NET object collections using LINQ to Objects.

LINQ to XML

LINQ to XML is implemented on top of the .NET Framework and provides comparable capabilities for the older Document Object Model (DOM) XML API. Link to XML is implemented on top of the .NET Framework XmlReader object

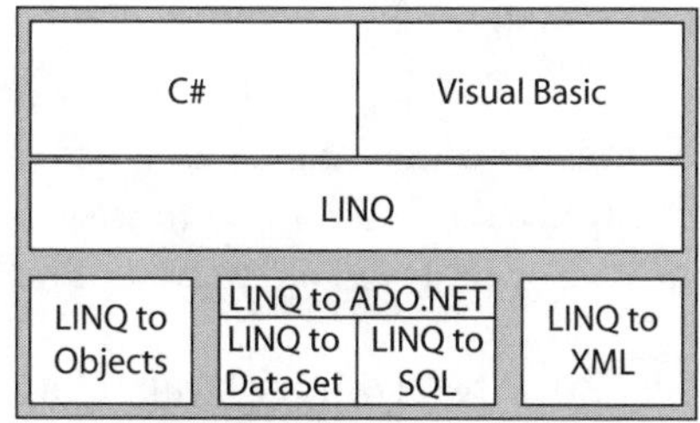

Figure 5-1 *LINQ architecture*

which provides fast forward-only XML parsing. LINQs query framework enables you to retrieve and update selected portions of the XML document.

LINQ to ADO.NET

As you can see from Figure 5-1, when LINQ is used for database access it is implemented as a layer on top of ADO.NET. For SQL Server developers, LINQ to ADO.NET is certainly the most significant of these different LINQ implementations. LINQ to ADO.NET enables access to either the data contained in an ADO.NET DataSet, or to data contained in a .NET-compatible database like SQL Server 2008. The LINQ# provider implemented by both LINQ to DataSet and LINQ to SQL surfaces the source data into IEnumerable-based object collections.

LINQ to DataSet The LINQ to DataSet implementation enables you to easily query the contents of a DataSet using LINQ expressions. LINQ to DataSet utilizes the ADO.NET DataSet object model for schema and data storage. The use of LINQ to DataSet enables greater flexibility in how data can be retrieved and manipulated in client applications. LINQ to DataSet is useful for n-tier caching in web applications.

LINQ to SQL LINQ to SQL enables developers to use the LINQ# programming model to directly query an existing database. LINQ to SQL is not limited to SQL Server 2008. Instead it can be used to connect to any ADO.NET-compliant data sources, including SQL Server 2000, SQL Server 2005, and even DB2 and Oracle. In order to use LINQ to SQL, the developer first needs to create .NET Framework classes that are an object-level representation of the underlying relational data. These classes map directly to database tables, views, stored procedures, and user-defined functions. The developer can generate these classes manually or by using the SQLMetal tool or Object Relational Designer (O/R Designer) tools that are a part of Visual Studio 2008. SQLMetal and the O/R Designer are presented in the next part of this chapter.

LINQ Operators

LINQ is defined by a set of general purpose standard query operators that you can use in .NET Framework 3.5 programming languages. These standard query operators enable you to propagate and traverse data contained in in-memory collections, XML documents, ADO.NET data sets, or tables in a database. The LINQ operators are listed in Table 5-1.

The LINQ operators work at the .NET object level. ADO.NET provides the underlying connection to the data source for LINQ to DataSet and LINQ to SQL.

Operator	Description
Aggregate	Computes a result over a sequence
Average	Computes the average of a sequence
Count	Counts the number of elements in a sequence, returns an int
LongCount	Counts the number of elements in a sequence, returns a Long
Max	Returns the maximum from a sequence
Min	Returns the minimum of a sequence
Sum	Computes the sum of a sequence
Concat	Concatenates two sequences
Cast	Casts the elements of a sequence to a given type
OfType	Filters the elements of a sequence based on a type
ToArray	Creates an array from a sequence
ToDictionary	Creates a Dictionary from a sequence
ToList	Creates a List from a sequence
ToLookup	Creates a Lookup from a sequence
ToSequence	Returns its argument typed as IEnumerable
DefaultIfEmpty	Supplies a default element for an empty sequence
ElementAt	Returns the element at a given index in a sequence
ElementAtOrDefault	Returns the element at a given index in a sequence, or a default value if the index is out of range
First	Returns the first element of a sequence
FirstOrDefault	Returns the first element of a sequence or a default value if no element is found
Last	Returns the last element of a sequence
LastOrDefault	Returns the last element of a sequence, or a default value if no element is found
Single	Returns the single element of a sequence
SingleOrDefault	Returns the single element of a sequence, or a default value if no element is found
SequenceEqual	Tests whether two sequences are equal
Empty	Returns an empty sequence of a given type
Range	Generates a sequence of integral numbers
Repeat	Generates a sequence by repeating a value a given number of times
GroupBy	Groups the elements of a sequence
GroupJoin	Performs a grouped join of two sequences based on matching keys
Join	Performs an inner join of two sequences based on matching keys

Table 5-1 *LINQ Operators*

Operator	Description
OrderBy	Orders a sequence according to one or more keys
ThenBy	Orders an ordered sequence according to one or more keys
OrderByDescending	Orders a sequence according to one or more keys in descending order
ThenByDescending	Orders an ordered sequence according to one or more keys in descending order
Reverse	Reverses the elements of a sequence
Skip	Skips a given number of elements from a sequence
SkipWhile	Skips elements from a sequence while a test is true
Take	Returns a given number of elements from a sequence and then skips the remainder of the sequence
TakeWhile	Returns elements from a sequence while a test is true and then skips the remainder of the sequence
All	Tests whether all elements of a sequence satisfy a condition
Any	Tests whether any element of a sequence satisfies a condition
Contains	Tests whether a sequence contains a given element
Where	Filters a sequence based on a predicate
Select	Performs a projection over a sequence
SelectMany	Performs a one-to-many element projection over a sequence
Distinct	Eliminates duplicate elements from a sequence
Except	Returns the set difference between two sequences
Intersect	Returns the set intersection of two sequences
Union	Returns the set union of two sequences

Table 5-1 *LINQ Operators (continued)*

Using LINQ to DataSet

LINQ to DataSet enables you to quickly and easily query the contents of an ADO. NET DataSet using the LINQ syntax. This can be particularly useful in an n-tiered architecture, because DataSets can be used as a local cache for data from a different data sources. No code generation step is required, as LINQ can be built directly over the DataSet's object model. The LINQ to DataSet functionality is provided by extension methods in the DataRowExtensions and a DataTableExtensions classes.

Prerequisites

In order to use the LINQ to DataSet functionality you first need to make sure that your Visual Studio 2008 project is targeting the .NET Framework 3.5.

NOTE

Technically, you can build LINQ projects without Visual Studio 2008. LINQ support is present in the .NET Framework 3.5 and you can use an alternate development environment in conjunction with the .NET Framework 3.5 Software Development Kit (SDK) to create LINQ projects. However, Visual Studio 2008 is the premier development environment for LINQ projects as it provides a number of useful productivity enhancements including integrated IntelliSense and LINQ debugging.

Visual Studio 2008 has the capability of targeting different versions of the .NET Framework. However, LINQ support was first added to .NET Framework 3.5, so in order to build a LINQ# project you must be sure that your project targets the .NET Framework 3.5 or higher. LINQ to DataSet can be used in a number of different Visual Studio 2008 project types, including Windows Forms Applications, ASP.NET Web Applications, and Smart Device Projects.

In the following example you'll see how to use LINQ in Windows Console applications. First, Open Visual Studio 2008 and then select the File, New, Project… option to display the New Project dialog that you see in Figure 5-2.

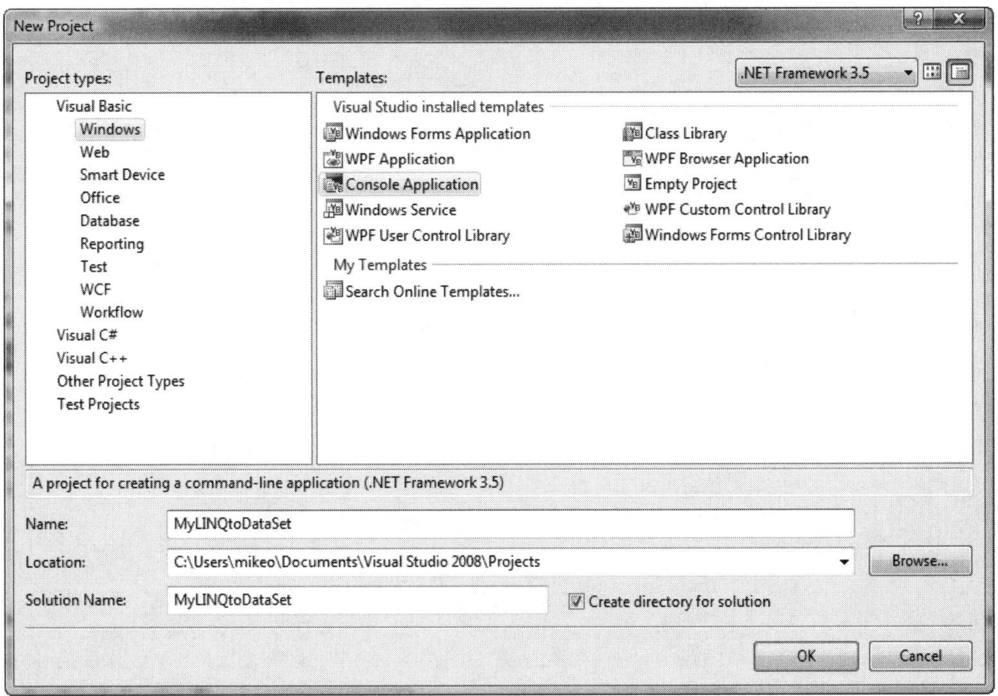

Figure 5-2 *Creating a new LINQ to DataSet project*

Make sure that the .NET Framework 3.5 is selected as the build target, as you can see in the upper right corner of Figure 5-2. Next, select Windows from the Project Types list and Console Application for the list of Templates. You can optionally change the location of the project's source code, or you can accept the default location. Finally, give your project a name and click on the OK button. The example shown in Figure 5-2 is named MyLINQtoDataSet.

The next step required to use the LINQ to DataSet functionality is to make sure that your project has references for System.Core.dll, System.Data.Linq, and the System.DataSetExtensions.dll. To add a reference to your Visual Studio 2008 project, use the Project, Properties… menu option. This will display the Visual Studio 2008 Add References dialog shown in Figure 5-3.

Scroll through the list and make sure that System.Core.dll, System.Data.Linq, and the System.DataSetExtensions.dll are all included in your project, as is illustrated in Figure 5-2. If they are not present, click the Add… button and scroll through the list of references and select them.

Next, after you add the required references to your project the next step is, add an Import statement for the System.Linq namespace using the either the VB Import or

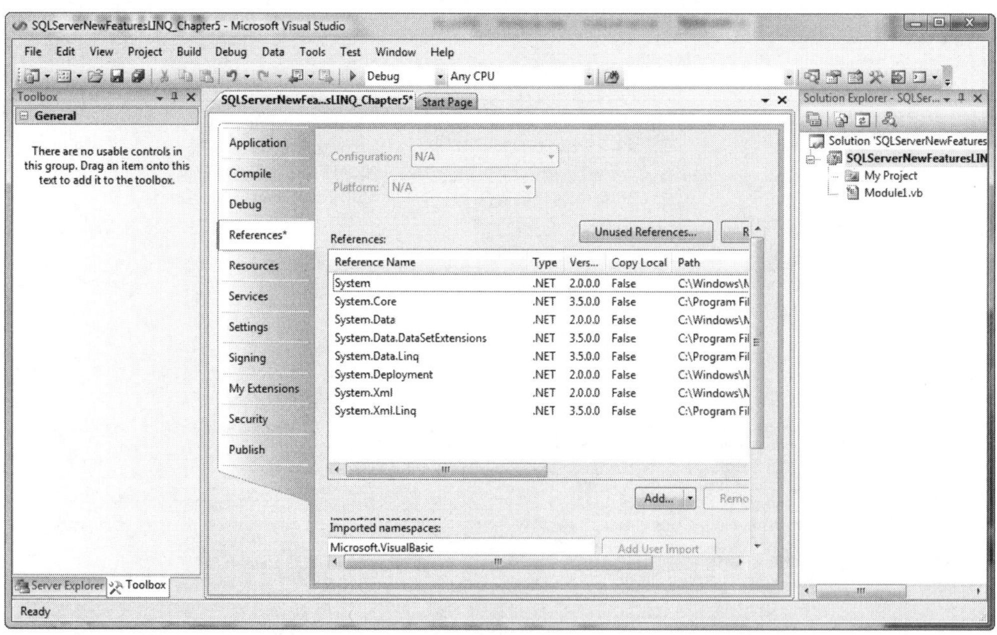

Figure 5-3 *Adding a reference for LINQ to DataSet*

the C# using directive. You can see an example of the VB Import statement for LINQ shown below:

```
Imports System.Data.SqlClient
Imports System.Linq
```

After your Visual Studio project is created and you've selected the .NET Framework 3.5 as the build target and added the prerequisite LINQ references and import statements, the next step is to create a DataSet and then connect LINQ to the dataset. In the following example, you can see how to connect LINQ to a DataSet that was created over the Product table in the sample AdventureWorks database. For reference, you can see the overall structure of the sample Windows Console application that demonstrates the LINQ to DataSet capabilities in the following listing:

```
Module Module1
    Public Const ERROR_CODE As Integer = -1

    Sub Main()
        Console.WriteLine("Beginning MyLINQtoDataSet...")

        ' Create and Load the DataSet
        Dim ds As New DataSet()

        If FillDataSet(ds) <> ERROR_CODE Then
            QueryDataSet(ds)
        End If

        Console.WriteLine("Press Enter to exit.")
        Console.ReadLine()

    End Sub
```

The overall structure of this sample application is straightforward. First, a constant is created to assist with some simple error handling. Next, a new DataSet object named ds is instantiated. Then a function named FillDataSet is executed. The purpose of this function is to populate a Dataset. If the FillDataSet function is successful, then the QueryDataSet subroutine is executed to run a simple LINQ to DataSet query over the ds DataSet object.

Connecting to the DataSet

Before you can make use of LINQ to DataSet you need to create and populate a DataSet. You saw how to create a DataSet in the previous example. In the following example you can see how to populate the DataSet in the FillDataSet subroutine shown in the following listing:

```
Function FillDataSet(ByRef ds As DataSet) As Integer
    Try
        Console.WriteLine("Filling the DataSet...")

        Dim cnString As String
        cnString = _
         "Server=sql2008-1;Initial Catalog=AdventureWorks;" & _
         ' "Integrated Security=true;"

        ' Create a new DataAdapter
        Dim da = New SqlDataAdapter( _
        "SELECT * FROM Production.Product", _
         cnString)

        ' Add a table mapping
        da.TableMappings.Add("Table", "Products")

        ' Fill the DataSet
        ' -- This simple dataset contains all the product data
        da.Fill(ds)

        Console.WriteLine("DataSet filled.")

    Catch ex As SqlException
        Console.WriteLine("FillDataSet error: " & ex.Message)
        FillDataSet = ERROR_CODE
    End Try
End Function
```

At the top of the FillDataSet function, you can see where the DataSet named ds is passed into the function. Next, a simple Console.WriteLine statement is used to output a status message to the console. Then a variable named cnString is created and assigned to an ADO.NET connection string. The connection string specifies that it will be used to connect to the AdventureWorks database on a system named SQL2008-1, and that integrated security will be used (in other words, the client application will send its associated Windows login information to SQL Server.)

Next, a new SqlDataAdapter object named da is created. The first parameter passes the da DataAapter a SQL SELECT statement that will retrieve all of the rows and columns for the Product table in the AdventureWorks database. The second parameter is used to pass the DataAdapter the SQL Server connection information contained in the cnString variable. Then, a new table mapping for the Products table is added to the DataAdapter.

NOTE

To facilitate understanding, this example uses a single table to populate the DataSet. However, you are not limited to using a single table. LINQ to Dataset is able to handle DataSets that are comprised of multiple tables – even tables from different data sources.

Finally, the da DataAdapter's Fill method is invoked to populate the ds DataSet object and a status line is output to the console.

If an error occurs within the routine, then the code in the Catch block will be executed and the error message will be output to the console window.

Querying the DataSet

After the DataSet had been populated, you can then use the new LINQ to DataSet support to query the contents of the DataSet. In the following QueryDataSet subroutine you can see how to query the DataSet using LINQ to DataSet:

```
Sub QueryDataSet(ByRef ds)
    Console.WriteLine("Querying the DataSet...")
    Try
        Dim products As DataTable = ds.Tables("Products")
        Dim query = _
        From product In products.AsEnumerable() _
            Where (product.Field(Of String)("Color") = "Blue") _
            Select New With _
            { _
               .ProductId = product.Field(Of Integer)("ProductID"), _
               .Name = product.Field(Of String)("Name"), _
               .Color = product.Field(Of String)("Color") _


            }

        For Each row In query
            Console.Write("Product ID: " & row.ProductId)
            Console.Write(" Name : " & row.Name)
            Console.WriteLine(" Color : " & row.Color)
        Next
```

```
            Console.WriteLine("Query complete.")
        Catch ex As SqlException
            Console.WriteLine("QueryDataSet error: " & ex.Message)
        End Try
    End Sub
```

The ds Dataset is passed into the beginning of the QueryDataSet subroutine and then the Console.WriteLine statement is used to write the status line to the console windows, showing that the LINQ query portion of the sample program has started. Next a Try-Catch block is set up to run the LINQ to DataSet query.

Within the Try block, a new DataTable names product is instantiated based on the Products table that is stored in the ds DataSet. Next, the results of a LINQ to DataSet query is assigned to a variable named query. The LINQ to DataSet query follows the standard LINQ syntax.

NOTE

While LINQ queries and SQL queries share many common elements, there are significant differences. For example, unlike a standard SQL query, which lists the selected columns first, a LINQ query lists the tables first. This structure enables IntelliSense to locate the tables in the data source and prompt the developer for that table's columns.

Remember, this example query uses the ds Dataset as a data source, and the ds Dataset has been populated with all of the rows and tables from the AdventureWorks Production.Product table. This query uses the ds DataSet as its data source, and in this example accesses the Products table that is contained in that DataSet. All LINQ queries work with the .NET IEnumerable interface. As the DataTable object doesn't directly support the IEnumerable interface, the AsEnumerable method is called to provide an IEnumerable interface over the products DataTable. Next, a Where clause is used to select just those rows where the column named Color contains the value Blue. Notice that because the DataSet is not strongly typed, this code needs to reference the DataTable's Field property and provide the type of column used by the Where clause. You'll notice that the same thing is true for the columns used in the Select clause that follows.

The Select clause is used to choose the columns that will be included in the result set. In this case, the DataSet contains all of the columns from the underlying Production.Product table. This Select statement only includes the ProductID, Name, and Color columns. Here again, because this code is dealing with data coming from a DataTable, the DataTable properties are used to identify the columns and the types of each column that need to be provided.

NOTE

This example also illustrates the new anonymous types feature that was added to the .NET Framework 3.5. In VB you use the New With clause to declare an anonymous type.

After the LINQ to DataSet query has executed, the query variable contains an IEnumerable collection of the query results. A For Each loop is then used to retrieve the contents of the query variable. Within the For Each loop, the values of each of the retrieved columns is output to the console window using the Console.Write and Console.WriteLine methods. Once all of the LINQ to DataSet query results have been processed, the Console.WriteLine method writes a query completion message to the console windows.

If an exception is raised by any of the operations in the Try block, the code in the Catch block is executed. Here you can see that the error message returned in the ex.Message property will be written to the console window. You can see the result of the MyLINQtoDataSet example shown in Figure 5-4.

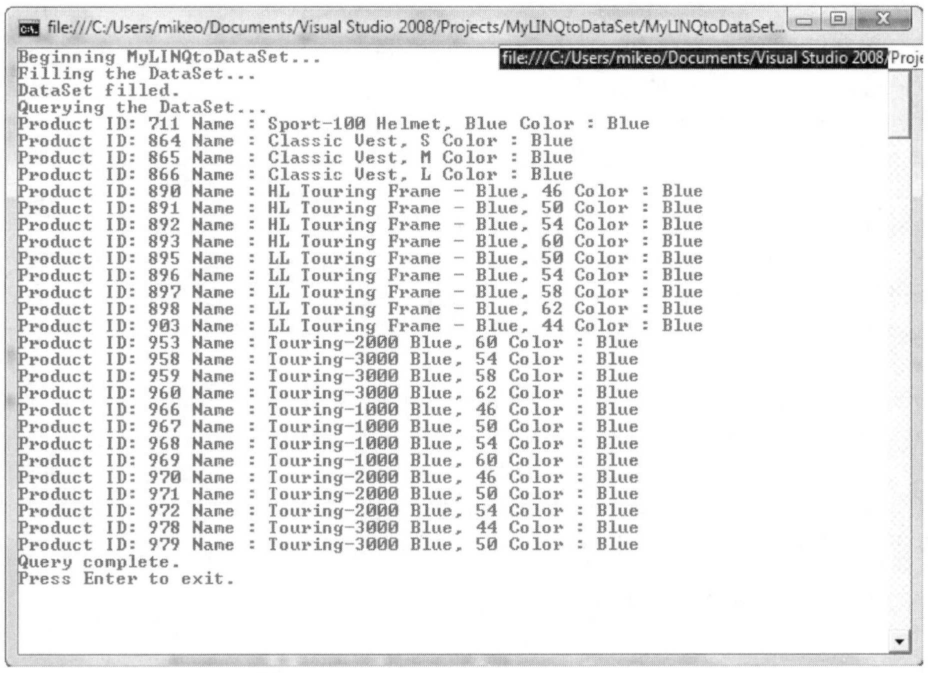

Figure 5-4 *Running the MyLINQtoDataSet example*

Using LINQ to SQL

In the previous section, you saw how LINQ to DataSet provided access to data that came out of SQL Server database by first populating that data into an ADO.NET DataSet and then using LINQ to DataSet to query the DataSet itself. That method is great for n-tier applications or applications that might need to centrally gather information from several disparate data sources. However, most of the time you'll want to be able access the SQL Server database directly without requiring any intermediate objects. That's where LINQ to SQL comes in. LINQ to SQL enables you to use LINQ queries directly against SQL Server and other relational databases.

Prerequisites

Like LINQ to DataSet, in order to use LINQ to SQL you first need to make sure that your Visual Studio 2008 project is targeting the .NET Framework 3.5. While Visual Studio 2008 supports previous versions of the .NET Framework, LINQ support is only available in the .NET Framework 3.5 or higher.

To create a new Visual Studio project using the .NET Framework 3.5, open Visual Studio 2008 then select the File, New, Project… option to display the New Project dialog that you can see in Figure 5-5.

First select .NET Framework 3.5 as the build target, as you can see in the upper right corner of Figure 5-5. Then select Windows from the list of Project Types and Console Application from the list of Templates. Finally, name your project. In Figure 5-5 you can see this LINQtoSQL example is named MyLINQtoSQL.

Next make sure that your project has references for System.Core.dll and System.Data.Linq.dll. To add a reference to your Visual Studio 2008 project use the Project, Properties… menu option. This will display the Visual Studio 2008 Add References dialog shown in Figure 5-6.

If the System.Data.Linq reference isn't present, click the Add… button, scroll through the list of references, and then select System.Data.Linq.

Next, add an Import statement for the System.Linq namespace using the either the VB Imports or the C# using directive. You can see an example of the VB Imports statement for the System.Linq namespace shown next:

```
Imports System.Data.SqlClient
Imports System.Linq
```

Creating the Object-to-Relational Mapping

Next, you'll need to create object-oriented mapping for the relational database tables that you want to use with LINQ queries. You can create the mapping manually, or you can use the command-line SQLMetal tool or the new O/R Designer.

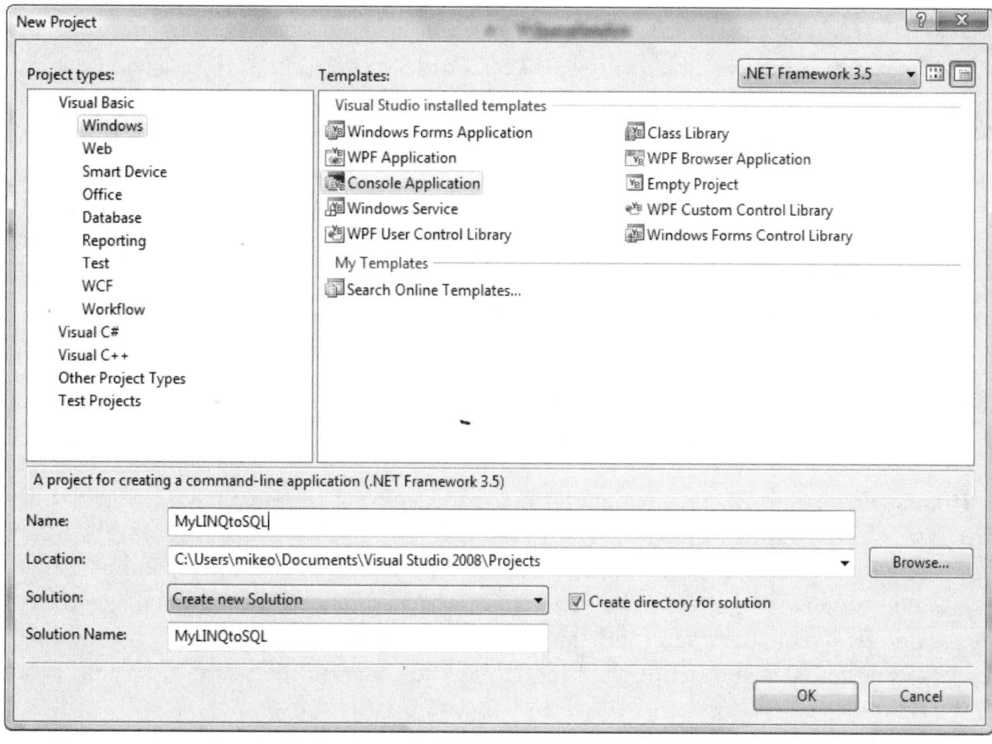

Figure 5-5 *Creating a new LINQ to SQL project*

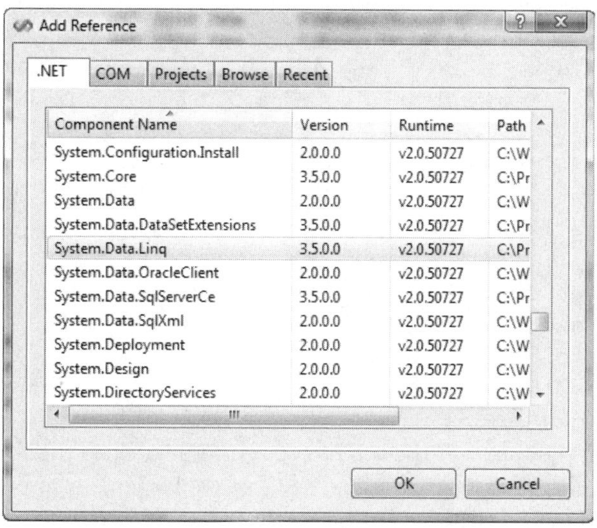

Figure 5-6 *Adding a reference for LINQ to SQL*

SQLMetal

SQLMetal is a command-line utility that's able to read the contents of a database and create an object mapping file that can be used by your LINQ to SQL applications. SQLMetal generates a VB or C# code module that can be included in your LINQ to SQL projects. The generated code includes the classes for each of the database objects, as well as the DataContext object that is used to connect to SQL Server. SQLMetal.exe is installed when you install Visual Studio 2008 and can be found in the c:\Program Files\Microsoft SDKs\Windows\V6.0a\bin directory.

The following listing shows how to use SQLMetal to create a VB class file containing the database mappings for the sample AdventureWorks database:

```
SQLMetal.exe /server:SQL2008-1 /database:AdventureWorks /sprocs /
functions /views /language:vb /code:c:\temp\AdW.vb
```

In this example, the /server parameter is used to identify the server system (which in this case is SQL2008-1). The /database parameter specifies that the AdventureWorks database will be processed. The /sprocs, /functions, and /views parameters indicate that in addition to tables, objects will be generated for stored procedures, functions, and views. The /language parameter indicates that SQLMetal will generate VB code. The /code parameter is used to name the file that will be generated. This example will result in the creation of a file named AdW.vb in the c:\temp directory.

While the entire contents of the AdW.vb file are too big to list, you can see a sampling of the relational object mapping used by LINQ to SQL in the following listing:

```
<Table(Name:="HumanResources.Department")>  _
  Partial Public Class HumanResources_Department _
      Implements System.ComponentModel.INotifyPropertyChanging, _
      System.ComponentModel.INotifyPropertyChanged

      Private Shared emptyChangingEventArgs As _
      PropertyChangingEventArgs = _
        New PropertyChangingEventArgs(String.Empty)

      Private _DepartmentID As Short
      Private _Name As String
      Private _GroupName As String
      Private _ModifiedDate As Date
```

The Table declaration used at the top of this listing identifies the name of the table in the target database. Here you can see that the table is HumanResources.Department and the class name used by the LINQ to SQL application is HumanResources_Department.

A little bit lower in the listing you can see where four, private, member variables are declared for internal storage of the column variables.

The actual declaration for each of the columns a little later in the generated AdW.vb file. Columns are defined as properties and occurs like you would expect for a property, each column has its own internet store and get and set methods. You can see the declaration for the first two columns shown in the following listing:

```
<Column(Storage:="_DepartmentID", AutoSync:=AutoSync.OnInsert,
DbType:="SmallInt NOT NULL IDENTITY", IsPrimaryKey:=true,
IsDbGenerated:=true)>  _
      Public Property DepartmentID() As Short
            Get
                  Return Me._DepartmentID
            End Get
            Set
                  If ((Me._DepartmentID = value) = false)  _
                  Then
                        Me.OnDepartmentIDChanging(value)
                        Me.SendPropertyChanging
                        Me._DepartmentID = value
                        Me.SendPropertyChanged("DepartmentID")
                        Me.OnDepartmentIDChanged
                  End If
            End Set
      End Property

<Column(Storage:="_Name", DbType:="NVarChar(50) NOT NULL", _
  CanBeNull:=false)>  _
      Public Property Name() As String
            Get
                  Return Me._Name
            End Get
            Set
                  If (String.Equals(Me._Name, value) = false) _
                  Then
                        Me.OnNameChanging(value)
                        Me.SendPropertyChanging
                        Me._Name = value
                        Me.SendPropertyChanged("Name")
                        Me.OnNameChanged
                  End If
            End Set
      End Property
```

A Column declaration is then used for each column in the table. For each column, the declaration specifies the private variable used for data storage, the data type, and whether the column is part of the primary key. Each column is then represented as a property with get and set methods that are used to access the column's data values. This partial listing shows the DepartmentID and Name properties.

After the source file containing the relational-to-object mapping has been created, you're ready to use LINQ to SQL to query the database. You can add the AdW.vb class file to your project using the Project | Add Existing Item option from the Visual Studio menu.

O/R Designer

SQLMetal is a great tool for generating a quick object-to-relational mapping for an entire database. However, if you just want to map a set of selected database objects (for example, tables, views, and stored procedures), or if you want to generate a more sophisticated mapping than the simple one-to-one mapping that is provided by SQLMetal, then you can use Visual Studio 2008's O/R Designer to generate the object-to-relational mapping.

To run the O/R Designer, first open up your Visual Studio 2008 project and right-click on your project name in the Solution Explorer window and then select the Add New Item... option from the Context menu. This will display the Add New Item dialog that you can see in Figure 5-7.

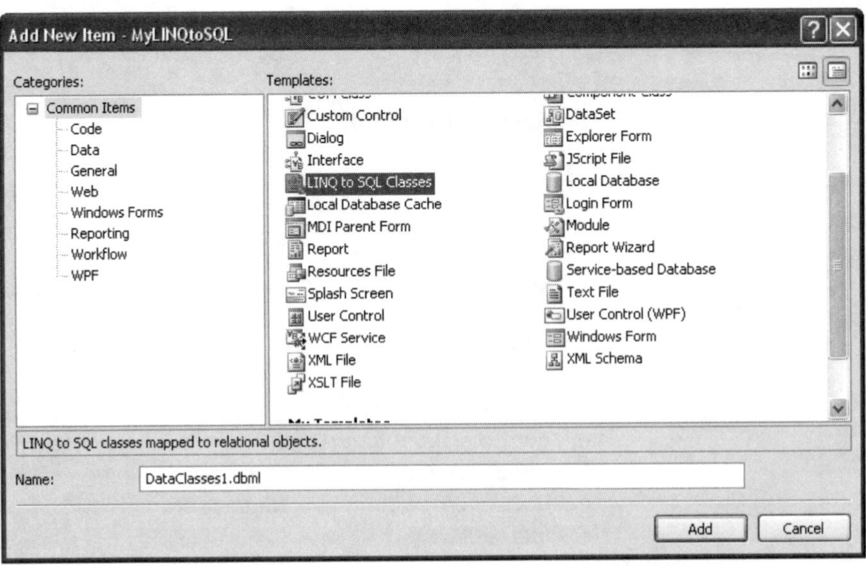

Figure 5-7 *Add New Item LINQ to SQL*

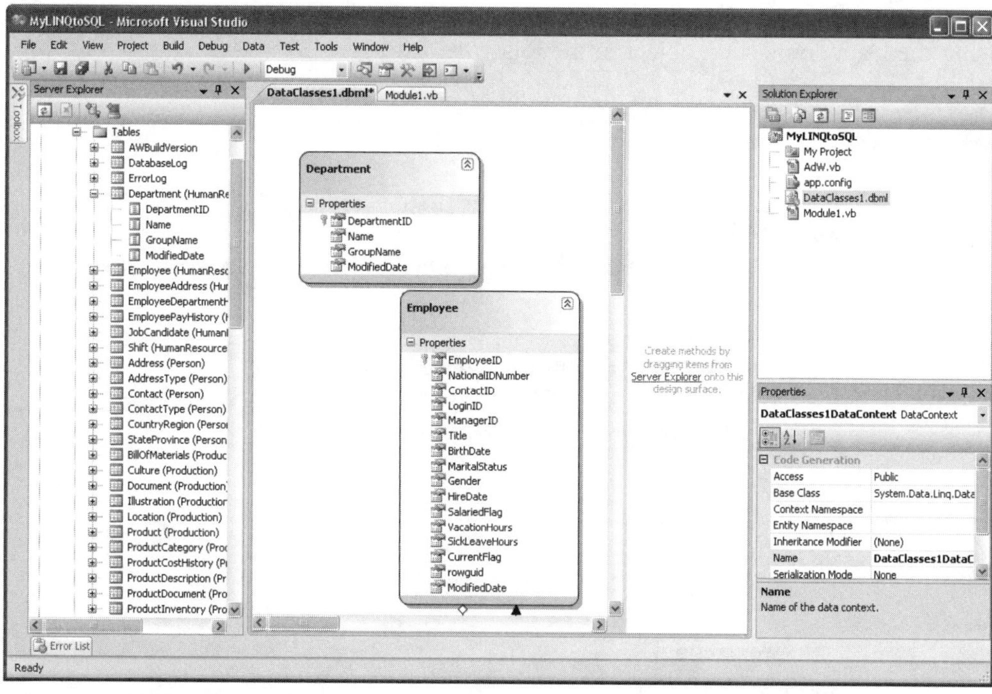

Figure 5-8 *O/R Designer*

From the Add New Item dialog, select the LINQ to SQL Classes option and then provide a name for the class file. By default the O/R Designer will store its classes in the DataClasses1.dbml file. Clicking the Add button will add the class file and display the Visual Studio 2008 O/R Designer that you can see in Figure 5-8.

To use the O/R Designer, you essentially create a new database connection using Visual Studio 2008's Server Explorer and then drag and drop the desired database objects from the Server Explorer window onto the O/R Designer. In Figure 5-8 you can see an example where the HumanResources.Department and HumanResources .Employee tables have been added to the designer. Saving the file generates the required LINQ object entity classes.

LINQ to SQL Example Application

To connect to SQL Server, you use the LINQ DataContext object. The data context object encapsulates the connection string used to connect to your data source and opens the connection to SQL Server. You can see an example of connecting to SQL Server using the DataConnection object in the following listing:

```
Imports System.Data.SqlClient
Imports System.Linq
Module Module1
    Private Department As HumanResources_Department
    Private cnString As String = _
     "server=SQL2008-1;database=AdventureWorks;Integrated Security=true;"
    Sub Main()
        Try
            Console.WriteLine("Beginning MyLINQtoSQL...")
            Dim AdWDC As MyLINQtoSQL.AdventureWorks = _
               New AdventureWorks(cnString)

            QueryAdW(AdWDC)
            InsertAdW(AdWDC)
            UpdateAdW(AdWDC)
            DeleteAdW(AdWDC)

            Cleanup(AdWDC)
            Console.WriteLine("Press Enter to exit.")

            Console.ReadLine()

        Catch ex As Exception
            Console.WriteLine("MyLINQtoSQL Ended in error:" & ex.Message)
            Console.ReadLine()
        End Try
    End Sub
```

At the top of this listing you can see import declarations for the LINQ System.Linq namespace along with the SQL Server .NET Data Provider, System.Data.SqlClient.

NOTE

LINQ to SQL is a layer on top of ADO.NET, making it possible to freely mix LINQ code with ADO.NET code. For instance, you can instantiate an ADO.NET Connection object and then pass that connection object to the LINQ DataContext object. All of the code that uses the LINQ DataContext object will use that ADO.NET connection.

You can see the framework of the example application in the previous listing. At the top, two private variables are declared. The first variable named Department is an instance of the HumanResources_Department class. The second variable holds the connection string for the application.

NOTE

You can also supply the connection using the Setting's tab of the project's Properties.

The overall application flow is directed by the Main subroutine. Here you can see that the sample LINQ to SQL application first creates an instance of the AdventuresWorks DataContext object from the class code that was generated by either SQLMetal or the O/R Designer. Next, that DataContext object is passed into a set of subroutines that illustrate the basic LINQ usage. Like their names suggest, the QueryAdW subroutine illustrates basic LINQ queries, while the InsertAdW, UpdateAdW, and DeleteAdW subroutines show how you can use LINQ to insert, update, and delete data. When all of the principle LINQ example functions have completed, a status message is displayed on the console and a Cleanup subroutine runs a T-SQL command to reset the status of the HumanResources.Department table that is used in these examples. The Console.Readline() method keeps the console window open, allowing the user to see the output of each of the example subroutines. If an error is encountered, the code in the Catch block will be executed and the error message will be output to the console. The LINQ code to query and update SQL Server is shown in the following sections.

Retrieving Data

After you've created a DataContext object you can use it with your LINQ query operations. The following example QueryAdW subroutine shows you the basic syntax for a LINQ query:

```
Sub QueryAdW(ByRef dc As AdventureWorks)
    Try
        Console.WriteLine("Beginning query ...")

        Dim query = From department In dc.HumanResources_Department _
            Where department.GroupName = "Manufacturing" _
            Select department

        For Each row In query
            Console.Write("Name : " & row.Name)
            Console.WriteLine(" Group : " & row.GroupName)
        Next

        Console.WriteLine("Query complete.")
        Console.ReadLine()
```

```
        Catch ex As SqlException
            Console.WriteLine("QueryAdW error: " & ex.Message)
        End Try
    End Sub
```

The DataContext object that was created in the Main subroutine is passed into the QueryAdW subroutine. Then a status message is output to the console.

The actual LINQ query can be seen in the assignment to the query variable. Unlike standard ADO.NET, there is no need to specify the SELECT statement in a text string that's passed to a command object. Instead, LINQ integrates the query operators directly into the .NET language. Unlike SQL which lists the columns first, the LINQ query must begin with the From clause. The From clause is an iterator over the variable that's used for the specified table object. Optional Join, Where, Orderby, Ascending, and Descending clauses can be added to filter and sort the results. The allowable LINQ operators are listed in the LINQ Architecture section. In this example, the Where clause is used to select just those rows where the value in the GroupName column is equal to "Manufacturing." Finally, the Select statement specifies the data that will be returned. In this case, all of the columns will be returned, but individual columns could be selected as well.

Next, the For Each statement is used to iterate over the contents of the collection returned by the LINQ query. In this example, the contents of the Name and GroupName columns are output to the console. You can see the results of the QueryAdW subroutine shown in Figure 5-9.

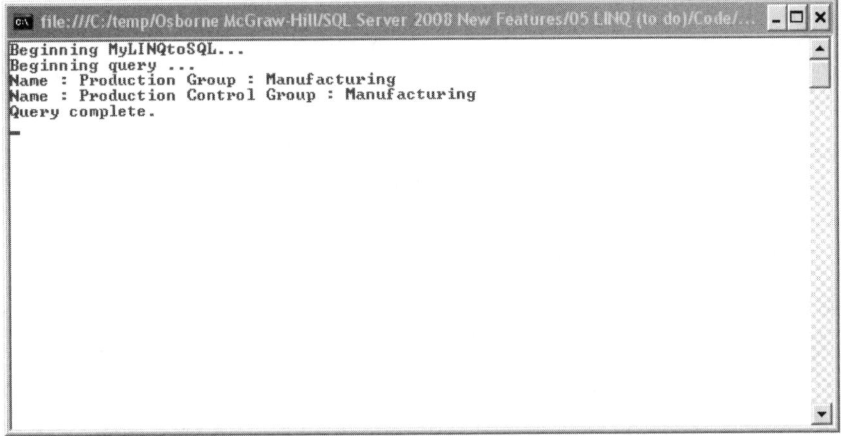

Figure 5-9 *LINQ to SQL query results*

In Figure 5-9 you can see that the LINQ query returned just those rows in the HumanResources.Department table where the GroupName column contained the value of "Manufacturing."

The remaining code in the Catch block would write an error message to the console window if an error were encountered by any of the code in the Try block.

Modifying Data

In addition to performing queries, you can also use LINQ to insert, update, and delete data from the target database. Just as you saw in the previous query examples, there's no need to change programming paradigms or drop back into T-SQL. All the update actions can be performed using the LINQ to SQL objects. The following sections illustrate how to perform insert, update, and delete operations using LINQ to SQL.

LINQ Insert Operations

Performing an insert operation using LINQ essentially requires inserting a row within the LINQ database entity object and then sending the changes to the underlying database using the DataContext object's SubmitChanges method. You can see a LINQ insert example in the following code list:

```
Sub InsertAdW(ByRef dc As AdventureWorks)
    Console.WriteLine("Beginning insert...")
    Try
        Dim query = From department In dc.HumanResources_Department _
            Select department

        'Insert a row
        Department = New HumanResources_Department With _
              {.Name = "Inserted Department", _
               .GroupName = "Inserted Row1", _
               .ModifiedDate = Now()}
        dc.HumanResources_Department.InsertOnSubmit(Department)
        dc.SubmitChanges()

        For Each row In query
            Console.Write("Name: " & row.Name)
            Console.WriteLine(" Modified: " & row.ModifiedDate)
        Next

        Console.WriteLine("Insert complete. " & query.Count & _
         " Rows. Press enter to continue")
        Console.ReadLine()
```

```
        Catch ex As SqlException
            Console.WriteLine("InsertAdW error: " & ex.Message)
        End Try
    End Sub
```

The InsertAdW subroutine begins by passing in a reference to the DataContext, writing a status line to the console window, and then querying the department table as you saw in the previous example. Next, values are assigned to the Department object's properties. Remember, each property represents a column in the target table. In this example, the Name column is set to "Inserted Department," the GroupName column is set to "Inserted Row1," and the ModifiedDate column is set to the current date and time. After the values have been assigned, the InsertOnSubmit method is used to add the row to the Department table object. This updates the object, but not the database. The HumanResources.Department table isn't updated until the SubmitChanges method is executed.

The remainder of the code in the listing queries the table in order to retrieve the new values, as you saw in the previous examples. The total count of the rows returned is also displayed in the status message. You can see the new row that was added to the HumanResource.Department table in Figure 5-10.

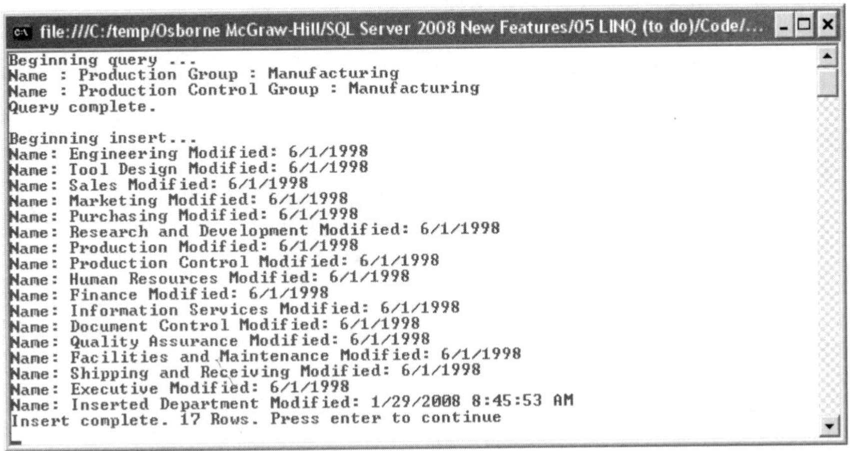

Figure 5-10 *Results of the LINQ to SQL Insert Operation*

LINQ Update Operations

The LINQ code needed to update a row is a bit different. The code shown in the following listing retrieves the newly added row and changes the value of the Name column from "Inserted Department" to "Updated Department:"

```
Sub UpdateAdW(ByRef dc As AdventureWorks)
    Console.WriteLine("Beginning update...")

    Try
        Dim query = From department In dc.HumanResources_Department _
          Where (department.Name = "Inserted Department") _
          Select department

        Department.Name = "Updated Department"
        Department.ModifiedDate = Now()

        dc.SubmitChanges()

        Dim query2 = From department In dc.HumanResources_Department _
                Select department

        For Each row In query2
            Console.Write("Name : " & row.Name)
            Console.WriteLine(" Modified : " & row.ModifiedDate)
        Next

        Console.WriteLine("Update complete. " & query2.Count & _
          " Rows. Press enter to continue")
        Console.ReadLine()

    Catch ex As SqlException
        Console.WriteLine("UpdateAdW error: " & ex.Message)
    End Try
End Sub
```

The subroutine to demonstrate LINQ updates begins by passing in a reference to the DataContext object, writing a status line to the console window, and then querying the department table as you saw in the previous example. However, in this example the query only retrieves the row where the value of the Department table's Name column has the value of "Inserted Department." After the result set is returned, its properties can be updated using a standard assignment operator. If you remember back

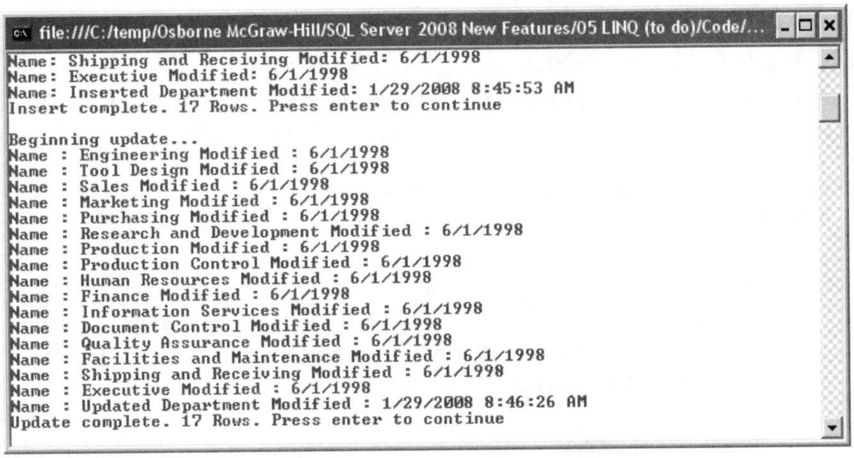

```
file:///C:/temp/Osborne McGraw-Hill/SQL Server 2008 New Features/05 LINQ (to do)/Code/...
Name: Shipping and Receiving Modified: 6/1/1998
Name: Executive Modified: 6/1/1998
Name: Inserted Department Modified: 1/29/2008 8:45:53 AM
Insert complete. 17 Rows. Press enter to continue

Beginning update...
Name : Engineering Modified : 6/1/1998
Name : Tool Design Modified : 6/1/1998
Name : Sales Modified : 6/1/1998
Name : Marketing Modified : 6/1/1998
Name : Purchasing Modified : 6/1/1998
Name : Research and Development Modified : 6/1/1998
Name : Production Modified : 6/1/1998
Name : Production Control Modified : 6/1/1998
Name : Human Resources Modified : 6/1/1998
Name : Finance Modified : 6/1/1998
Name : Information Services Modified : 6/1/1998
Name : Document Control Modified : 6/1/1998
Name : Quality Assurance Modified : 6/1/1998
Name : Facilities and Maintenance Modified : 6/1/1998
Name : Shipping and Receiving Modified : 6/1/1998
Name : Executive Modified : 6/1/1998
Name : Updated Department Modified : 1/29/2008 8:46:26 AM
Update complete. 17 Rows. Press enter to continue
```

Figure 5-11 *Results of the LINQ to SQL Update Operation*

to the previous object entity listing, each property has its own Get and Set methods. Assigning a value to the property will result in the execution of the column object's Set method. The target database table is then updated using the SubmitChanges method.

The next section of code requeries the table to show the updated values in the Name and Modified date columns. You can see the updated row in Figure 5-11.

Deleting Data

The LINQ code that deletes a row is very similar in concept to the update example that was shown in the previous listing. The DeleteAdW subroutine shown next deletes the row where the Name column contains the value of "Updated Department."

```
Sub DeleteAdW(ByRef dc As AdventureWorks)
    Console.WriteLine("Beginning delete...")

    Try
        Dim query = From department In dc.HumanResources_Department _
          Where (department.Name = "Updated Department")

        dc.HumanResources_Department.DeleteOnSubmit(Department)
        dc.SubmitChanges()

        Dim query2 = From department In dc.HumanResources_Department _
              Select department
```

```
            For Each row In query2
                Console.Write("Name : " & row.Name)
                Console.WriteLine(" Modified : " & row.ModifiedDate)
            Next

            Console.WriteLine("Delete complete. " & query2.Count & _
              " Rows. Press enter to continue")
            Console.ReadLine()

        Catch ex As SqlException
            Console.WriteLine("DeleteAdW error: " & ex.Message)
        End Try
    End Sub
```

The subroutine begins by passing in a reference to the DataContext object. Then you can see where it writes a status line to the console window and then queries the department table to retrieve the row where the value of the Department table's Name column has the value of "Updated Department." After the result set is returned, the DeleteOnSubmit method is called to delete the row. This method deletes the row from the local collection. Calling the dc DataContext object's SubmitChanges method then sends the update to SQL Server.

The next section of code requeries the Department table to show the remaining values in the Name and Modified date columns. You can see the updated contents of the HumanResources.Department table in Figure 5-12.

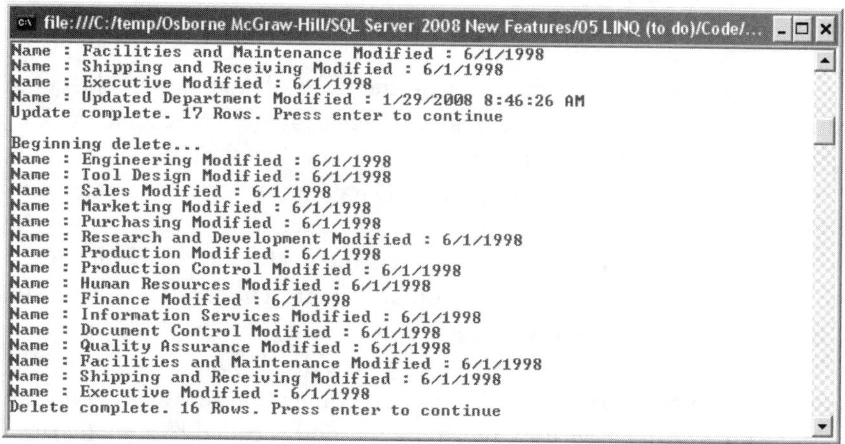

Figure 5-12 *Results of the LINQ to SQL delete operation*

Executing DDL Commands

LINQ can also be use to execute commands on SQL Server or the backend data source that you are connected to. The following example illustrates how to execute a command using the LINQ DataContext object. The purpose of the Cleanup subroutine shown in the following listing is to reset the Identity seed property for the department_id column in the HumanResources.Department table that was used by the previous insert example. Performing an insert operation increments the identity seed value, and this subroutine resets it to is orginal value. To do so, the LINQ example uses the DataContext object to execute the T-SQL DBCC CHECKIDENT command as you can see next:

```
Sub Cleanup(ByRef dc As AdventureWorks)
    Try
        Dim cmd As SqlCommand = dc.Connection.CreateCommand()
        cmd.CommandText = _
        "DBCC CHECKIDENT('HumanResources.Department', RESEED, 16)"
        dc.Connection.Open()
        cmd.ExecuteNonQuery()

        Console.writeline("Cleanup complete. Press enter to
continue")
        Console.readline()
    Catch ex As SqlException
        Console.WriteLine("Cleanup error: " & ex.Message)
        Console.readline()
    End Try
End Sub
```

At the top of this listing you can see where the LINQ DataContext object named dc is passed into the Cleanup subroutine as a parameter. Then a Try-Catch block is used to execute the T-SQL DBBCC command. Within the Try block, a new SqlCommand object named cmd is instantiated using the dc DataContext object's CreateCommand method. Next, the cmd SqlCommand object's CommandText property is assigned the T-SQL DBCC command. This command resets the seed value for the department_id column in the HumanResource.Department table to 16. The result of this command is that the next row that is inserted will have a department_id value of 17. After setting the SqlCommand object's CommandText property, the dc DataContext object's Connection Open method is executed to open a connection to SQL Server. Then the SqlCommand object's ExecuteNonQuery method is called to actually run the command on the SQL Server system.

Summary

Microsoft's LINQ is the biggest paradigm change for database developers since the advent of ODBC. LINQ eliminates the language-database disconnect and enables object-oriented database access via SQL-like extensions to VB or C# languages. For more information about LINQ# you can refer to: http://msdn2.microsoft.com/en-us/netframework/aa904594.aspx.

Chapter 6

New Data Types

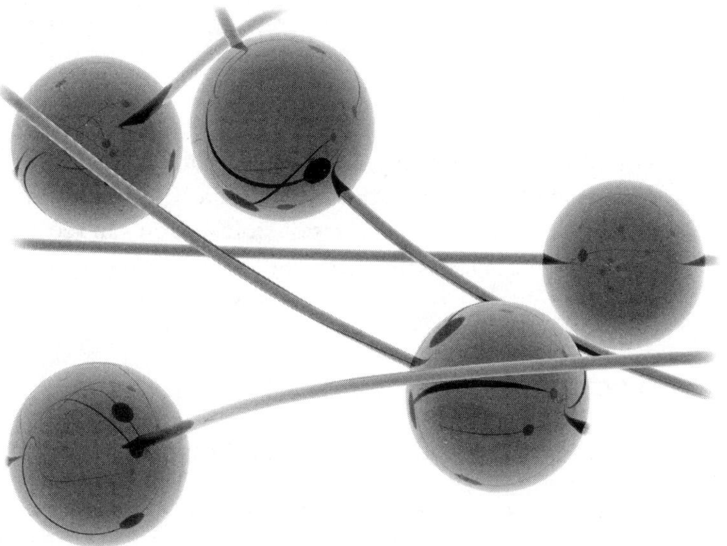

SQL Server 2008 adds a number of important new data types that extend the functionality of SQL Server beyond the realm of a traditional relational database server, transforming it into an enterprise level data platform. Most of these new data types are native SQL Server data types, but a few of the new data types are SQLCLR-based data types as well. In this chapter you'll learn about the new SQL Server 2008 data types and see some examples of how they are used.

Date /Time Data Types

The new date and time data types are undoubtedly the most important new data types that Microsoft added to SQL Server 2008. Previous releases of SQL Server provided the DATETIME and SMALLDATETIME data types. While these data types were functional, many database designers didn't care for the way that they combined the date and time values. This also introduced complications in writing queries that accessed date or time values, as well as formatting issues in retrieving those values. In addition, the fact that there were no discreet date and time column values was often a problem point when converting data from other systems like Oracle and DB2, which *did* make use of separate date and time data types. To address these issues, SQL Server 2008 introduced four new date and time data types: DATE, TIME, DATETIME2, and DATETIMEOFFSET.

DATE

The new DATE data type uses the format YYYY-MM-DD and is ANSI-compliant. A native SQL data type, the DATE data type can contain values from 0001-01-01 to 9999-12-31 and it uses 3 bytes of storage. You can see an example of using the DATE data type in the following listing:

```
DECLARE  @MyDate DATE
SET @MyDate = '12/25/07'
PRINT @MyDate
```

The results of this listing are shown next:

```
SQL2008-1(SQL2008-1\Administrator):
2007-12-25
```

TIME

TIME is another native SQL data type. The new TIME data type complements the new DATE data type. TIME is ANSI compliant and it uses an hh:mm:ss[.nnnnnnn] format. TIME can contain values from 00:00:00.0000000 to 23:59.59.9999999, and it requires 3 to 5 bytes of storage. You can see how to use the new TIME data type in the following example:

```
DECLARE  @MyTime TIME
SET @MyTime = '22:18:48.123'
PRINT @MyTime
```

You can see the results of running this code using the Time data type in the following listing:

```
SQL2008-1(SQL2008-1\Administrator):
22:18:48.1230000
```

You might notice from the output that by default the TIME data type utilizes the maximum amount of storage and is created with seven nanosecond decimal places. To reduce the storage, you can specify the number of decimal positions in the declaration. The following example shows show to create a new TIME data type which uses three decimal positions:

```
DECLARE @MyTime TIME(3)
SET @MyTime = '22:18:48.123'
PRINT @MyTime
```

This changes the output to the following:

```
SQL2008-1(SQL2008-1\Administrator):
22:18:48.123
```

Notice that the trailing decimals after the third position are now gone. This same technique also applies to the new DATETIME2 and DATETIMEOFFSET data types.

DATETIME2

The new DATETIME2 data type is designed to address the need for more precise time storage requirements. The DATETIME2 data type is accurate up to 100 nanoseconds and uses the format YYYY-MM-DD hh:mm:ss[.nnnnnnn]. The DATETIME2 data type can store values ranging from 0001-01-01 00:00:00.0000000 through 9999-12-31 23:59.59.9999999 and uses 6 to 8 bytes of storage. You can see how to use the new DATETIME2 data type in the following listing:

```
DECLARE  @MyDateTime2 DATETIME2
SET @MyDateTime2 = '2007-12-25 11:04:18.1234567'
PRINT @MyDateTime2
```

You can see the results of using the DATETIME2 data type in the following listing:

```
SQL2008-1(SQL2008-1\Administrator):
2007-12-25 11:04:18.1234567
```

DATETIMEOFFSET

The DATETIMEOFFSET is the most sophisticated of the new date and time data types. Unlike DATETIME2, the DATETIMEOFFSET is time zone aware. DATETIMEOFFSET use the format YYYY-MM-DD hh:mm:ss[.nnnnnnn] and can store values ranging from 0001-01-01 00:00:00.0000000 through 9999-12-31 23:59.59.9999999. You can see an example of using the new DATETIMEOFFSET data type in the following example:

```
DECLARE  @MyDateTimeOffset DATETIMEOFFSET
SET @MyDateTimeOffset = '2007-12-31 23:59:59.1234 -5:00'
PRINT @MyDateTimeOffset
```

The results of using the new DATATIMEOFFSET data type is shown in the following listing:

```
SQL2008-1(SQL2008-1\Administrator):
2007-12-31 23:59:59.1234000 -05:00
```

LOB Data Types

Storing large unstructured data like photos, documents, and video files (also known as Large Objects or LOBs) in a relational database has always been a problem. The earlier editions of SQL Server implemented a number of different data types that were designed to solve this problem. SQL Server 7 and SQL Server 2000 used the IMAGE, TEXT, and NTEXT data types for LOB storage. Using the TEXT and IMAGE data types, SQL Server could store up to 2GB of data, but using them was difficult because they required a different access mechanism than the other relational data. In addition, accessing these data types was slower then retrieving them from the raw file system. In addition, accessing large IMAGE, TEXT, and NTEXT data values disrupted the contents of SQL Server's buffer pool (the cache where relational data is stored to improve subsequent query performance).

With SQL Server 2005, Microsoft took steps to resolve some of these issues by adding the VARBINARY(MAX) data type. While theVARBINARY(MAX) data type enabled the use of a single development model for both LOB and relational data, it didn't address the performance and buffer cache issues. These issues typically caused developers to store LOB data in the file system and then store pointers or access paths to that data in SQL Server's database columns. This scenario enabled faster data access, but it also put data integrity at risk because the links between the file system data and the SQL Server column pointers needed to be maintained manually. Operations like backing up and restoring the database did not include any data in the file system.

Designed to solve the problem of storing and accessing LOB data, SQL Server 2008 introduces the new FILESTREAM data type. The FILESTREAM data type combines the performance of file system data access with the transactional integrity of the relational database.

FILESTREAM

Unlike the earlier IMAGE, TEXT, and VARBINARY(MAX) data types, the FILESTREAM data type stores the raw unstructured data in the server's NTFS file system. SQL Server 2008 manages the association between the FILESTREAM columns and the raw files in the file system. Unlike earlier alternatives where the developer needed to manually maintain links between external objects and SQL Server columns, with the new FILESTREAM data type SQL Server 2008 is responsible for data integrity. Operations, including database backup and restore, include the raw data stored in the file system. Unlike the older IMAGE and VARBINARY(MAX) data types, the SQL Server buffer pool is not affected by the retrieval of the LOB data.

To work with the new FILESTREAM data type you first need to enable it at the server level using the sp_ configure stored procedure as shown next:

```
EXEC sp_configure filestream_access_level, 2
RECONFIGURE
```

By default, filestream access is disabled. The sp_configure filestream_access_level stored procedure can enable the access capabilities for T-SQL, the local file system, or remote file system using the following option shown in Table 6-1.

filestream_access_level Value	Description
0	Disabled (Default)
1	T-SQL access
2	T-SQL and local file system access
3	T-SQL, local file system access, and remote file system access

Table 6-1 *sp_configure filestream_access_level options*

Next, any database that uses the new FILESTREAM objects must be created using the new CONTAINS FILESTREAM keywords. The following example shows how to create a new database called MyFileStream:

```
CREATE DATABASE MyFileStream ON PRIMARY
  ( NAME = FileStream_data,
    FILENAME = N'C:\FileStream\MyFileStream_data.mdf',
    SIZE = 10MB,
    MAXSIZE = 50MB,
    FILEGROWTH = 15%),
      FILEGROUP MyDBData
  ( NAME = MyFileStream_group,
    FILENAME = N'C:\FileStream\MyFileStream_stream.ndf)',
    SIZE = 10MB,
    MAXSIZE = 50MB,
    FILEGROWTH = 5MB),
FILEGROUP MyFileStreamGroup1 CONTAINS FILESTREAM
  ( NAME = MyFileStream,
    FILENAME = N'C:\FileStream\MyFileStream')
LOG ON
  ( NAME = 'MyFileStream_log',
    FILENAME = N'C:\FileStream\MyFileStream_log.ldf',
    SIZE = 5MB,
    MAXSIZE = 25MB,
    FILEGROWTH = 5MB);
```

After the database is created you can then create tables that use the new FILESTREAM data type.

NOTE

Tables using the FILESTREAM data type require one column of the UNIQUEIDENTIFIER data type.

The following listing shows how to declare and use the new FILESTREAM data type.

```
USE MyFileStream
CREATE TABLE dbo.MyFileStreamTable
(
  FileStream_ID UNIQUEIDENTIFIER ROWGUIDCOL NOT NULL UNIQUE,
  FileStream_Row INT,
  FileStream_Data VARBINARY(MAX) FILESTREAM
);
```

In this listing, the USE statement changes the current database to the MyFileStream database that was created earlier using the new CONTAINS FILESTREAM keywords. Next, the CREATE TABLE statement is used to create a new table named MyFileStreamTable. The MyFileStream table contains three columns: one for the UNIQUEIDENITIER that's needed to use the FILESTREAM data type, one INTEGER, and the FILESTREAM data type.

Inserting FILESTREAM Data

You can use T-SQL to manipulate the data in the FILESTREAM column. The following example shows you how to insert a row into the MyFileStream table:

```
INSERT into dbo.MyFileStreamTable
    VALUES(newid(), 1, CAST ('My File Stream data' As VARBINARY(MAX)))

SELECT FileStream_Row, CAST( FileStream_Data As varchar(35))
  FROM dbo.MyFileStreamTable WHERE FileStream_Row = 1;
```

Here you can see that the INSERT statement casts a string as a VARBINARY(MAX) data type in order to insert it as FILESTREAM data. The next line executes a SELECT statement that retrieves the FILESTREAM data. In the following SELECT statement, another CAST is used to convert the FILESTREAM data from the column FileStream_Data into a VARCHAR data type for display. You can see the results in the following listing:

```
FileStream_Row
-------------- -----------------------------------
1              My File Stream data

SQL2008-1(SQL2008-1\Administrator): (1 row(s) affected)
```

Updating FILESTREAM Data

You can also use T-SQL to update the contents of the FILESTREAM data after it has been added to the database. Here again, using the T-SQL UPDATE statement to work with the FILESTREAM data is very much like working with standard relational data types. You can see an example of using UPDATE statement in the following listing:

```
UPDATE dbo.MyFileStreamTable
SET FileStream_Data = CAST ('My updated file stream data' as
varbinary(max))
WHERE FileStream_Row = 1;
```

```
SELECT FileStream_Row, CAST( FileStream_Data As varchar(35))
  FROM dbo.MyFileStreamTable WHERE FileStream_Row = 1;
```

In this listing, the UPDATE statement changes the contents of the FileStream_Data column in the row that was just added (the row where the value of the FileStream_Row column is equal to 1). The SELECT statement is then used to retrieve the updated FileStream_Data value, which you can see in the following results:

```
FileStream_Row
-------------- -----------------------------------
1              My updated file stream data

SQL2008-1(SQL2008-1\Administrator): (1 row(s) affected)
```

Deleting FILESTREAM Data

Just as you can use the INSERT and UPDATE statements to add and modify FILESTRAM data, you can use the DELETE statement to delete rows containing the FILESTREAM data. One important point to remember about using the DELETE statement with FILESTREAM data is that it deletes both the row stored in the SQL Server relational database, and the LOB data stored in the NTFS file system. The following listing illustrates using the DELETE statement to delete FILESTREAM data:

```
DELETE dbo.MyFileStreamTable
  WHERE FileStream_Row = 1;

SELECT FileStream_Row, CAST( FileStream_Data As varchar(35))
  FROM dbo.MyFileStreamTable WHERE FileStream_Row = 1;
```

The first line in the listing uses the DELETE statement to delete the row from the dbo.MyFileStreamTable table where the value of the FileStream_Row column is equal to 1. This will delete the row as well as the externally stored FILESTREAM data. The next line attempts to retrieve the row, but since it has been deleted no results will be returned. You can see this for yourself in the following listing:

```
SQL2008-1(SQL2008-1\Administrator): (1 row(s) affected)
FileStream_Row
-------------- -----------------------------------

SQL2008-1(SQL2008-1\Administrator): (0 row(s) affected)
```

Organizational Data Types

Dealing with organizational data has always been challenging in relational databases. The traditional solution to this type of storage problem lies in performing recursive queries; but recursive queries are both difficult to write as well as understand. SQL Server 2008's new HIERARCHYID data type is designed to address the problem of dealing with hierarchical organizational data like the kind you find in organization charts.

HIERARCHYID

SQL Server 2008's new HIERARCHYID data type is designed to address the problem of storing hierarchically structured data containing relationships like manger and employee. HIERARCHYID is a variable length system data type. The HIERACHYID data type can store data optimized for either depth or breadth. The following table illustrates how HIERACHYID encodes values that represent a tree.

/	Root
/1/	The first node from the root
/1/2/	The second node from the root
/1/2.5/	Node inserted between the second and third node
/1/3/	The third node

The values used for HIEARCHYID columns do not automatically represent a hierarchy. Instead, it is the responsibility of the application developer to assign and store the proper HIERARCHYID values in a way that properly represents the desired hierarchy. To help you work with the new HIERARCHYID data type, Microsoft has included a number of methods to query and modify the hierarchical data. The following table shows HIERARCHYID data type methods:

GetAncestor	Retrieves this node's nth ancestor
GetDescendant	Retrieves this node's x child node
GetLevel	Returns an integer representing the distance from the root
GetRoot	Returns the root node
IsDescendant	Returns a value of TRUE if this node is a descendant of the current node
Parse	Converts a string to a HIERARCHYID value
Read	Reads the binary representation of a node
Reparent	Changes the parent node for the current node
ToString	Converts the node value to a string
Write	Assigns a value to a node

The code in the following example shows how to declare a new HIERARCHYID data type and the GetLevel method is used to create a breadth-first ordering. Then a primary index is created by making a composite of the Emp_Level and Emp_Node columns:

```
CREATE TABLE dbo.EmpMaster
(
     Emp_ID INT UNIQUE NOT NULL,
     Emp_Node HIERARCHYID PRIMARY KEY CLUSTERED,
     Emp_Level as Emp_Node.GetLevel(),
     Emp_Name VARCHAR(50)
);
CREATE UNIQUE INDEX EmpMasterOrgIdx ON dbo.EmpMaster(Emp_Level, Emp_Node);
```

The code in the following example shows how to declare a new HIERARCHYID data type using the GetLevel method to create a breadth-first ordering:

```
INSERT dbo.EmpMaster (Emp_Node, Emp_ID, Emp_Name)
  VALUES (hierarchyid::GetRoot(), 1, 'Michael') ;
SELECT Emp_Node.ToString() AS Text_Emp_Node,
  Emp_Node, Emp_Level, Emp_ID, Emp_Name
  FROM dbo.EmpMaster ;
```

You can see the contents of the HIERARCHYID column for the root node shown in the following listing:

```
Text_Emp_Node       Emp_Node            Emp_Level Emp_ID       Emp_Name

/                   0x                  0         1            Michael

SQL2008-1(SQL2008-1\Administrator): (1 row(s) affected)
```

Spatial Data Types

The integration of mapping capabilities into many applications makes the new spatial data types a valuable and useful addition to SQL Server 2008. SQL Server 2008 adds two new spatial data types: GEOGRAPHY and GEOMETRY.

GEOGRAPHY

The new GEOGRAPHY data type uses a geodetic (round earth) model. It can store points, lines, polygons, and collections of latitude and longitude coordinates. You can see an example of how to declare and assign values to the new GEOGRAPHY data types in the following listing:

```
CREATE TABLE dbo.MyGeography
(
     Location_Name VARCHAR(50),
     Location_Point GEOGRAPHY
);
```

After creating a table containing the new GEOGRAPHY data type you can then store spatial values in the column. The following code example illustrates how you can store a point value in the new GEOGRAPHY column named Location_Point:

```
INSERT into dbo.MyGeography
  VALUES('MICROSOFT', geography::Point(47.643583, -122.128585, 4326))
```

GEOMETRY

GEOMETRY uses a planar (flat earth) model, unlike GEOGRAPHY, which is primarily designed for navigation and mapping on a round earth model. GEOMETRY complies with Open Geospatial Consortium standards for the representation of geographic features. You can see an example of how to declare and assign values to the new GEOMETRY data type in the following example:

```
CREATE TABLE dbo.MyGeometry
(
   Location_Name VARCHAR(50),
   Location_Poly GEOMETRY
);
```

The following example illustrates how you can store polygon data into the new GEOMETRY data type:

```
INSERT into dbo.MyGeometry
  VALUES('This Polygon',
   'POLYGON ((0 0, 300 0, 300 150, 100 150, 0 150, 0 0))')
```

Summary

The new data types introduced in SQL Server 2008 solve some old problems and at the same time provide several new capabilities. These new data types extend SQL Server 2008 beyond the realm of a traditional relational database server into an enterprise data platform. In particular, the new Date and Time data types are both easier to use and more compatible with other databases than the older DateTime data type. In addition, the new FileStream data type combines the advantages of relational database retrieval with the high performance of the raw NTFS file system. In the next chapter, you'll learn about some of the additional T-SQL language enhancements found in SQL Server 2008.

Chapter 7

New T-SQL Features

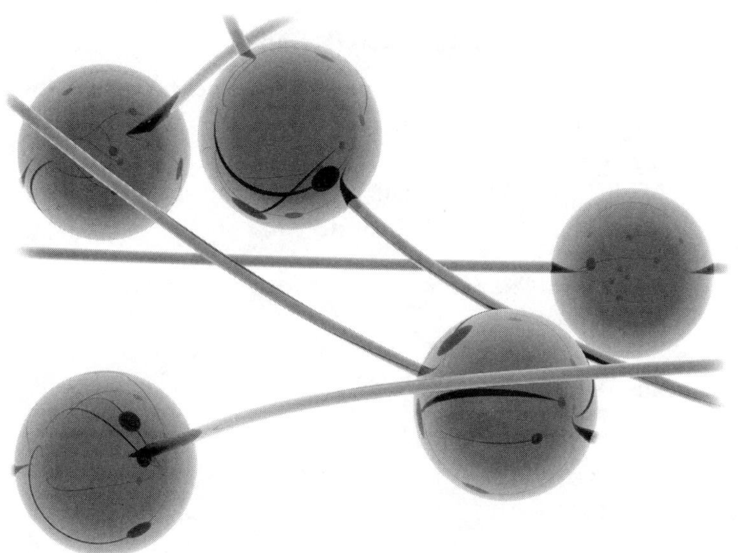

T-SQL continues to be the core development and administration language for SQL Server 2008. Microsoft has made a number of important enhancements to T-SQL in the SQL Server 2008 release. These changes affect many different aspects of the language, from the way you can declare variables to new ways of working with result sets. In this chapter, you'll get an introduction to the new T-SQL features in SQL Server 2008.

Variable and Assignment Enhancements

Variables are one of the most fundamental aspects of the T-SQL language. For SQL Server 2008, Microsoft has made some useful enhancements to the way that you declare variables, as well as to the way that you can assign values to variables using compound assignment operators. These changes mean that some features found in other, more modern languages have been brought to T-SQL. In addition, Microsoft has also added a new feature called Row Constructors, which really changes the way that you can assign row values. In this section, you'll get a look at using SQL Server 2008's new DECLARE statement, compound assignment operators, and Row Constructors.

The DECLARE Statement

One of the most fundamental enhancements to the T-SQL *DECLARE statement* is the ability to assign values to the variables being declared. You can assign values to most data types including SQLCLR data types. However, you can't assign values to TEXT, NTEXT, or IMAGE data types. You can see several examples of the SQL Server 2008's new DECLARE statement next:

```
DECLARE @MyName varchar(20)='Michael'
PRINT @MyName

DECLARE @MyInt int = 20
PRINT @MyInt

DECLARE @MyDate date = '07/04/08'
PRINT @MyDate
```

The results of the dilatation and assignments are shown next:

```
Michael
20
2008-07-04
```

Compound Assignment Operators

The ability to perform compound assignments is another new and fundamental T-SQL enhancement in SQL Server 2008 that follows the lead of other modern languages. SQL Server 2008 supports the *compound operators* shown in the following table:

Operator	Description
+=	Addition for numbers, Concatenation for strings
−=	Subtraction
/=	Division
%=	Percentage
&=	Bitwise And
|=	Bitwise Or
^=	XOR

The following listing illustrates the use of the new T-SQL compound operators:

```
/** Compound assignment operators **/
PRINT 'Compound Assignment Examples'
DECLARE @MyNumber int = 10
PRINT 'Start value:'
PRINT @MyNumber

-- Addition the old way
SET @MyNumber = @MyNumber + 1
PRINT 'Addition, standard assignment:'
PRINT @MyNumber

-- Addition using compound assignment
SET @MyNumber += 1
PRINT 'Addition, compound assignment:'
PRINT @MyNumber

-- Subtraction
SET @MyNumber -= 1
PRINT 'Subtraction, compound assignment:'
PRINT @MyNumber

-- Multiplication
SET @MyNumber *= 2
```

```
PRINT 'Multiplication, compound assignment:'
PRINT @MyNumber

-- Division
SET @MyNumber /= 2
PRINT 'Division, compound assignment:'
PRINT @MyNumber

-- Percentage
SET @MyNumber %= 10
PRINT 'Percentage, compound assignment:'
PRINT @MyNumber

-- Bitwise AND operation
SET @MyNumber &= 2
PRINT 'Bitwise AND, compound assignment:'
PRINT @MyNumber

-- Bitwise OR operation
SET @MyNumber |= 2
PRINT 'Bitwise OR, compound assignment:'
PRINT @MyNumber

-- XOR operation
SET @MyNumber ^= 2
PRINT 'XOR, compound assignment:'
PRINT @MyNumber

-- Concatentation
DECLARE @MyString varchar(40) = 'Michael'
SET @MyString += ' Otey'
PRINT 'Concatentation, compound assignment:'
PRINT @MyString
```

You can see the results of the previous example in the following listing:

```
Compound Assignment Examples
Start value:
10
Addition, standard assignment:
11
Addition, compound assignment:
12
Subtraction, compound assignment:
11
```

```
Multiplication, compound assignment:
22
Division, compound assignment:
11
Percentage, compound assignment:
1
Bitwise AND, compound assignment:
0
Bitwise OR, compound assignment:
2
XOR, compound assignment:
0
Concatentation, compound assignment:
Michael Otey
```

I'll now take you through this code listing step by step.

1. At the top of the first listing you can see the basic variable declaration using the assignment capability that was discussed in the previous section.
2. In this case, the integer data type variable named @MyNumber is first assigned a value of 10 and then that initial value is output to the client.
3. Next, to illustrate the difference between the new compound operators and the older standard assignment operators, an addition statement is performed using the standard assignment operator. The result, shown in the second listing, is 11.
4. Next, the new compound addition assignment operator is used to add 1 to the @MyNumber variable then that variable is printed.
5. At this point you can see that the value of @MyNumber is now 12 in the second listing. Then, the subtraction compound assignment operator is used to subtract 1 from @MyNumber.
6. Now you can see that in the second listing the value of @MyNumber has been changed back to 11.
7. Next, the multiplication compound operator is used to multiply the contents of @MyNumber by 2. The results shown in the second listing demonstrates that the value of the @MyNumber variable has been changed to 22.
8. Now the division compound assignment operator is used to divide the @MyNumber variable by 2. In the results listing you can see that the result of the division operation sets the value of @MyNumber back to 11.
9. At this point, the compound percentage operator is used to calculate 10 percent of the value of the @MyNumber variable. In the results listing you can see that the value of @MyNumber has been rounded to 1.
10. The use of the compound bitwise AND and OR component operators is now illustrated. The results are 0 and 2 respectively.

11. In the next part of the first listing you can see the results of the using the compound XOR assignment operator and the results in the second listing show that the result is 0.
12. Finally, near the end of the first listing you can see how the compound addition operator can be used for string concatenation. In this example a new varchar variable named @MyString is declared and assigned the initial value of Michael. Then the compound assignment operator is used to add the string Otey to that initial value. The results shown in the second listing show that the resulting value is Michael Otey.

Row Constructors

Sometimes called Table Value Constructors, SQL Server 2008's new *Row Constructors* allow you to insert multiple rows with a single statement. This new feature can help make your data loading tasks more concise and readable. The following example shows how you can use SQL Server 2008's new Row Constructor feature to insert three rows with a single INSERT statement into a table variable named MyTableVar:

```
/** Row Constructors  **/
CREATE TABLE MyTableVar (ID int, Vehicle varchar(20))
INSERT INTO MyTableVar VALUES (1, 'Car'), (2, 'Truck'), (3, 'Van')

SELECT * FROM MyTableVar
```

In the previous listing you can see the creation of a table variable named MyTableVar. This table variable contains two columns consisting of an integer data type and a varchar data type. You can also see the Row Constructor used in the subsequent INSERT statement. The INSERT statement uses the typical VALUES clause to identify the data that will be inserted. However, unlike the older-style INSERT statement, the new INSERT statement using Row Constructors contains multiple sets of values, where each set of values is contained within a set of parenthesis and is separated by comma. This example inserts three separate rows into the MyTableVar table variable. Then, a SELECT statement is used to show the contents of the table variable.

As you can see in the following listing, the results of using SQL Server 2008's new Row Constructor is exactly like performing three separate insert operations:

```
(3 row(s) affected)
ID          Vehicle
----------- --------------------
1           Car
2           Truck
3           Van
```

Table-Valued Parameters

Like their name implies, *table-valued parameters* allow you to pass a table as a parameter to a stored procedure or function. Table-valued parameters can be a very clean way to pass a number of variables into a stored procedure or function without needing to use a large unwieldy collection of parameters. In addition, because it's a table, the different values will all be strongly typed. In order to use table-valued parameters, you first need to create a table type, and then you need to instantiate a table or table variable of that type. Next, you'll need to create a stored procedure or function that accepts a table type as a parameter. Finally, you must execute that stored procedure or function, passing in the instantiated table type. The following example illustrates how you can use SQL Server 2008's new table-valued parameters feature:

```
/** Table-valued parametere **/
-- Create an new Table Type
CREATE TYPE MyTableType AS TABLE (ID int, Vehicle varchar(20))
GO

-- Create an SP that uses a table-valued parameter
CREATE Procedure usp_MyProc(@MyTableIn MyTableType READONLY)
AS
SELECT * FROM @MyTableIn
GO

-- Create and populate a table variable
DECLARE @MyTableIn MyTableType;

-- Execute the SP with the table-valued parameter
INSERT INTO @MyTableIn VALUES (10, 'Bike')
EXEC usp_MyProc @MyTableIn
```

In the beginning of this listing you can see where new table type called MyTableType is created. This table type defines the schema of the table that will be passed as a parameter.

Next, you can see where a stored procedure named usp_MyProc is created. This stored procedure accepts the MyTableType table as a parameter. Only table objects of the MyTableType can be passed into the stored procedure. SQL Server will generate an error if you attempt to pass in another table object. In addition, you should note that the table-valued parameter must be declared as read-only. The stored procedure cannot change the contents of the table-valued parameter. Inside the body of the usp_MyProc stored procedure, you can see that in this case a SELECT statement simply reads the contents of the table-valued parameter.

In the next part of the previous listing you can see where a new table variable named @MyTableIn is created. The @MyTableIn table variable is declared as a MyTableType using the table type that was created previously. After the new @MyTableIn variable is created, an INSERT statement populates it with a single row. While this simple example only used one row, table-valued parameters allow very large tables containing hundreds or even thousands of rows to be used as parameters.

NOTE

Passing table variables as parameters causes SQL Server to materialize the tables in the tempdb database. This enables SQL Server to effectively work with large table variables without placing the entire contents of the table variable in memory.

At the end of the listing you can see where the usp_MyProc stored procedure is executed and the table @MyTableIn is passed into the stored procedure as a parameter. You can see the results of running this table-valued parameter example in the following listing:

```
ID          Vehicle
----------- --------------------
10          Bike

(1 row(s) affected)
```

New Statements, Operators, and Functions

In addition to the basic language enhancements that you saw in the first part of this chapter, SQL Server 2008 also provides several new statements. The most significant of which are the new MERGE statement which can synchronize the contents of two tables, and the new GROUPING SETS capability which enables you to have more control over data sorting and aggregation.

The MERGE Statement

The *MERGE statement* enables you to selectively merge the contents of two tables together based on the contents of those tables. MERGE combines the ability to perform INSERT, UPDATE, and DELETE actions in a single statement. In the following example you can see how to use the new MERGE statement to merge together the data from two tables. If rows exist in the table defined as the MERGE target that are the same as the rows in the source table used for the MERGE operation, then those rows will be updated in the MERGE target table. If there are rows in the MERGE source table that are not present in the MERGE target table, then those rows will be added to the table defined as the MERGE target. If there are rows in the MERGE target table that are not present in the table used as the MERGE source table, then those rows will be deleted:

```
/** MERGE **/
CREATE TABLE MyMergeSourceTable (ID int, Vehicle varchar(20))
INSERT INTO MyMergeSourceTable
  VALUES (1, 'Bicycle'), (2, 'Car'), (3, 'Truck')

CREATE TABLE MyMergeTargetTable (ID int, Vehicle varchar(20))
INSERT INTO MyMergeTargetTable
  VALUES (1, 'Bicycle'), (2, 'Sedan'), (4, 'Van')
GO

-- Show original tables
PRINT 'Source table before MERGE.'
SELECT * FROM MyMergeSourceTable
PRINT 'Target table before MERGE.'
SELECT * FROM MyMergeTargetTable

-- Perform MERGE
MERGE MyMergeTargetTable AS TargetTable
USING (SELECT ID, Vehicle FROM MyMergeSourceTable) SourceTable
ON (TargetTable.ID = SourceTable.ID)
WHEN MATCHED THEN UPDATE SET Vehicle = SourceTable.Vehicle
WHEN NOT MATCHED BY TARGET THEN INSERT VALUES (ID, Vehicle)
WHEN NOT MATCHED BY SOURCE THEN DELETE;
GO

-- Show merged tables
PRINT 'Source table after MERGE.'
SELECT * FROM MyMergeSourceTable
PRINT 'Target table after MERGE.'
SELECT * FROM MyMergeTargetTable
```

At the top of this example you can see where the table named MyMergeSource Table is created and then populated with three rows. Each of the new rows has an ID number of 1, 2, or 3. Next a second table named MyMergeTargetTable is created and it is populated with three rows. However, you should note the difference between the row values in the tables MyMergeSourceTable and MyMergeTargetTable. You can see that the row values for the row with the ID of 1 are the same. However, the rows values for the row with ID of 2 are different: MyMergeSourceTable has the value of Car, while MyMergeTargetTable has the value of Sedan. Next, note that MyMergeSourceTable has a row with the ID of 3, while MyMergeTargetTable does not. Further, the table MyMergeTargetTable has a row that begins with the ID of 4, while MyMergeSourceTable does not.

NOTE

The schema of the two tables being merged must match.

After the source and the target tables have been created, two SELECT statements are used to display the contents of each of the tables. This allows you to see the pre-merged contents of each table.

The next section of the code is where the actual MERGE operation is performed. This example takes the MyMergeTargetTable and then merges it with the contents of the existing MyMergeSourceTable. The MERGE target table is the table that will be updated with merged data (i.e., MyMergeTargetTable). The source table (in this example MyMergeSourceTable) will be used as a source for data but it will not be modified. The USING clause identifies the columns from the source table that will be used by the merge operation. The ON clause specifies that the two tables will be merged based on the ID column. The MERGE statement's WHEN clause controls the actions that SQL Server will take according to the different merge conditions. In this example, if the value in the ID column is matched, then the value in the Vehicle column of the MyMergeTargetTable will be updated with the value from the Vehicle column value from the MyMergeSourceTable. Or, if the ID column in the MyMergeTargetTable is not matched , indicating that there is a row in the source table that is not in the target table, then an INSERT statement is executed that will insert the missing row into the MyMergeTarget table. Otherwise, the NOT MATCHED BY SOURCE clause indicates that if there is a row in the target table (for example, MyMergeTargetTable) that is not present in the source table (such as MyMergeSourceTable), then that row will be deleted from the MyMergeTargetTable table.

Finally, after the MERGE operation has completed, two SELECT statements are used to show the contents of the MyMergeSourceTable and the "MyMergeTargetTable". You can see the results of the MERGE example shown in the following listing:

```
(3 row(s) affected)
(3 row(s) affected)
Source table before MERGE.
ID          Vehicle
----------- --------------------
1           Bicycle
2           Car
3           Truck

(3 row(s) affected)

Target table before MERGE.
ID          Vehicle
----------- --------------------
1           Bicycle
2           Sedan
4           Van

(3 row(s) affected)

(4 row(s) affected)

Source table after MERGE.
ID          Vehicle
----------- --------------------
1           Bicycle
2           Car
3           Truck

(3 row(s) affected)

Target table after MERGE.
ID          Vehicle
----------- --------------------
1           Bicycle
2           Car
3           Truck

(3 row(s) affected)
```

In the previous listing, you can see the contents of the MyMergeSourceTable and the MyMergeTargetTable after the example MERGE operation has completed. Here you can see that the MyMergeSourceTable is unchanged. Because the MyMergeSourceTable was designated as the source of the merge, no modifications were made to the table and its original three rows stayed the same. However, that isn't the case for the MyMergeTargetTable; the first row in the MyMergeTargetTable matched in both the source and the target tables, so no changes were made to it. However, the second row had matching values in the ID column but the values in the Vehicle column were different. In this case, the value in the MyMergeTarget table was overridden with the value from the Vehicle column of the MyMergeSourceTable. Next, there was no matching row in the MyMergeTargetTable with an ID value of 3. The contents of the row from the MyMergeSourceTable with the value of 3 in the ID column were inserted into the MyMergeTargetTable. Finally, the row in the MyMergeTargetTable with an ID value of 4 had no matching row in the MyMergeSourceTable and was deleted.

GROUPING SETS

SQL Server 2008 also provides a new GROUPING SETS operator. *GROUPING SETS* are an extension to the GROUP BY clause. The new GROUPING SETS operator allows you to specify multiple groupings of data returned by a single query. GROUPING SETS enable you to have more control over the aggregations that are returned by a query. You can use GROUPING SETS to create multiple aggregation levels within the same result set. The new GROUPING SETS operator returns a single result set that is essentially equal to the use of the UNION ALL statement of different grouped rows. GROUPING SETS add to the power and flexibility of SQL Server 2008's reporting capabilities. You can see an example of using the GROUPING SETS operator in the following listing:

```
Use AdventureWorks
GO
SELECT Name, DATEPART(yy,DueDate) As Year, SUM(TotalDue) As Total
FROM Sales.SalesOrderHeader O
 JOIN Sales.Store AS S ON S.CustomerID = O.CustomerID
GROUP BY GROUPING SETS
(
      (Name, DATEPART(yy,DueDate)),
      (Name),
      ()
)
```

In this example, you can see how GROUPING SETS are used to aggregate the total due for each customer per year, as well as to produce the totals due for each customer.

At the top of the listing you can see that the AdventureWorks database is set as the current database. Then, a SELECT statement is used to return the values from first the Customer's Name column, then the year portion of the DueDate column, and finally a summary of the amount in the TotalDue column. A JOIN to the Sales.Store column is used to retrieve the customer's name.

Next you can see where the GROUP BY clause uses the new GROUPING SETS extension to create three new grouping sets. The first set groups the results by the customer name and the year portion of the due date—creating a summary of the customer orders due for that year. The next set produces a total for the group by customer. The final set will aggregate the total due for the entire result set.

NOTE

You cannot nest a GROUPING SET inside other GROUPING SETs.

You can see the partial results of this query in the following listing:

```
Name                                      Year        Total
----------------------------------------- ----------- -------------
A Bike Store                              2001        40732.6067
A Bike Store                              2002        72366.1284
A Bike Store                              NULL        113098.7351
A Great Bicycle Company                   2001        6279.5691
A Great Bicycle Company                   2002        5053.3945
A Great Bicycle Company                   2003        673.7178
A Great Bicycle Company                   NULL        12006.6814
A Typical Bike Shop                       2001        43166.2766
A Typical Bike Shop                       2002        67585.3448
A Typical Bike Shop                       NULL        110751.6214
Acceptable Sales & Service                2001        556.2026
Acceptable Sales & Service                2002        1112.405
Acceptable Sales & Service                NULL        1668.6076
Accessories Network                       2003        1092.6354
Accessories Network                       2004        1903.3829
Accessories Network                       NULL        2996.0183

….(code cut from from to the end of the result set)
Yellow Bicycle Company                    2001        29696.8428
Yellow Bicycle Company                    2002        72951.8988
Yellow Bicycle Company                    2004        50.2703
```

```
Yellow Bicycle Company                         NULL        102699.0119
NULL                                           NULL        108266245.7018

(2271 row(s) affected)
```

With these results you can see where the GROUP SETS query produced a summary from each customer per year. This is output for the first GROUPING SET. Next, if you scan through the listing you'll see various rows where the Year column contains a NULL. This is the total for the customer and it is produced by the second GROUPING SET. Finally, at the end of the listing you can see where both the Name and the Year columns contain the value of Null. This is total for the entire result set and it is produced by the third GROUPING SET.

Enhanced CONVERT Function

SQL Server 2008's *CONVERT function* has been enhanced to support multiple conversion styles. This gives you more control over the output of the CONVERT function. You can see how the new styles are used in the following example:

```
SELECT CONVERT(char(8), 0x4D69636861656C, 0) AS 'Style 0'
SELECT CONVERT(char(8), 0x4D69636861656C, 1) AS 'Style 1'
SELECT CONVERT(char(8), 0x4D69636861656C, 2) AS 'Style 2'
```

In this example you can see where binary data is converted using one of three different styles. For the BINARY data type style 0, the data is converted to ASCII on a character by character basis. Style 2 converts the data to character with no conversion. The length of the data matches the size of the target field. Style 1 added the prefix of 0x to its binary data. Style 2 does the same thing as style 1, but it doesn't add the 0x prefix.

NOTE

There are different styles for each of the different data types. This example shows the styles for the BINARY data type.

You can see the results of using the enhanced CONVERT function in the following listing:

```
Style 0
--------
Michael

(1 row(s) affected)
```

```
Style 1
--------
0x4D6963

(1 row(s) affected)

Style 2
--------
4D696368

(1 row(s) affected)
```

Summary

In this chapter you've learned about the most important new T-SQL–related enhancements that Microsoft has made to SQL Server 2008. In the first part of the chapter, you saw how the enhanced DECLARE statement and new compound operators bring a couple of useful language features from other modern languages into T-SQL. You also saw how the new table-valued parameters feature can be used to pass large amounts of variable data to stored procedures and functions. In the second part of this chapter, you saw the new T-SQL MERGE statement and GROUPING SETS operators. MERGE is useful for BI and ETL data loading scenarios as it enables you to synchronize the contents of two tables. The new GROUPING SETS statement gives you more control over how query data can be sorted and aggregated. In the next chapter we'll jump into the BI side of things where you'll get to learn about the new features found in SQL Server 2008 Integration Services.

Part III

Business Intelligence Features

Chapter 8

Business Intelligence

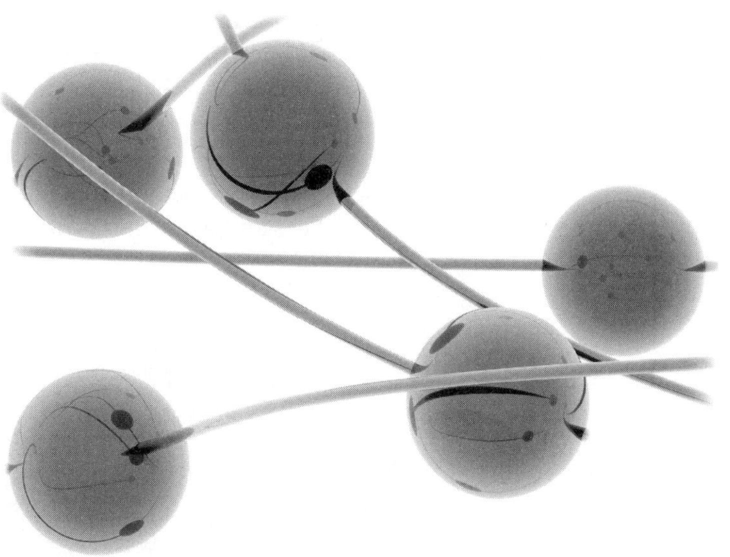

SQL Server's built-in Business Intelligence (BI) suite is one of the main factors that set it apart from the competing enterprise database platforms, such as Oracle and IBM's DB2. While both Oracle and IBM offer BI components to their respective relational database platforms for a substantial additional cost, SQL Server 2008 includes full BI functionality in both the SQL Server 2008 Standard Edition and the SQL Server 2008 Enterprise Edition. The inclusion of the full BI stack gives SQL Server a tremendous edge in value over these competing database platforms.

BI enables a business to get more meaningful information out of the operational data that it currently uses in its line of business applications. By taking the operational data from their order entry, shipping, and sales applications, OLAP, data warehousing, and data mining technologies enable businesses to accumulate and aggregate important pieces of information in ways that are not possible with pure relational data access techniques. The end result uncovers more meaningful information about your business and the important factors that influence it.

SQL Server's BI stack consists of three main subsystems: SQL Server Integration Services (SSIS), SQL Server Analysis Services (SSAS), and SQL Server Reporting Services (SSRS). Together they provide end-to-end BI functionality. You can see an overview of SQL Server 2008's BI implementation in Figure 8-1.

The stack starts with ability to pull data into the data warehouse from the OLTP relational database systems that typically run your organization's Line of Business (LoB) applications. That's where SSIS fits in. SSIS is an Extraction Transfer Load (ETL) tool that's capable of transferring and transforming data as it is sent between two data sources. SSIS can be used between relational data sources, but it is primarily designed as a data warehouse data cleansing and loading tool. Analysis Services

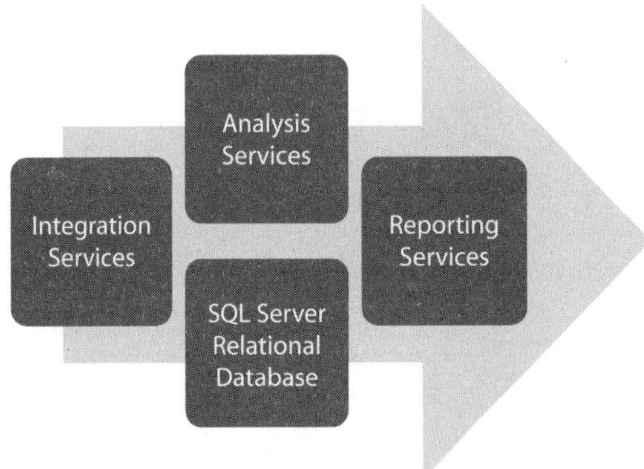

Figure 8-1 *An overview of SQL Server 2008 Business Intelligence Implementation*

takes off from that point by providing tools to perform Online Analytical Processing (OLAP) queries on the data sources. Analysis Services enables you to create OLAP cubes that aggregate the data generated from your LoB systems, which in turn enables you to rapidly perform ad-hoc queries. Analysis Services and OLAP queries enable businesses to better turn their data into information that can be used to make better business decisions. Reporting Services is at the other end of SQL Server 2008's BI stack. While SSIS is about populating the data warehouse, and SSAS is about providing the ability to query the data warehouse, SQL Server Reporting Services is about presenting that information to the end users and business decision makers. Reporting Services enables you to build reports from both relational data sources and Analysis Services cubes. These reports can be delivered to the end users in a variety of formats, including web pages, applications, or email. In addition, Reporting Services provides tools to enable end users to build their own reports.

In this chapter you'll learn about the new features in each of SQL Server 2008's BI subsystems. First you'll learn about the enhancements to SQL Server 2008 Integration Services. In the central part of this chapter you'll learn about the improvements in SQL Server 2008 Analysis Services. Finally, you'll get a tour of the new features in SQL Server 2008 Reporting Services.

Integration Services

SQL Server Integration Service was first introduced with SQL Server 2005 as a replacement for the older Data Transformation Services (DTS) supplied with SQL Server 7 and SQL Server 2000. Unlike DTS, which was a basic data transfer engine with limited control flow and logic, SQL Server 2008's Integration Services was redesigned from the ground up as an enterprise capable ETL platform. With SQL Server 2008, Microsoft has continued to enhance SSIS with several significant performance and programming improvements.

Performance Enhancements

Performance-wise, SSIS has benefited from several major improvements to the Data Flow Task, which is the SSIS component responsible for moving data between two data sources. The Data Flow engine is the core component of SSIS.

Asynchronous Components

One of the important performance enhancements to the SQL Server 2008 Data Flow engine is the use of asynchronous components. With SQL Server 2008, the Data Flow components that create rows and allocate new data buffers now operate asynchronously, freeing the Data Flow Engine from waiting on the completion of these tasks before beginning the actual data transfers.

Improved Parallelism of Execution Trees

Probably the biggest performance improvement in the SQL Server 2008 Data Flow engine is the incorporation of parallelism in the processing of execution trees. The execution tree essentially defines the flow of the data from the originating data source to the destination. However, this isn't necessarily a straight path because transformation and other tasks can split the data flow into multiple paths. With SQL Server 2005, each execution tree used a single thread. For SQL Server 2008, the Data Flow engine was redesigned to utilize multiple threads and take advantage of dynamic scheduling to execute multiple components in parallel, including components within the same execution tree. The use of parallelism for SQL Server 2008's Data Flow execution trees improves the performance of the Data Flow engine and enables it to take better advantage of the multiple processing cores available in today's high performance servers.

Programmability Enhancements

The other major category of enhancements for SSIS is in the area of programmability. SSIS uses a new scripting engine that enables the use of .NET languages for scripting tasks, as well as the use of ADO.NET tasks for SSIS package source and targets.

New Visual Studio Tools for Applications Scripting Engine

One of the biggest changes for SSIS is the incorporation of the new Visual Studio Tools for Applications (VSTA) scripting engine. The VSTA scripting engine replaces the older Visual Studio for Applications (VSA) scripting engine. The biggest advantage of this change is the fact that it enables you to use .NET languages like C# and VB as scripting languages. SQL Server 2005 only supported the use of VB. It also makes it easier for you to reference .NET assemblies in your script tasks. You can see the new Integration Services Script Task with VSTA support shown in Figure 8-2.

Components Improvements

Several of the Integration Services components have been enhanced in SQL Server 2008. These include a new ADO.NET source and destination components, as well as an improved Cached Lookup Transformation and a new Data Profiling Task.

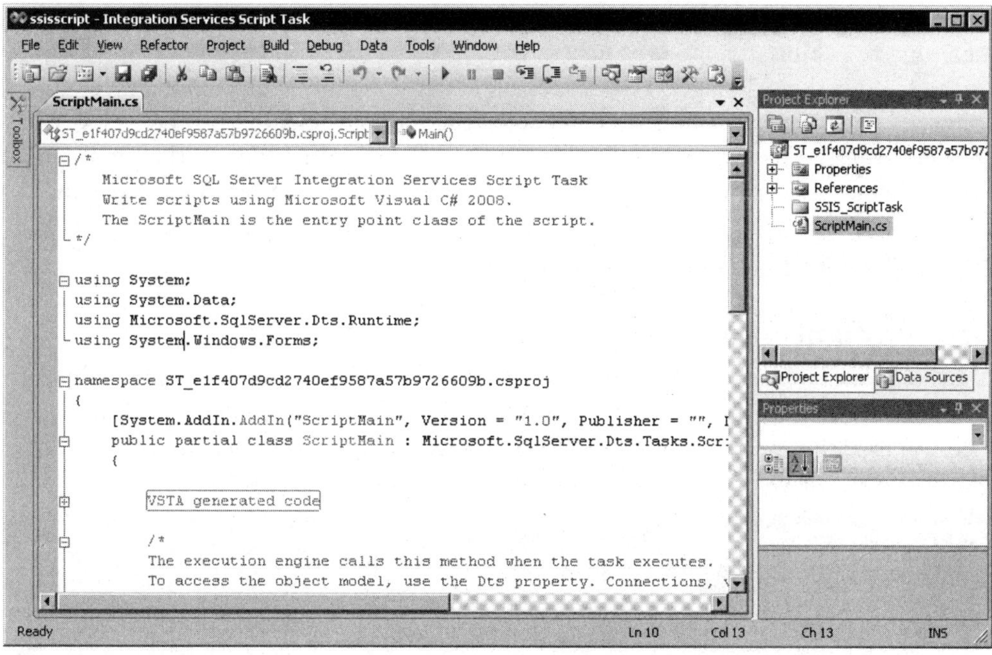

Figure 8-2 *Integration Services new Visual Studio Tools for Applications*

ADO.NET Tasks and Source and Destination Components

Another new development feature in SQL Server 2008's SSIS is the ability to use ADO.NET sources and destinations. An ADO.NET source takes data from an ADO.NET connection and makes it available to the data flow. For example, an ADO.NET source connection could be an ADO.NET connection object created with a `SELECT * FROM HumanResources.Department` statement. This would enable the HumanResources.Departmant table to act as the package source. Likewise, you can also use ADO.NET components for an SSIS destination where the package can output to a specific table or other ADO.NET connection.

Cached Lookup Transformations

In addition to improvements in the Data Flow engine, the performance of the Lookup Transformation has also been improved. With SQL Server 2008 SSIS, the Lookup Transformation has faster cache loading and lookup operations.

The new Lookup Transformation features a number of new caching options, including the ability for the reference dataset to use a cache file (.caw) accessed by the Cache Connection Manager. The referenced dataset can be a connected data source accessed by the Cache Connection Manager, the reference dataset can be a table, view or query accessed by the OLE DB Connection Manager. In addition, the same cache can be shared between multiple Lookup Transformations in the same package and you now have the option of deploying the cache along with the SSIS package. You can see the new Cache Connection Manager shown in Figure 8-3.

Data Profiling Task

Another new enhancement to Integration Services in SQL Server 2008 is the addition of the new Data Profiling Task. The Data Profiling Task is a debugging aid that can help you to analyze the data flows occurring in your Integration Services packages.

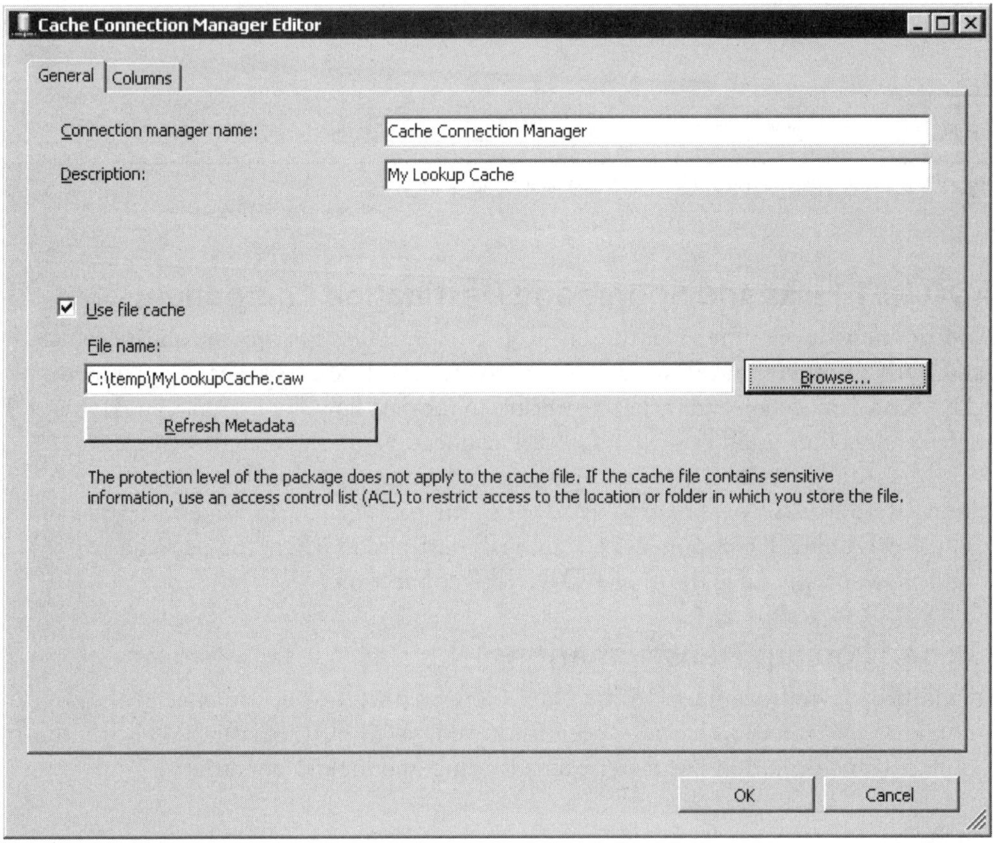

Figure 8-3 *Cache Connection Manager*

In many cases, Integration Services' package execution errors are caused by unexpected variations in the data that is being transferred. The Data Profiling Task can help you to discover the source of these errors by giving you better visibility into the data flow that's occurring in your packages. Adding the Data Profiler to your Integration Services Package enables you to generate reports showing the transferred data that you can later view using the Data Profile Viewer. You can see the properties of the new Data Profiling Task shown in Figure 8-4.

The drop-down menu that you can see in figure 8-4 shows the available profiling types. Table 8-1 summarizes these types.

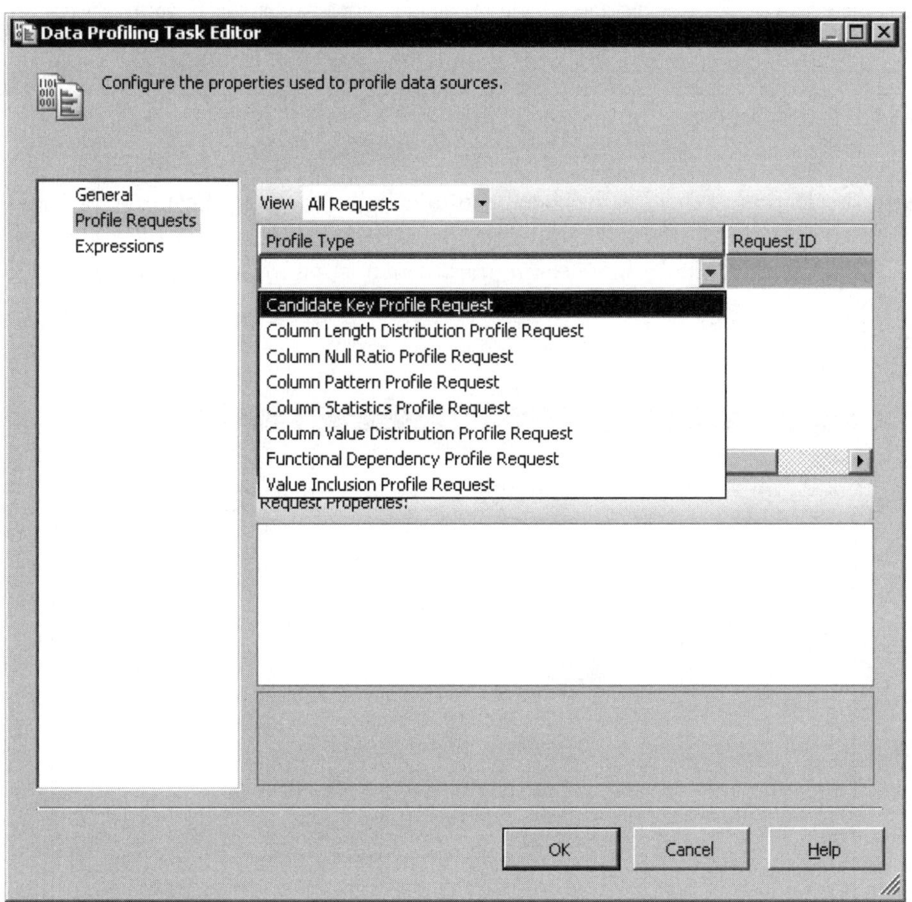

Figure 8-4 *Data Profiling Task*

Profile type	Description
Candidate Key	Determines a column's suitability to act as a key
Column Length Distribution	Determines the lengths of the string values and the ratio of values that share the length value
Column Null Ratio	Determines the number of null values
Columns Pattern	Determines the number of rows that match a regular expression
Column Statistics	Provides statistical information about a column's values like the minimum and maximum values
Column Value Distribution	Determines the distinct values in a column
Function Dependency	Determines the number of values that depend on values in another column
Value Inclusion	Determines if a value is suitable for use as a foreign key

Table 8-1 *Data Profiling Types*

After a selection of the data has been captured using the Data Profiling Task you can use the Data Profile Viewer to examine the data. To run the Data Profile Viewer you need to execute the DataProfiler.exe program which is found in the C:\Program Files\Microsoft\SQL Server\100\DTS\Binn directory. The Data Profile Viewer is shown in Figure 8-5.

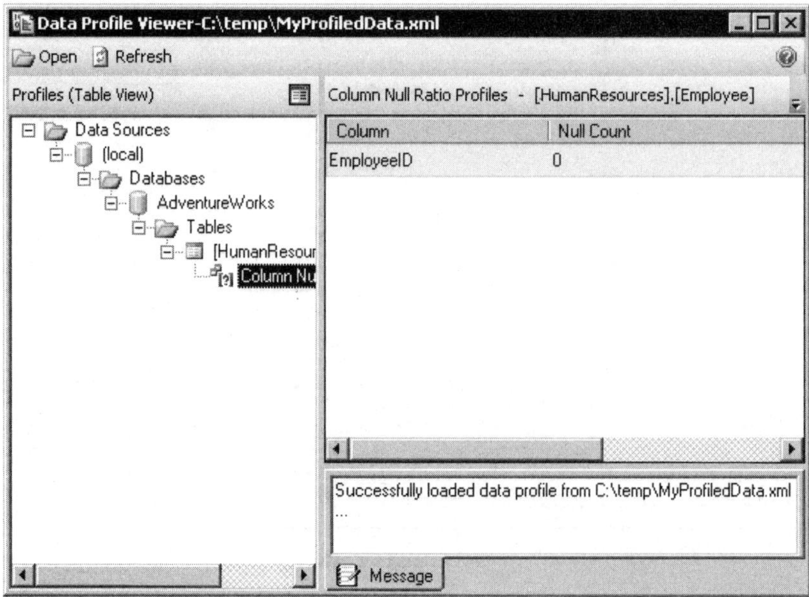

Figure 8-5 *Data Profile Viewer*

After launching the Data Profile Viewer, you use the Open option to open the saved .xml file that was generated by the Data Profiling Task. Then, you can expand the nodes for the server and report and find the display the saved profile values.

Usability Enhancements

In addition to performance and development enhancements, SQL Server 2008 Integration Services also has several enhancements that improve its usability.

New Connections Project Wizard

One of the main usability enhancements that Microsoft added to Integration Services in SQL Server 2008 is the new Connections Project Wizard. The Connections Project Wizard guides you through the steps required to create source and destination connections within an Integration Services designer. You launch the new Connections Project Wizard by opening the Business Intelligence Development Studio and then selecting the File | New | Project menu option. This displays the New Project dialog box, where you can select the Integration Services Connections Project Wizard from the list of displayed templates. You can see the Connections Project Wizard in Figure 8-6.

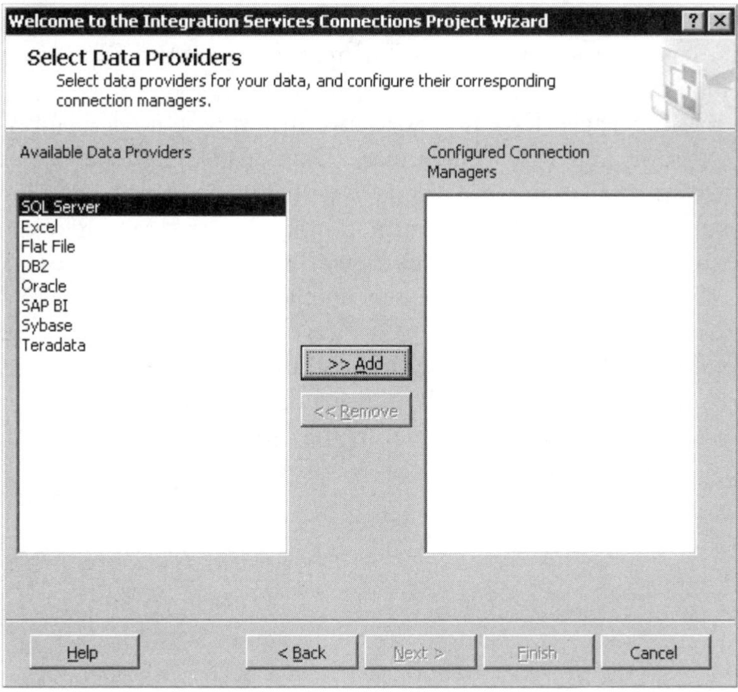

Figure 8-6 *Connections Project Wizard*

The Connections Project Wizard essentially walks you through the steps of setting up your SSIS packages' source and target connections before displaying the SSIS Designer.

Enhanced Import and Export Wizard

The SSIS Import and Export Wizard also has several new features that enhance its usability. First, Microsoft sensibly added the wizard back into the Start menu from where they incomprehensibly removed it in SQL Server 2005. With SQL Server 2008, you can start the Import and Export Wizard using the Start | All Programs | Microsoft SQL Server 2008 | Import and Export Data option.

The Import and Export wizard now allows you to review the data type mapping for the tables that are selected for either import or export. If the Import and Export Wizard can directly convert all of the data types, then the Review Data Type Mapping dialog is not shown. However, if the Import and Export Wizard either can't perform the data type mapping or isn't sure if the correct data type mapping is being used, it will automatically display the new Review Data Type Mapping dialog, which enables you to verify and change the data type mappings that are in use. For example, if you are importing a flat file that has a date value defined as a string and you are trying to import that value to a SQL Server Data column, the Import and Export Wizard will display the Review Data Type Mapping dialog showing you the potential data type conversion problem. The new Review Data Type Mapping dialog is shown in Figure 8-7.

Data that the Import and Export Wizard can convert with no problem is displayed prefixed with a green circle with a check mark. Data that is questionable, such as the string-to-date conversion example is displayed with a prefix showing a yellow triangle with an exclamation point. This is the warning icon. Data that cannot be converted without an error is displayed with a red circle with x icon. This is the error icon. You can view the specific warning or error text by double clicking on the line to display the Column Conversion Details dialog. SQL Server Integration Services uses the C:\Program Files\Microsoft SQL Server\100\DTS\binn\DtwTypeConversion.xml file to control how data will be converted. If there are data type mappings that you require that are not present in the file, you can modify the DtwTypeConversion.xml file and add your own custom data conversions.

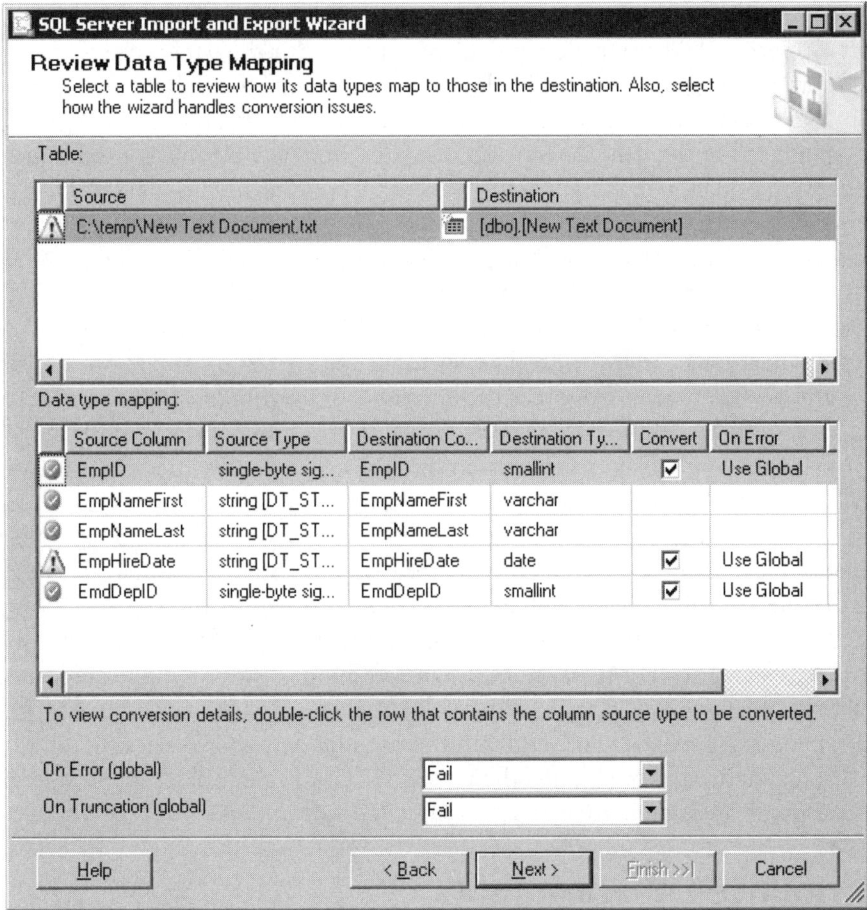

Figure 8-7 *The Import and Export Wizard's Review Data Type Mapping dialog*

Analysis Services

Analysis Services is the core of the Microsoft BI stack. To help you understand the significance of some of the new features in Analysis Services, it's important to understand a little bit about the background of Analysis Services and a few of the key concepts of Online Analytical Processing (OLAP).

SQL Server 2008 Analysis Services, and its predecessor OLAP Services, are decision support tools that enable rapid ad-hoc queries for the data typically stored in a data warehouse or data mart. The decision support information is not typically stored in a relational database form, but rather in a cube form. Unlike relational data, which contains all of the detailed transaction data, cube data is typically summary data consisting of data points built using the data from many relational database transactions. This summary data is stored using a cube model that's optimized for flexible and fast ad-hoc reporting. The cube is optimized to quickly navigate the summary data to return results. Improved query performance is the reason behind the emergence of Online Analytical Processing (OLAP). For example, to come up with the local, regional, national, and worldwide sales totals for a given organization, a relational query might have to process hundreds of thousands or even millions of rows—a process that could be quite lengthy even on the fastest of systems. In contrast, an OLAP query might need to read only two or three data points in order to come up with the same answer. This makes OLAP queries an order of magnitude faster than relational queries because they are primarily performed on summary information. OLAP's much faster performance enables ad-hoc querying and processing of data that just isn't feasible using traditional means of relational data access.

OLAP queries work with cubes, consisting of dimensions and measures. A *dimension* is a descriptive category. For instance, a dimension might be a geographical location or a product type. A *measure* is a quantitative value such as sales dollars, inventory amount, or total expenses. Aggregates derived from the original data source are stored in each cube cell. This method of organizing data makes it easy to filter data, as well as making subsequent queries fast and efficient.

Performance Enhancements

With SQL Server 2008, Analysis Service has received a couple of important performance enhancements. First, for improved scalability, Analysis Services is able to make better use of parallelism for queries of partitioned tables. Plus, the SQL Server 2008 query engine uses bitmap filters to improve the performance of join queries over star schema. There are also improvements to MOLAP write back and MDX block computation capabilities.

Improved Parallelism for Partitioned Table Queries

Fact tables are often partitioned because they typically contain very large numbers of rows. SQL Server 2005 queries used a single thread for each partition. SQL Server 2008 Enterprise Edition is now able to use multiple threads to query a single partition potentially improving query response time for partitioned tables.

Improved Query Performance over Star Schema

Most data warehouses use the star schema for the data warehouse tables. SQL Server Analysis Services uses bitmap filtering to eliminate joined rows from the second table for star schema tables where the values don't match the values in the base table. With SQL Server 2008 the query optimizer can apply bitmap filtering during the generation of the query execution plan. In contrast SQL Server 2005 applied the bitmap filters following the generation of the query plan. Applying the bitmap filters earlier results in improved performance for queries over star schemas.

Improved MOLAP-enabled Write Back

MOLAP-enabled write back enables organizations to quickly perform what-if analyses by allowing them to change cube values on the fly and then requery the cube. SQL Server 2008 Analysis Services improves the performance of MOLAP write back by removing the need to requery the underlying data for the cube's Relational Online Analytical Processing (ROLAP) relational partitions. This enables the use of MOLAP write-back with no loss of OLAP query performance.

MDX Performance Enhancements

MDX query performance has also been enhanced for SQL Server 2008 with the improved ability to perform *block computations*. Also called subspace computations, MDX block computations can increase the performance of certain MDX queries. SQL Server 2005 evaluated most MDX queries on a cell-by-cell basis. Higher performance block computation mode was available in SQL Server 2005, but its usage was limited. MDX in Analysis Services 2008 extends the applicability of MDX block computational mode to a much wider larger number of scenarios. With block computational mode, more operations can be pushed down the query engines enabling it to process MDX queries much more effectively.

Backup and Restore Performance Enhancements

Analysis Services in SQL Server 2008 also uses a new storage structure that can significantly improve the backup and restore time for your Analysis Services databases.

Development Enhancements

Some of the biggest changes in SQL Server 2008 Analysis Services are in the area of BI development. With the SQL Server 2008 release, Microsoft has made numerous enhancements to the development tools provided for Analysis Services including a new Cube Designer, an improved Dimension Designer, an improved Aggregate Designer, and a new Attribute Designer.

New Cube Designer

One of the most prominent new features in the development tools for Analysis Services 2008 is the new Cube Designer. Cube design is probably the most central feature to Analysis Services because cubes are the foundation of OLAP functionality. The new Analysis Services 2008 Cube Designer enables you to edit various properties of a cube, including cube measures, cube dimensions, dimension relationships, calculations, key performance indicators (KPIs), partitions, actions, perspectives, and translations. The new Cube Designer is simpler because it makes it easier to create cubes. Likewise, an enhanced Cube Wizard streamlines the initial creation of a cube allowing you to design better cubes in fewer steps. The Cube Wizard is typically used to create cubes, while the Cube Designer is used to update cubes.

You open the Cube Designer by first starting the Business Intelligence Development Studio (BIDS) and then either creating or opening an existing Analysis Service project. To open the new Cube Designer, right-click a cube in the BIDS Solution Explorer and then select the View Designer option. Analysis Services' updated Cube Designer is shown in Figure 8-8.

Analysis Services 2008's new Cube Designer also links to the improved Aggregation Designer.

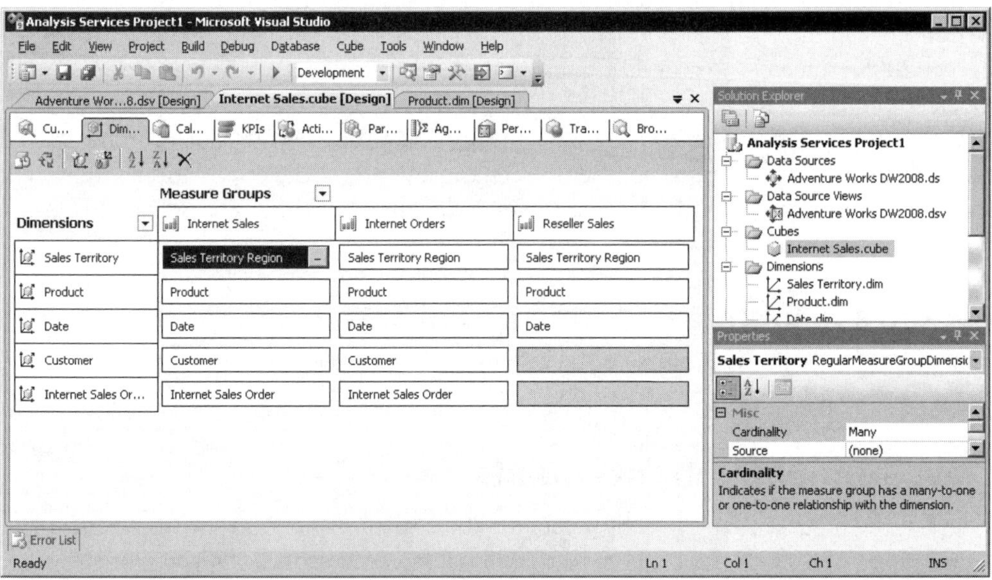

Figure 8-8 *The Cube Designer*

Enhanced Aggregation Designer

Analysis Services in SQL Server 2008 also features several important improvements to the Aggregation Designer. The Aggregation Designer makes it easier for you to view and change aggregations. To use the Aggregation Designer start, the Cube Designer from BIDS and then click on the Aggregations tab. Finally, click on the Advanced button in the toolbar. The new Aggregation Designer is shown in Figure 8-9.

Enhanced Dimension Designer

Analysis Service in 2008 also sports a new Dimension Designer. You can use the Dimension Designer to create and update the attributes, hierarchies, and levels of a cube's dimensions. The Dimension Wizard has also been simplified and improved. The new Dimension Wizard is able to identify parent-child hierarchies as well as supporting

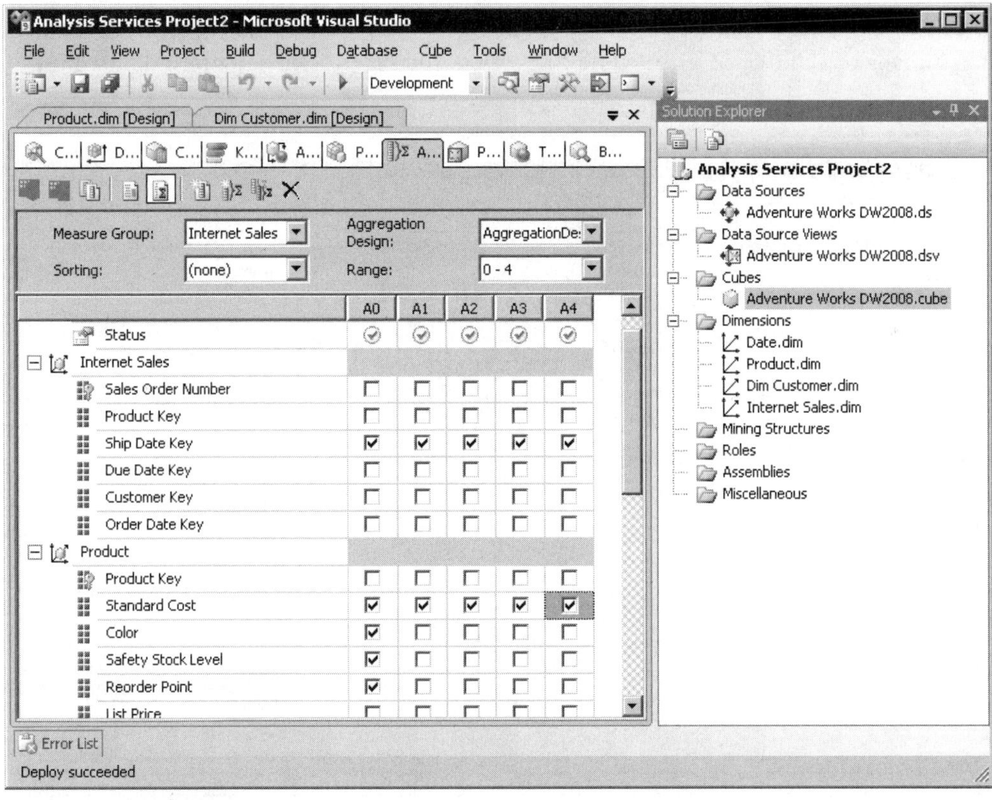

Figure 8-9 *The Aggregation Designer*

the definition of member properties. As with the Cube Designer and Cube Wizard, the Dimension Wizard is typically used to create dimensions, while the Dimension Designer is used to modify existing dimensions.

The Dimension Designer can be started by opening a dimension in the BIDS Solution Explorer, right clicking on the dimension to be edited, and then selecting the View Designer option from the Context menu. You can see the new Dimension Designer in Figure 8-10.

The enhanced Dimension Designer features a new Key Columns dialog box for editing key columns. In addition, key columns can also be updated in the dimension properties dialog. The new Dimension Designer has an updated Dimension Structure editor that enables you to more easily work with dimension hierarchies. The Dimension Structure tab also displays the dimension's attributes. In addition, the Dimension Designer includes a new Attribute Relationship Designer.

New Attribute Relationship Designer The new Attribute Relationship Designer makes it easier to view and modify the relationships between the different attributes in a dimension. Unlike SQL Server 2005, where you essentially need to link attributes

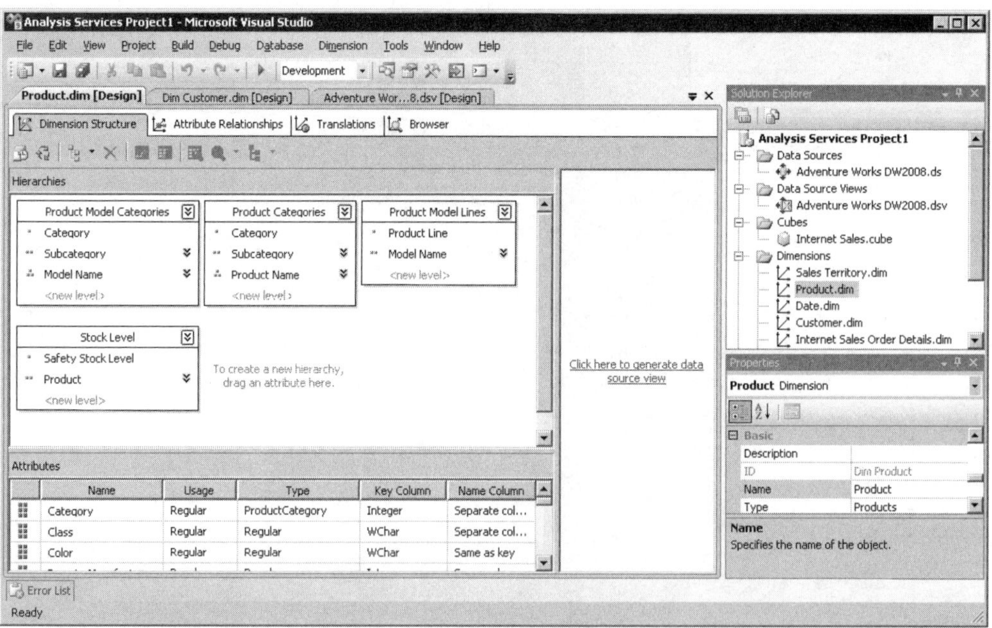

Figure 8-10 *The Dimension Designer*

in a bottom-up fashion, the new attribute designer shows a visual representation of the relationship between attributes making it much easier to create an understand the relations of a dimension's attributes. You can open the key Attribute Relationship Designer by first opening the Dimension Designer and then clicking on the Attribute Relationships tab. You can see the new Attribute Relationship Designer shown in Figure 8-11.

Best Practice Design Alerts

Another useful development feature in Analysis Services 2008 is the new best practices warning. The best practices warning is shown with a yellow icon that displays a message alerting you about any cube design attributes that don't follow best practices. You can see an example of the best practices warning for the Cube Wizard shown in Figure 8-12.

Dynamic Named Sets

Dynamic named sets are another new development feature in Analysis Services 2008. Named sets enable you to specify a set of dimension members with a common retrieval query. For instance, you could use a named set to identify the top ten products by sales.

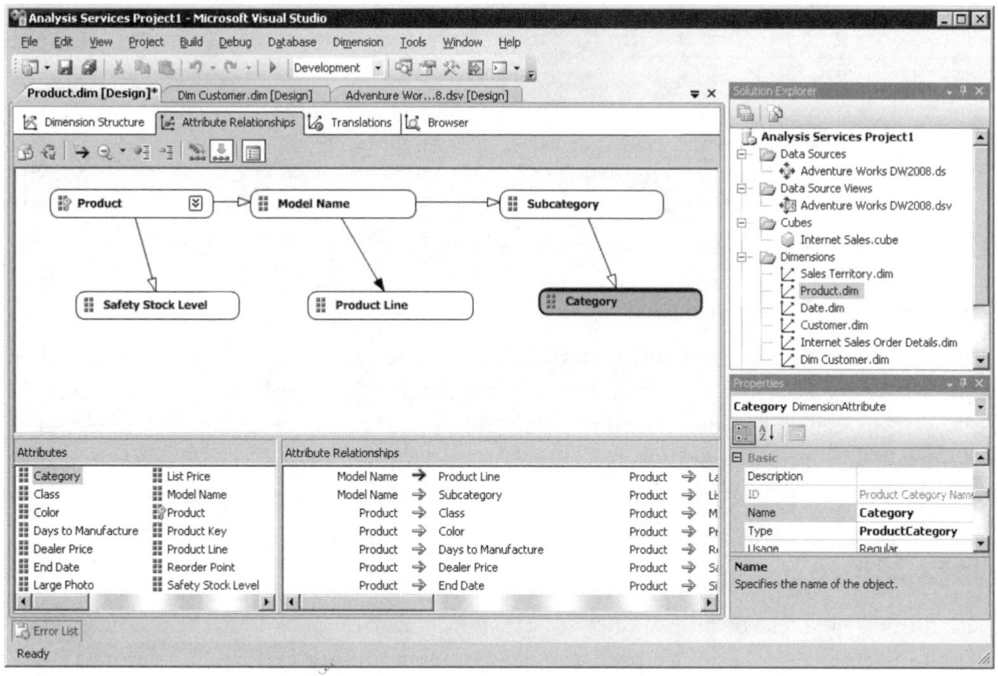

Figure 8-11 *Attribute Relationship Designer*

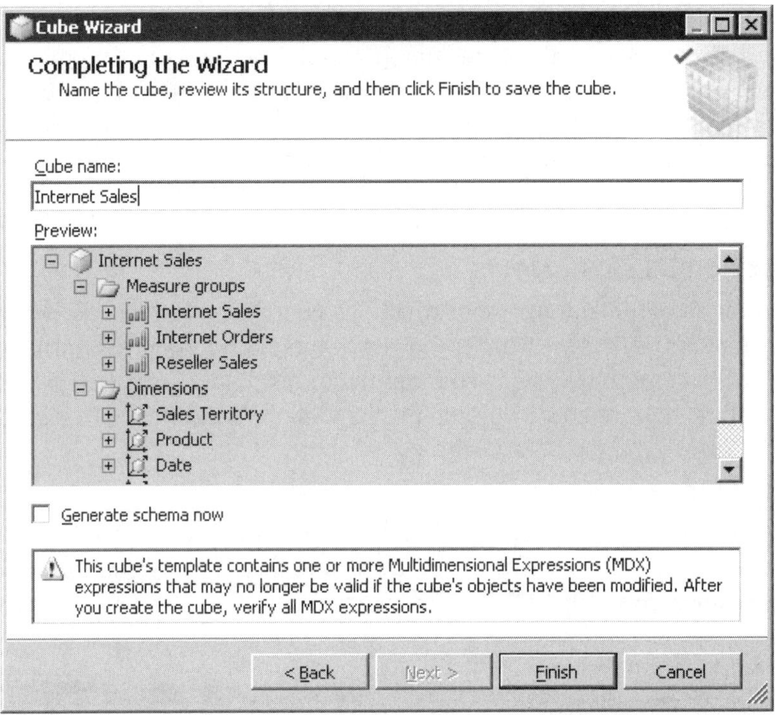

Figure 8-12 *AMO Best Practice Design alert*

SQL Server 2005 possessed a named set feature. However, with SQL Server 2005 you needed to define the named set statically at design time. For SQL Server 2008, named sets can be dynamic and they can be specified and evaluated when they are used.

Personalized Extensions

Another new feature in the development side of analysis services in SQL Server 2008 is the new *personalized extensions*. Personalized extensions enable you to create new Analysis Services objects dynamically within the context of a user session. Personalization extensions are not persistent objects in the database. Rather, they are created dynamically for each user and are only visible to that user during the duration of the user's sessions.

Data Mining

Data mining enables you to use the data in your data warehouse to make predictions about future behavior based on past data trends. Data mining was first introduced to SQL Server with the SQL Server 2000 release. With SQL Server 2008 the most important new data mining feature is the new Time Series algorithms.

Improved Time Series Support

With Analysis Services 2008 Microsoft added a new, time series data mining algorithm based on the Auto-Regressive Integrated Moving Average (ARIMA) algorithm. This algorithm is intended to provide better predictions than the existing Auto Regression Tree algorithm that was in SQL Server 2005. The new Time Series algorithm permits custom weighting to provide improved accuracy of predictions.

Reporting Services

First introduced as a web download for SQL Server 2000 and then later bundled in with SQL Server 2005, Reporting Services quickly became one of the biggest driving forces behind SQL Server adoption. Working with both relational and OLAP data sources, Reporting Services provides an out-of-the-box reporting solution that goes far beyond the capabilities of simple reporting solutions like Access. Reporting Services is an enterprise-capable reporting system that not only provides the ability to graphically design reports, but also enables you to securely deploy those reports across the enterprise, rendered in a variety of different formats including web-based HTML reports, Windows-based rich client reports, and reports rendered for mobile devices.

With the SQL Server 2008 release, Microsoft has added a number of architectural-, performance-, management-, and development-oriented features.

Architectural Enhancements

Without a doubt, the biggest change to Reporting Services for SQL Server 2008 is in the architecture. Reporting Services in SQL Server 2008 no longer requires IIS, which is welcome news to just about all SQL Server DBAs who were reluctant to install IIS on their database server. In addition, the new release combines the Reporting Services applications into a single service which provides better performance and scalability.

Native Support for HTTP.SYS and ASP.NET – No Need for IIS

Previous versions of Reporting Services all required IIS to be installed on your SQL Server system. IIS was needed both for Reporting Services administration and the delivery of reports. This was a requirement that most DBAs didn't care for because it increased the server overhead, as well as the overall system management requirements and attack surface. However, the benefits offered by Reporting Services made it worthwhile for most organizations to add IIS in order to gain the benefits of Reporting Services.

SQL Server 2008 Reporting Services removes the dependency on IIS. Reporting Services now leverages the HTTP support in the operating system to provide a native HTTP listener with support for running

- Report Manager
- Report Server Web Service
- ASP.NET

The ability to handle incoming web requests allows Reporting Services to function as a true middle-tier application because it is separated from the IIS front-end. In conjunction with this change, Reporting Services now includes a new hosting layer, which handles authentication requests, memory management, logging, and support for tracing.

The removal of IIS and the incorporation of the HTTP.SYS and ASP.NET capabilities into Reporting Services makes the installation of SQL Server 2008 easier and faster. It also reduces the management overhead and improves system reliability.

Consolidated Services

The other major architectural change in Reporting Services 2008 is that the Reporting Services server applications have been combined into a single service. The combined Reporting Services service supports

- The Report Server Web Service
- The Report Manager
- The reporting delivery background process

Consolidating the Reporting Services server applications simplifies configuration and system management. It also increases scalability as the service has more control over the use of system resources.

Performance Enhancements

Reporting Services in SQL Server 2008 contains some important performance enhancements, allowing it to provide better report rendering performance, increased scalability, and support for a higher number of users.

Re-engineered On-Demand Report Processing Model

Reporting Services in SQL Server 2005 could become memory bound because the report processing rendered the reports in memory. SQL Server 2008 Reporting Services uses a new on-demand report processing model, which enables the report processing to use a file system caching system to adapt to memory demands. This re-engineered architecture ensures that adequate memory is available to process complex reports and resource intensive workloads from large numbers of concurrent users.

Management Enhancements

In conjunction with the architectural changes, Microsoft has also made several changes to the Reporting Services management tools that enable you to fully manage Reporting Services.

Enhanced Reporting Service Configuration Manager

In order to completely replace IIS, the Reporting Services Configuration Manager has been enhanced to enable it to address the configuration settings that were formerly performed using the IIS Manager. Reporting Services 2008's Reporting Service Configuration Manager now enables you to configure the Report Manager virtual directory and the Report Server Web Service URL as well as the SSL certificate and port. You can see the Reporting Services Configuration Manager's web service URL configuration illustrated in Figure 8-13.

New Default URLs for Named Instances

Reporting Services 2008 has also changed the default URLs used by SQL Server Reporting Services for named instances. The new Report Server and Report Manager URLs are shown in the following table.

Management Tool	URL
Report Server	http://localhost/reportserver
Report Manager	http://localhost/Reports
Report Server for named instance	http://localhost/reportserver_[Instance Name]
Report Manager for a named instance	http://localhost/Reports_[Instance Name]

New My Reports Folder

Another new feature for Reporting Services in SQL Server 2008 is the addition of the My Reports folder. The new My Reports folder enables you to create a customized reports folder for each different login. If the My Reports feature is enabled, then the users that log in to the server will only see the reports that are in their own My Reports folder.

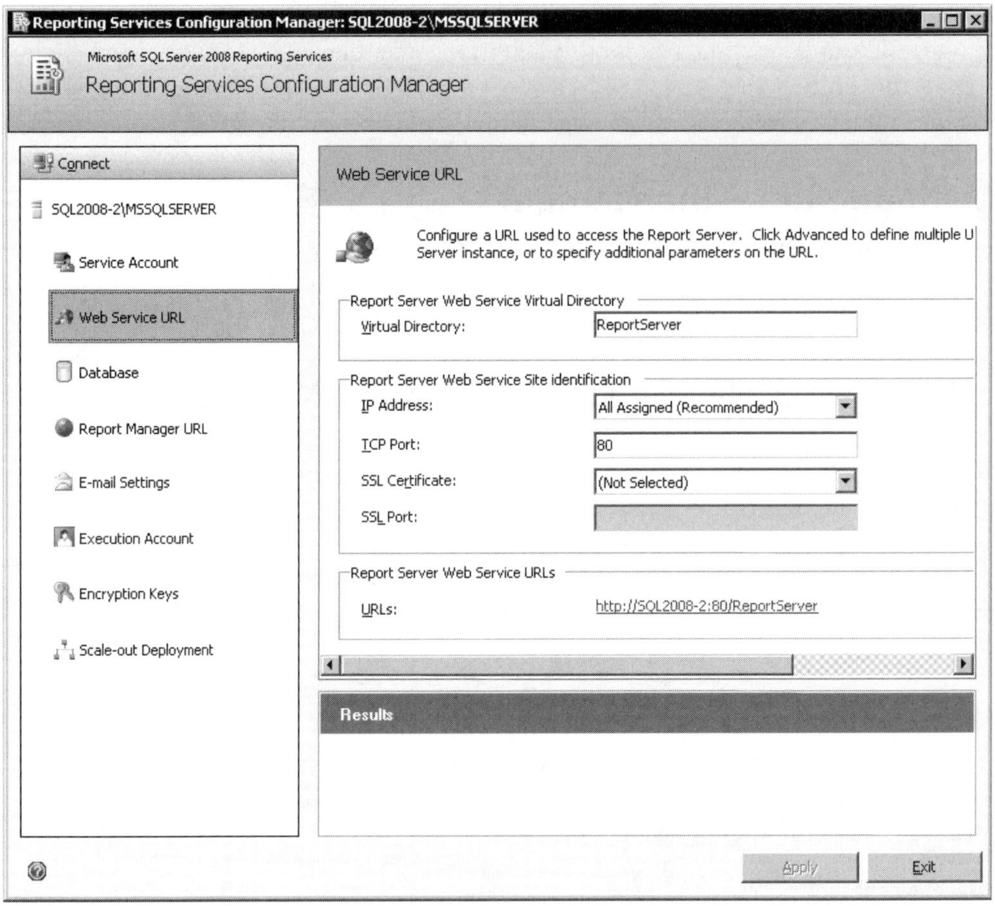

Figure 8-13 *Reporting Services Configuration Manager*

You can enable the new My Folders feature by first opening SQL Server Management Studio (SSMS) and then connecting to the Reporting Services Server type. This will display your Report Server in the SSMS Object Explorer. Right click on your Reporting Server and then select Properties from the pop-up menu. This will display the Server Properties dialog that you can see in Figure 8-14.

To enable the new My Folder feature, check the Enable a My Report folder for each user and then click OK.

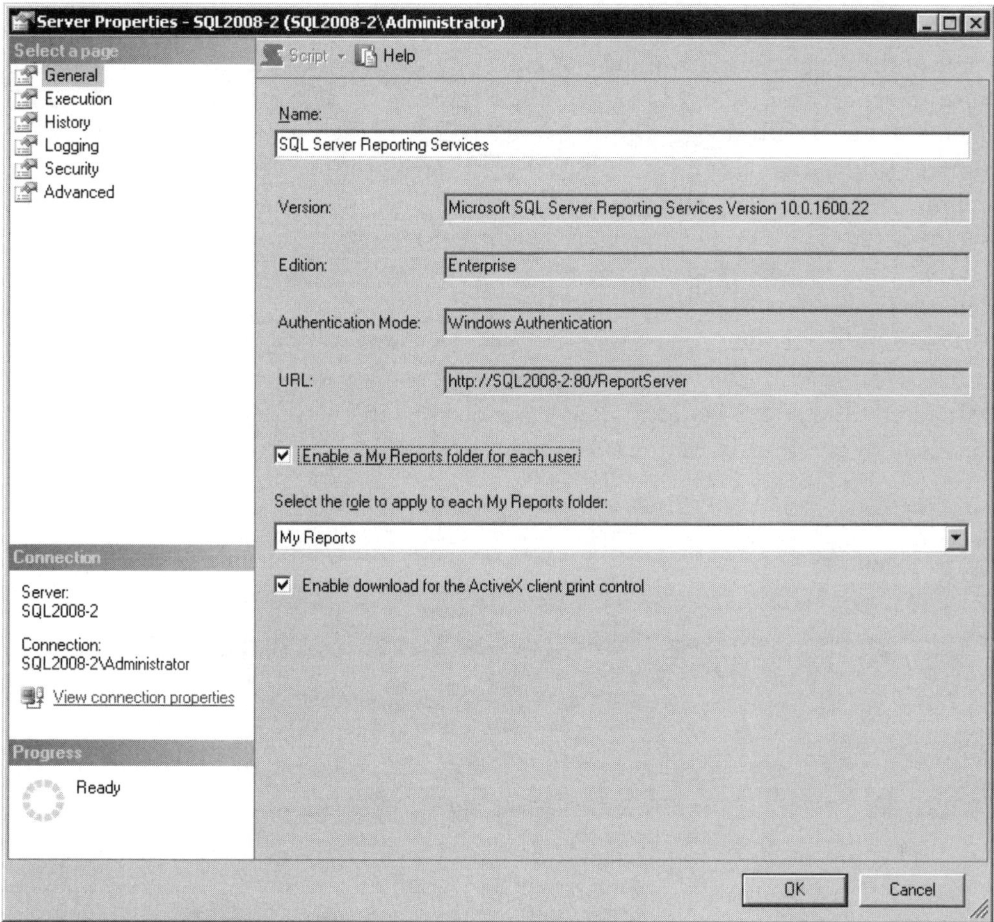

Figure 8-14 *Enabling My Folders*

Development Enhancements

Reporting Services has several new features that enhance the development process. Some of the most important new development features include enhancements to the Report Designer, the new Tablix data region, and an updated end user Report Builder tool.

New Teradata Data Source

SQL Server 2008 Report Services has a new Teradata data source. Teradata is a specialized data warehousing system, and the new Teradata data source enables you to access Teradata data warehouses in your Report Services reports.

New Report Designer

Some of the biggest changes in the development side of Reporting Services include enhancements to the Report Designer. The Reporting Services Report Designer enables you to visually design reports, as well as control their deployment. To start the Report Designer, you first open up SQL Server 2008's Business Intelligence Studio and then select the File | New | Project | Report Server Project option to create a new Report Services project. Then, to open the Report Designer, you select the Project | Add New Item | Report option. You can see an example of the Reporting Services Report Designer in Figure 8-15.

The SQL Server 2008 Report Designer includes a number of important enhancements.

Enhanced Chart Data Region Reporting Services in SQL Server 2008 also features an enhanced set of the chart types. The new Reporting Services chart types include:

- Bar/column
- Pyramid

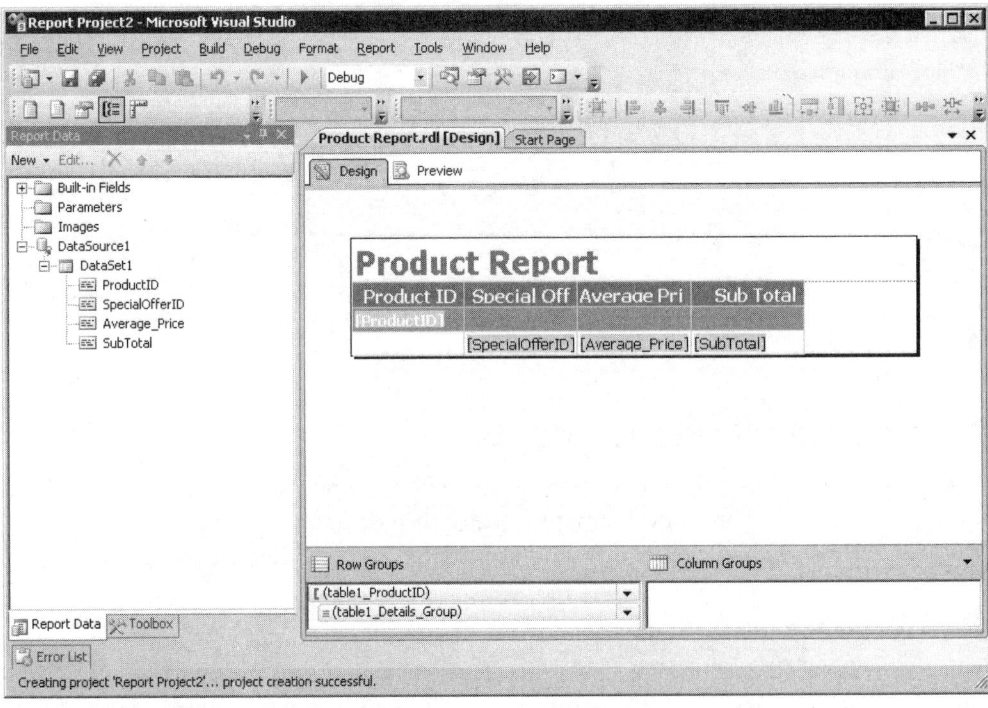

Figure 8-15 *Report Designer*

- Funnel
- Polar
- Radar
- Stock
- Candlestick
- Range column
- Range bar
- Smooth area
- Smooth line
- Stepped line
- Box plot
- Pareto
- Histogram

With Reporting Services 2008, you have more control over how chart data can be labeled and displayed. You can now display a series on any chart area. You can insert empty points to replace missing data points. You can combine multiple chart areas, legends, and titles in the same chart. Plus, there is support for secondary axes.

Enhanced Gauge Data Region The new Gauge Data Region in Reporting Services 2008 enables you to group multiple gauges together in a single report panel. You can select either radial or linear gauge types. Gauges display a single data point indicated with a pointer, a scale, and a label.

New Tablix Data Region Another important new feature in Reporting Services 2008 is the addition of the new Tablix data region. The new Tablix data region replaces the Table, Matrix, and List data regions. The new Tablix support provides more flexibility in your ability to layout reports. In many cases, this has been referred to as Tablix control. However, Tablix is not actually a control; rather it is a data region. As its name implies, Tablix is a combination of table and matrix type data regions. It supports both row groups and column groups. Groups can be nested, adjacent, or even recursive. You can embed any type of report item within a Tablix cell.

Enhanced Rendering Extensions

Another development improvement in Reporting Services 2008 is support for report rendering in both Microsoft Word and Excel. More detailed information about this new Office integration feature is found in Chapter 9.

Report Builder

SQL Server 2008 still includes Report Builder 1.0. However, Report Builder 2.0 is available as a part of the SQL Server 2008 Feature pack. You can download Report Builder 2.0 from http://www.microsoft.com/downloads/details.aspx?FamilyId=9F783224-9871-4EEA-B1D5-F3140A253DB6&displaylang=en Report Builder 2.0 will have a new user interface built using the Office Ribbon UI. You can see the new Report Builder 2.0 in Figure 8-16.

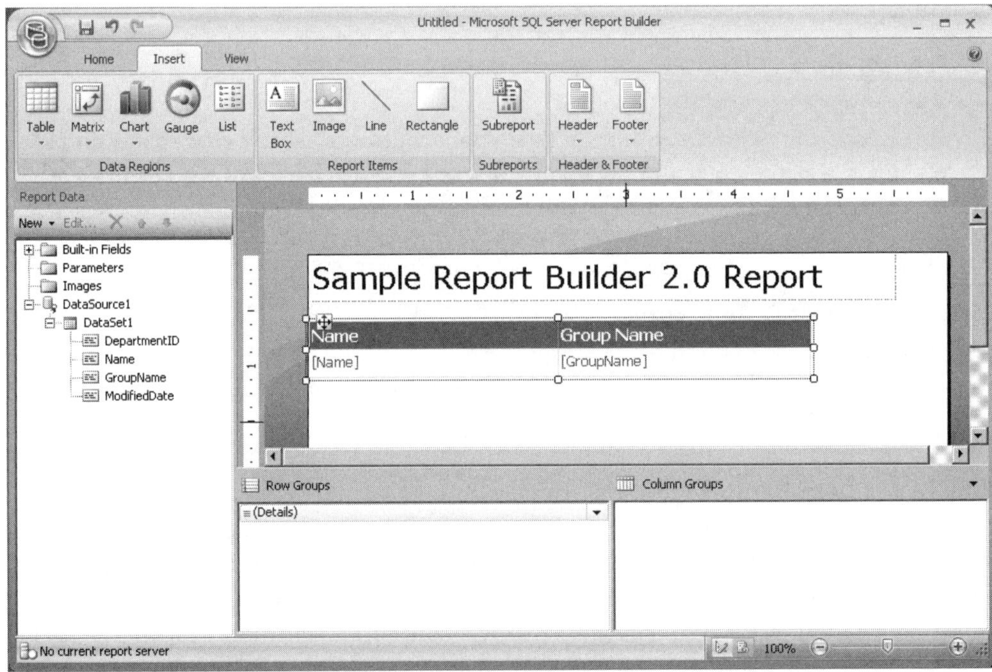

Figure 8-16 *Report Builder 2.0*

Summary

In this chapter you've learned about the new enhancements to SQL Server 2008's Business Intelligence suite. Here you saw how the performance of Integration Services has been improved through the use of asynchronous components and improved parallelism. In addition, you saw how the inclusion of Visual Studio Tools for Applications has been used to revamp the scripting capabilities in Integration Services. Next, you learned about the performance enhancements in Analysis Services, as well as the new Cube, Dimension, and Aggregation designers that enhance the Analysis Services development experience. Finally, you saw how the new architectural changes in Reporting Services eliminated the need for IIS, and how the enhancements to the Report Designer and Report Builder make the creation of reports easier and more effective.

In the next chapter you'll see how the new extensions to Reporting Services enable tight integration with Microsoft Office.

Chapter 9

Office Integration

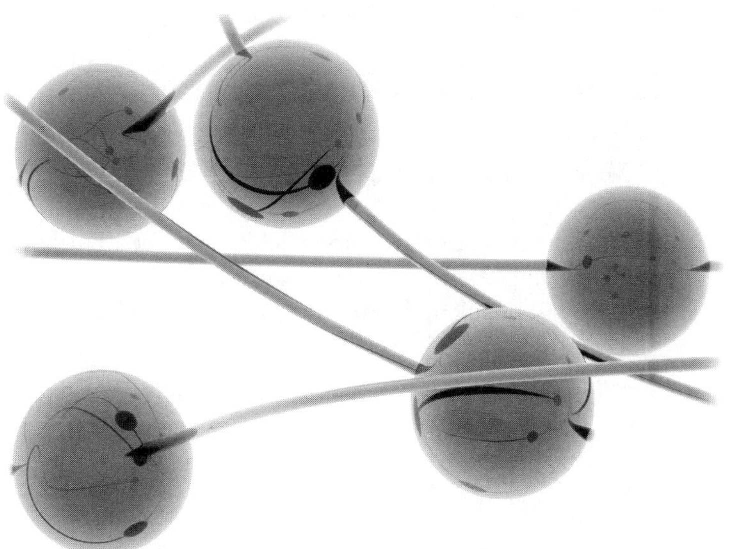

Without a doubt, Microsoft Office is one of the most widely used tools in virtually all organizations, both large and small. SQL Server 2008's tighter integration with Office goes a long way toward breaking down the barriers of information in the enterprise by taking the information in your relational databases and data warehouses and delivering it into the hands of your users. For the SQL Server 2008 release, Microsoft has added a couple of important pieces to the Office integration picture. In the first part of this chapter, you'll see how enhancements to Reporting Services in SQL Server 2008 enable you to export reports to Microsoft Office. In the second part of this chapter, you'll see how SQL Server 2008 can be used with Office SharePoint for publishing reports and how Reporting Services can be incorporated into a SharePoint infrastructure.

Exporting Reports to Excel and Word

Exporting reports into the Microsoft Office formats is the most fundamental level of SQL Server 2008 and Microsoft Office integration. SQL Server 2008 supports exporting reports from the web-based Report Server, as well as from Report Builder, into either Microsoft Word 2000 or Excel 2000 format. The newer Office 2007 formats are not supported in this release.

Exporting from Report Server

In this section, you'll see how to export a report from SQL Server 2008's Report Server to Microsoft Excel. To export a report, you first need to create the report using either Report Designer or the Report Wizard and then deploy the report to Report Server. To export the report to Excel, first click the Select a Format drop-down menu that you can see in the upper left portion of Figure 9-1.

This will populate the dropdown with the value of Excel and will activate the Export link as is shown in Figure 9-2.

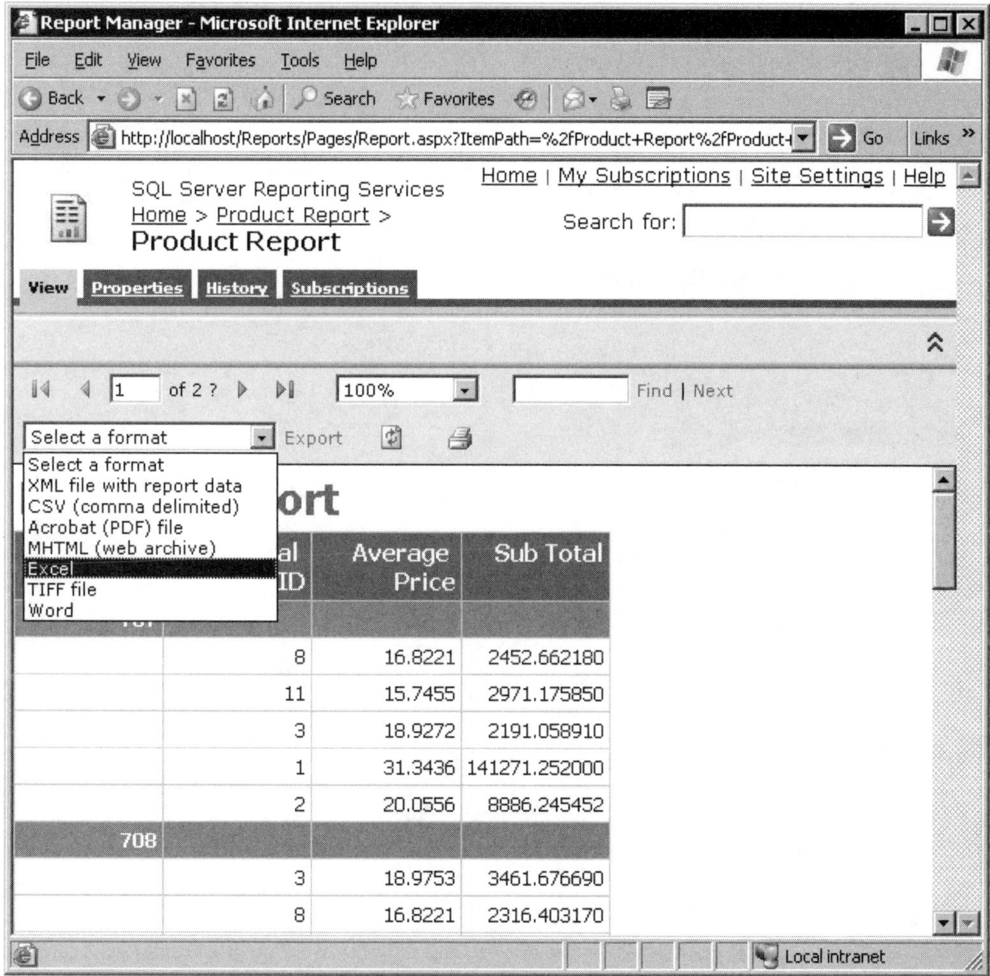

Figure 9-1 *Selecting the Excel export format*

After the export format of Excel has been selected and the Export link has been activated, you can click the Export link to export the report. This will display the File Download dialog box that you can see in Figure 9-3.

On the File Download dialog click Save to display the Save As dialog shown in Figure 9-4.

From the Save As dialog box, you can select the path and file name that you want to use to save the Excel file. The default file name provided by Report Services uses the report name and the Excel file extension of .xls. Clicking Save will export the

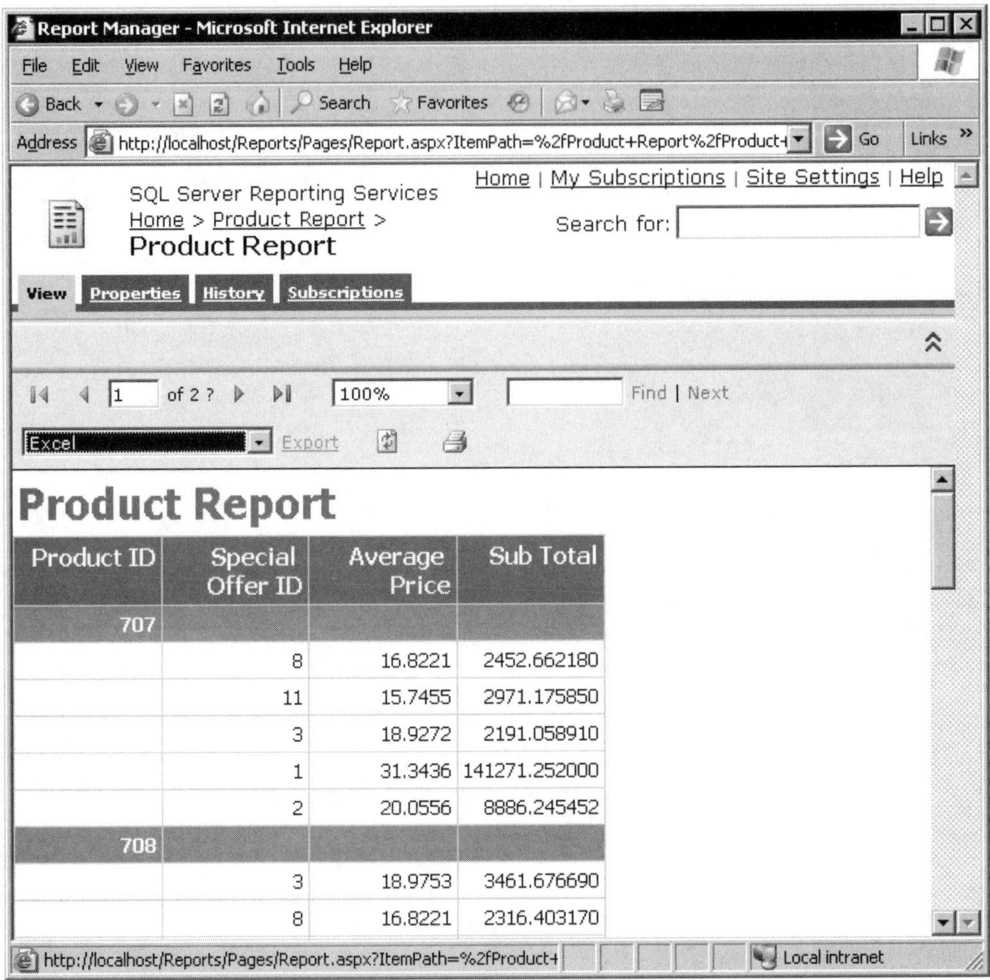

Figure 9-2 *Selecting the Export link*

Excel spreadsheet to the directory and file name of choice. You can see a sample of an exported Excel report shown in Figure 9-5.

This section showed an example of exporting from Report Services to Excel. However, you can also export from Report Server to Word. The only real difference is in the selection of export formats, which you saw listed in Figure 9-1.

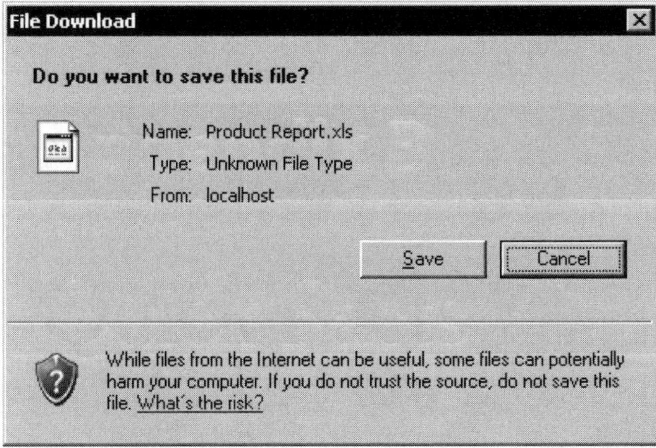

Figure 9-3 *Download the Excel file from Reporting Services*

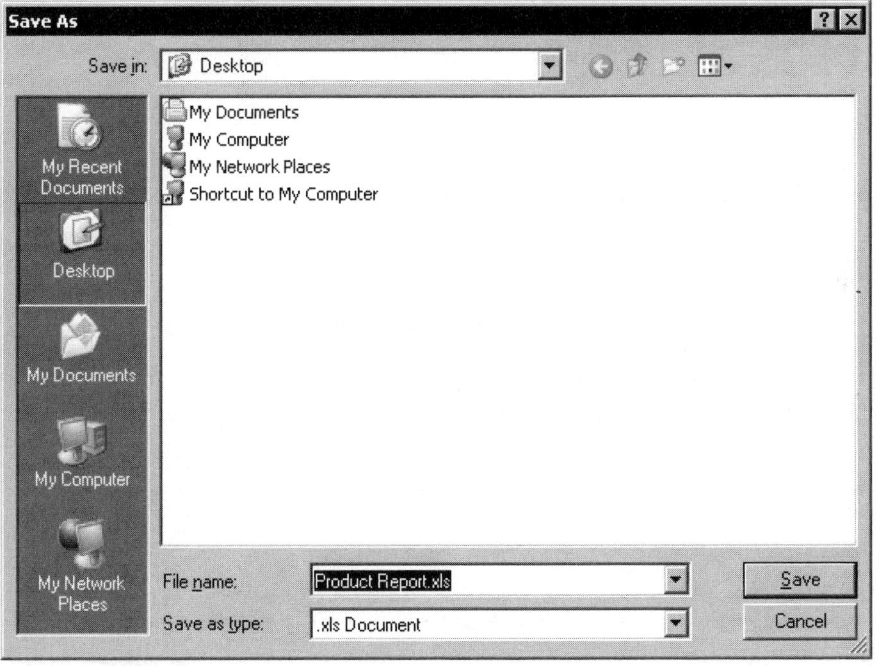

Figure 9-4 *Save the Excel file*

Product Report

Product ID	Special Offer ID	Average Price	Sub Total
707			
	8	16.8221	2452.66218
	11	15.7455	2971.17585
	3	18.9272	2191.05891
	1	31.3436	141271.252
	2	20.0556	8886.245452
708			
	3	18.9753	3461.67669
	8	16.8221	2316.40317
	11	15.7455	2997.9432
	2	20.0502	11689.73028
	1	30.9648	140403.7645
709			
	2	5.51	723.5732
	3	5.225	853.765
	1	5.7	4235.1
	4	4.75	247.95
710			
	1	5.7	513
711			

Figure 9-5 *The exported Excel report*

Exporting Reports from Report Builder 2.0

In this next section, you'll see how to export a report from Report Builder to Microsoft Word. To export a report using Report Builder, you first need to open the report using Report Builder. This will display the Report Builder user interface shown in Figure 9-6.

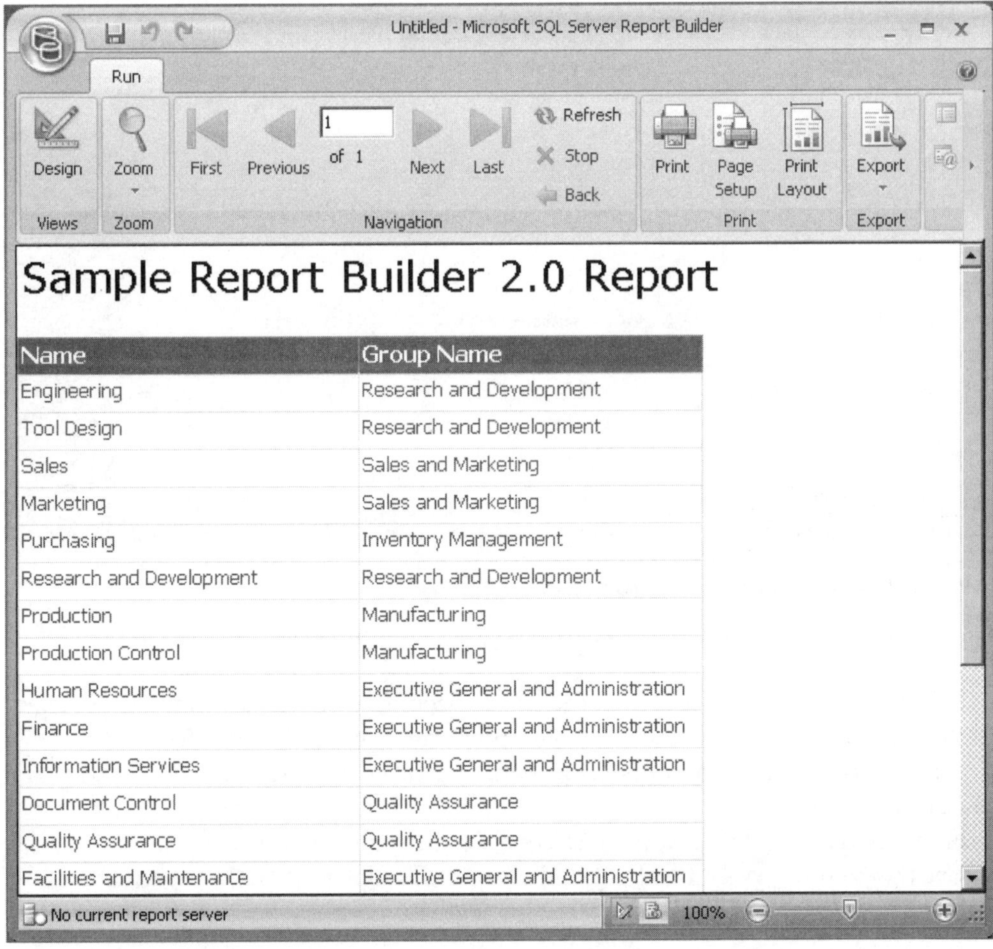

Figure 9-6 *Starting Report Builder*

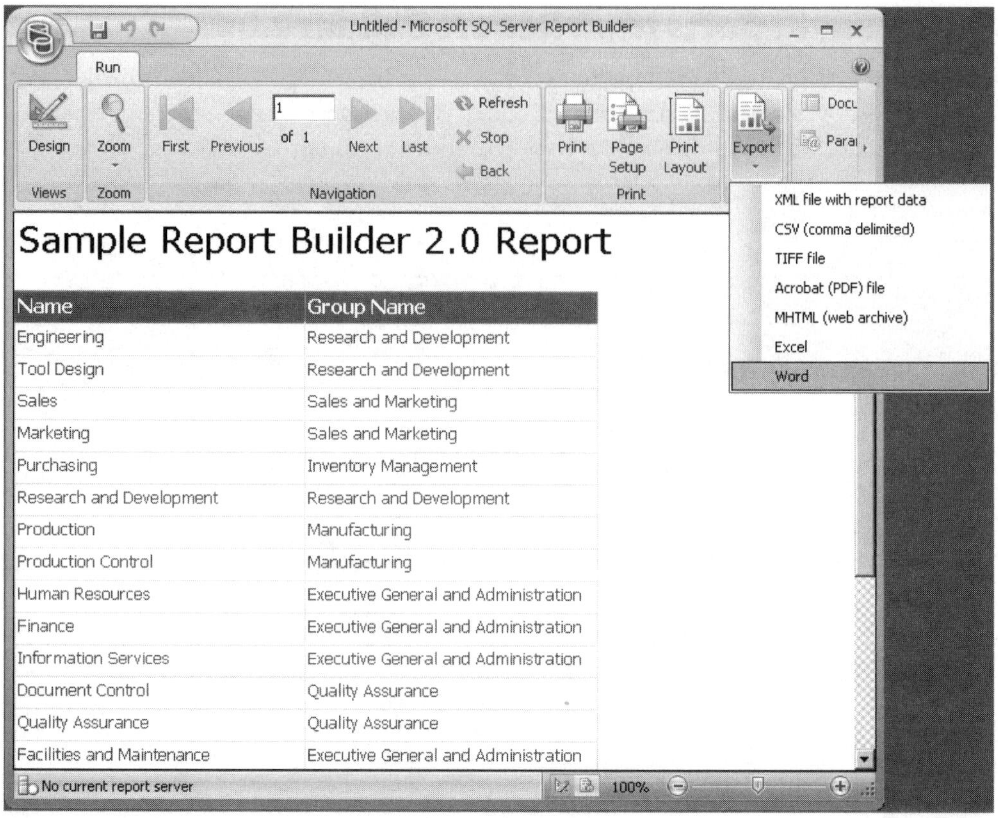

Figure 9-7 *Exporting a Word report from Report Builder*

To export a report to Word, click the Export icon that you can see in the upper right section of the ribbon and select the Word option you can see in Figure 9-7.

Selecting the Word Export option will immediately display the Save As dialog that you can see in Figure 9-8.

From the Save As dialog, you can select the path and file name that you want to use to save the exported Word file. By default, Report Builder will use the report name

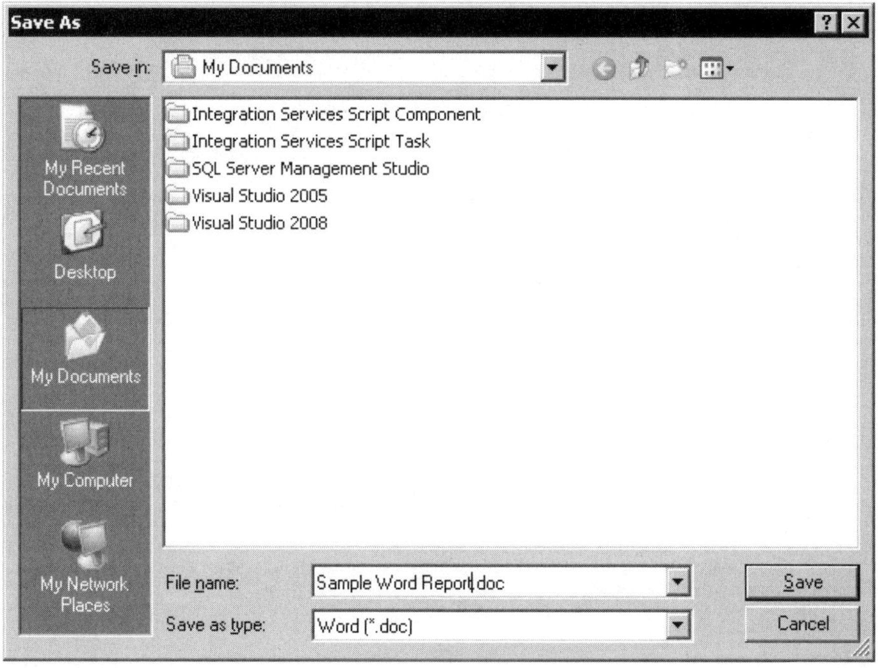

Figure 9-8 *Save the Word file*

and the Word file extension of .doc. Clicking Save will export the report to a Word document in the directory that you selected. You can see the exported Word document shown in Figure 9-9.

This section showed how to export from Report Builder to Microsoft Word. However, you can also export from Report Builder to Excel. To do so change the export format selection that you saw in Figure 9-7.

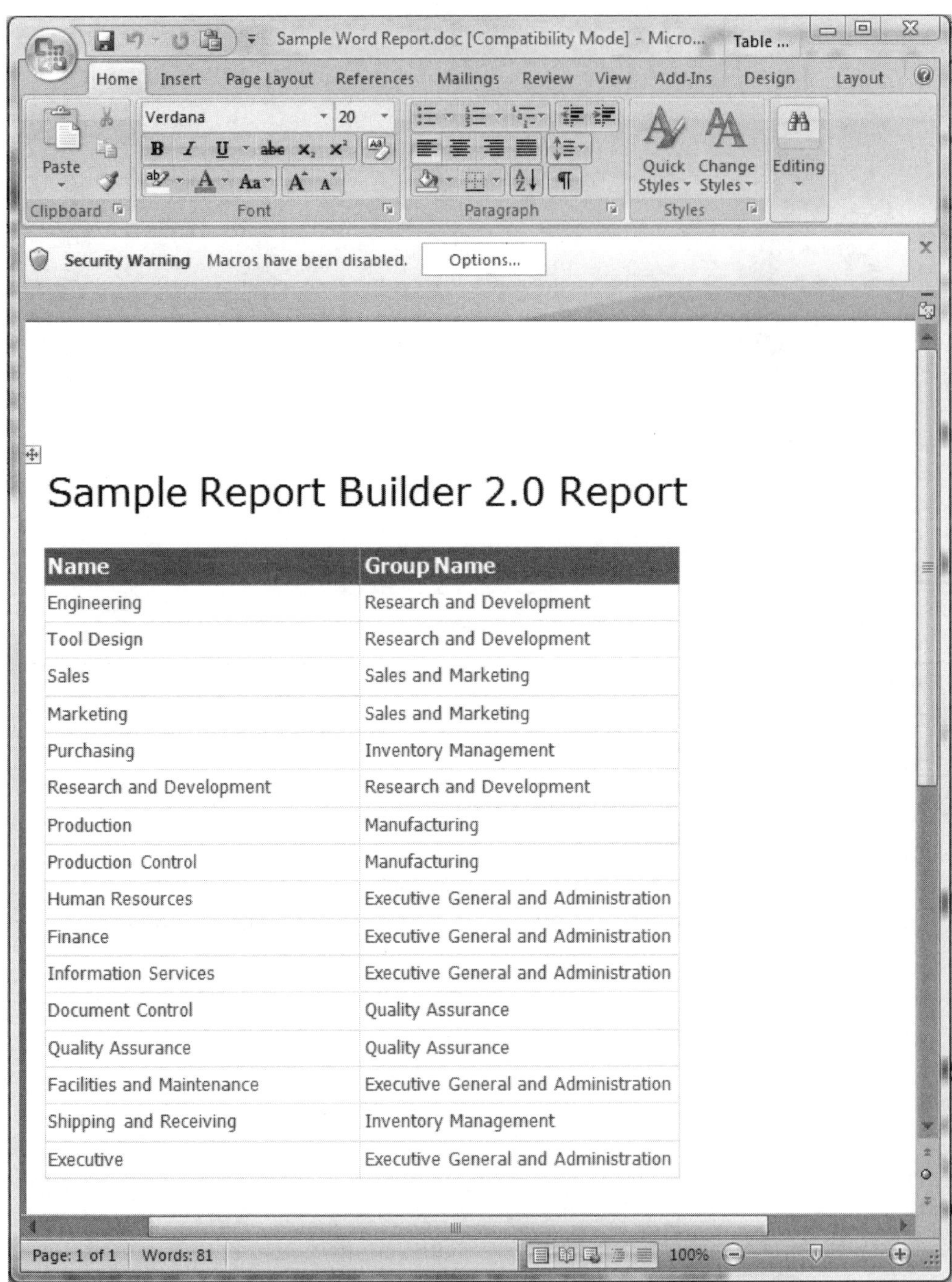

Figure 9-9 *The exported Word document*

Integrating Reporting Services with SharePoint

In addition to exporting reports in Microsoft Office formats, SQL Server 2008 can also be integrated with Windows SharePoint Services 3.0 or Microsoft Office SharePoint Server 2007. Integrating SQL Server 2008 and SharePoint provides several advantages. First, SharePoint provides a standard way for the employees of an organization to access the information from SQL Server Reporting Services reports, just as they would access their shared office documents and spreadsheets. Employees can use the same SharePoint front-end to access all of the important information that they need in their daily jobs. Integrating SQL Server 2008 and SharePoint allows you to publish reports to a SharePoint report library, or include reports into your portals by using the Reporting Services Report Viewer Web Part for renderings within SharePoint. The integration of SQL Server and SharePoint enables greater management and operations efficiency. The organization can gain the advantages of shared storage between the two platforms, reducing disk requirements and making backup operations more efficient. In addition, SharePoint integration mode enables a shared security model and central administration for SharePoint and Reporting Services, streamlining the organization's administration requirements.

Reporting Services and SharePoint Integration Architecture

When Reporting Services is installed in SharePoint integration mode, all of the Reporting Services items and properties are stored in the existing SharePoint content databases. This allows all of the Reporting Services items to be accessed and secured using the authentications and permissions that SharePoint uses. This also enables the SharePoint collaboration features to be used with Reporting Services. For example, this enables check in and check out of reports, as well as the sending of a notification when a report has changed. SharePoint also controls the setting and configuration for SharePoint and Reporting Services. While SharePoint controls the storage and security, the Reporting Services report server still performs all of the report processing, rendering, and delivery. You can see an overview of the Reporting Services and SharePoint integration architecture shown in Figure 9-10.

End users access the SharePoint site using browser requests. When a user requests a Reporting Services report on the SharePoint site, SharePoint uses the Reporting Service's web service to connect to the Reporting Services report server. The report server opens the user sessions, retrieves the data from the different data sources used by the report, renders the report, and then displays it in the Report Viewer Part installed on the SharePoint server. Likewise, any subsequent actions, such as drilling down into

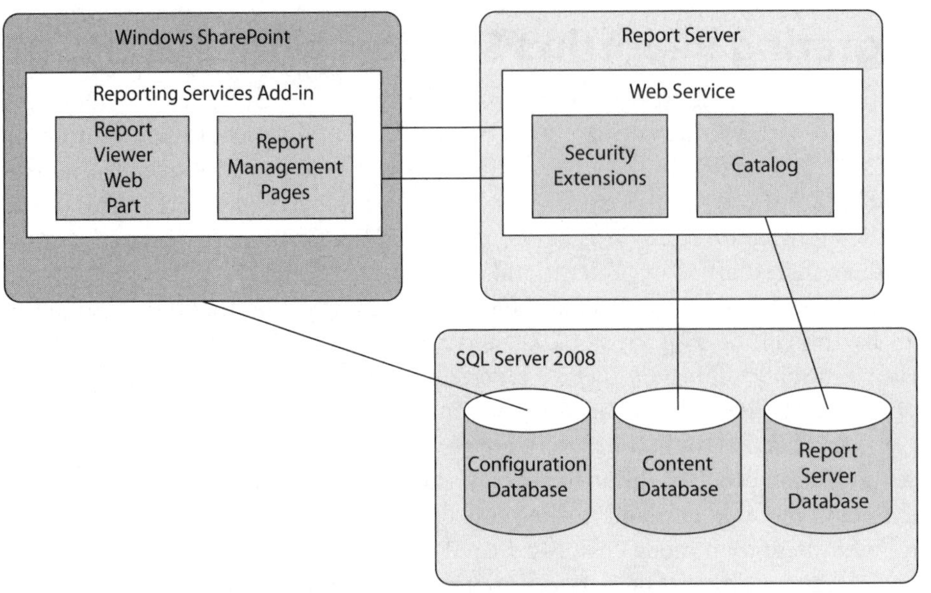

Figure 9-10 *Reporting Services and SharePoint Integration Architecture*

a report or opening a linked report, are sent from the Report Viewer Web Part back to the Reporting Services report server that processes the request. This then renders the result back to the Report Viewer Web Part in SharePoint.

Requirements

In order to integrate SQL Server 2008 and SharePoint, you must first have either Windows SharePoint Services 3.0 or Microsoft Office SharePoint Server 2007. While Microsoft Office SharePoint Server 2007 is a licensed product, Windows SharePoint Services 3.0 is a free download that can be found at: http://www.microsoft.com/downloads/details.aspx?FamilyId=D51730B5-48FC-4CA2-B454-8DC2CAF93951&displaylang=en.

SharePoint must be installed and a SharePoint site must be created before you can enable Reporting Services and SharePoint integration. The SharePoint installation would typically be on a separate system from the SQL Server 2008 Reporting Services installation, although this doesn't have to be the case.

Next, the SharePoint integration mode is installed as an option of the SQL Server 2008 setup program. However, only the SQL Server 2008 Standard, Enterprise, or Developer Editions support SharePoint Integration. You can see the setup screen that controls Reporting Servers and SharePoint Integration in Figure 9-11.

You can learn more about the SQL Server 2008 setup process in Appendix A.

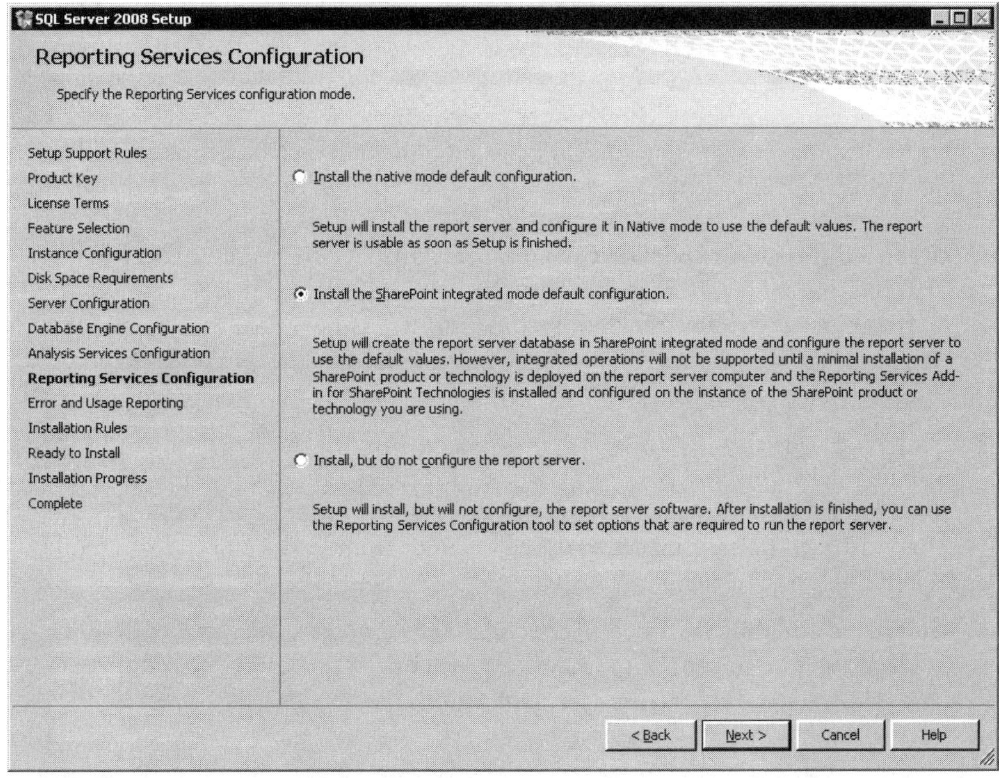

Figure 9-11 *Setting up Reporting Services in SharePoint Integration Mode*

The Reporting Services Add-in for SharePoint Technologies must be installed on the SharePoint front-end server. The Reporting Services Add-in for SharePoint is a free download from Microsoft and can be obtained from: http://www.microsoft.com/downloads/details.aspx?FamilyId=200FD7B5-DB7C-4B8C-A7DC-5EFEE6E19005&displaylang=en.

Finally, if you want Reporting Services to be able to join a SharePoint farm, SharePoint must be installed on the same system as Reporting services. This installation can happen either before or after the Reporting Services installation.

Using SQL Server 2008 as a SharePoint Backend

Regardless of whether or not you take advantage of SQL Server 2008 and SharePoint integration features, you can still gain benefits by running SharePoint with SQL Server 2008. SharePoint uses SQL Server as a data store. It can use an existing SQL Server implementation, or if there isn't a SQL Server instance available, it will install and use SQL Server Express as it data store. In any event, SharePoint always uses a SQL Server database. By using SQL Server 2008 as a backend for SharePoint, you can take immediate advantage of many of the new SQL Server 2008 features with no change whatsoever required for your SharePoint front-end implementations. Some of the immediate advantages that you can gain by using SQL Server 2008 as the back-end database for SharePoint include:

- **Reduced storage and backup time requirements** SQL Server 2008's built-in database compression can reduce the disk requirements for SharePoint and also significantly reduce the backup and restore time needs for your SharePoint implementations. You can find more details about SQL Server 2008's database compression in Chapter 1.
- **Enhanced security** SQL Server 2008's Transparent Data Encryption (TDE) can be used with your SharePoint databases, adding a level of security on top of the user authentication level. TDE can encrypt all of your SharePoint data and it doesn't require any changes to the SharePoint front-end. You can learn more about TDE in Chapter 1.
- **Improved scalability** The SQL Server 2008 Resource Governor can be used with SharePoint to control the resources used by SharePoint. You can learn more about the Resource Governor in Chapter 1.

To move an existing SharePoint SQL Server database to SQL Server 2008, you need to run the SQL Server setup program and then select the option to upgrade to an existing instance. Here you do need to be sure that you upgrade to the appropriate SQL Server 2008 edition. For example, if you are running SQL Server Express 2005 you can't upgrade to the SQL Server 2008 Enterprise Edition. Instead, you would upgrade to the SQL Server 2008 Express Edition. Conversely, if you are running the SQL Server 2005 Enterprise Edition, you couldn't upgrade to the SQL Server 2008 Standard or Express editions. You would need to upgrade to the SQL Server 2008 Enterprise Edition. You can see an example of running the SQL Server 2008 upgrade process in Appendix A.

Summary

Integrating SQL Server 2008 with Microsoft Office helps brings the information contained in SQL Server 2008's relational databases or data warehouses to the end users in the organization who can use that information to make better decisions about the business. In this chapter, you saw how to export reports from Reporting Services to both Microsoft Excel and Microsoft Word. You also saw how SharePoint can take advantage of the new features in SQL Server 2008 and how you can make use of Reporting Services in a SharePoint infrastructure.

Part IV

Appendixes

Appendix A

Installation and Upgrade

In this appendix you'll get an overview of the SQL Server 2008 editions as well as SQL Server 2008's installation and upgrade options. The first step to either installing or upgrading SQL Server is to select the edition of the product that you want to use. In the first section of this chapter, you'll learn about the different editions of SQL Server 2008. In the second part of this appendix you'll get a guide to installing a new SQL Server 2008 instance. In the final part of the appendix you see how to upgrade from SQL Server 2005 to SQL Server 2008.

SQL Server 2008 Editions

As with the previous releases of SQL Server, Microsoft makes several different editions of SQL Server 2008. Microsoft will provide the following different versions of SQL Server 2008.

SQL Server 2008 Enterprise Edition

The Enterprise Edition provides the full feature set available in SQL Server 2008. The SQL Server 2008 Enterprise Edition is designed for large, highly scalable enterprise implementations. The Enterprise Edition is priced at $24,999 per processor, or $13,969 per server including 25 CALs. The features that are available in the SQL Server 2008 Enterprise Edition are

- Support for 32 – bit and 64 – bit processors
- Support for up to 64 CPUs – OS Max
- Support for up to 2TB of RAM – OS Max
- Database size limited only by available storage
- Support for 50 instances
- Hot add CPU
- Hot add RAM
- Database partitioning
- Database compression
- Transparent database encryption
- Resource Governor
- Partition table parallelism
- All database mirroring modes
- Failover clustering support for up to 16 nodes

- Database snapshots
- Fast recovery
- Online indexing
- Online restore
- Distributed, partitioned views
- Parallel index operations
- Fine grained auditing
- Oracle replication publishing
- P2P transactional replication
- Integration Services advanced transformations
- Change Data Capture
- Analysis Services shared and scalable databases
- Analysis Services start join query optimization
- Analysis Services proactive caching
- Analysis Services partitioned cubes and distributed partitioned cubes
- Analysis Services writeback dimensions
- Analysis Services linked measures and dimension
- Reporting Services scale out web farms
- Reporting Services infinite click through
- Reporting Services data-driving subscriptions

SQL Server 2008 Standard Edition

The Standard Edition provides the core SQL Server 2008 feature set but does not provide the enterprise-oriented features found in the SQL Server 2008 Enterprise Edition. The SQL Server Standard Edition is priced at $5,999 per processor, or $1,849 per server with 5 CALs. The SQL Server 2008 Standard Edition includes a number of features that are not available in the Workgroup, Web, or Express editions of SQL Server 2008. The SQL Server 2008 Standard Edition features include

- Support for 32-bit and 64-bit processors
- Support for up to 4 CPUs
- Support for up to 2TB of RAM – OS Max

- Database size limited only by available storage
- Support for 16 instances
- Analysis Services
- Integration Services
- Reporting Services
- SharePoint Integration

SQL Server 2008 Web Edition

As the newest addition to the SQL Server family, Microsoft introduced the SQL Server 2008 Web Edition to meet the database needs of web hosting providers. The SQL Server 2008 Web Edition is designed to provide a highly scalable relational database platform for web hosting providers. It includes support for Report Services, but not for the other BI subsystems. It is also licensed differently than the other editions of SQL Server. The SQL Server 2008 Web Edition is priced at $15 per processor per month. Some of the notable features in the SQL Server 2008 Web Edition include

- Support for 32-bit and 64-bit processors
- Support for up to 4 CPUs
- Support for up to 2TB of RAM – OS Max
- Support for 16 instances
- Database size limited only by available storage
- Reporting Services

SQL Server 2008 Workgroup Edition

The SQL Server 2008 Workgroup Edition is designed to provide a relational database for departments and branch offices. The SQL Server 2008 Workgroup Edition is priced at $3,899, or $739 per server including five CALs. The main features of the SQL Server 2008 Workgroup edition are

- Support for 32-bit and 64-bit processors
- Support for up to 2 CPUs
- Support for up to 4GB of RAM on 64-bit, OS Max on 32-bit

- Database size limited only by available storage
- Support for 16 instances
- Reporting Services

SQL Server 2008 Express Edition

The SQL Server 2008 Express Edition is the low end of the SQL Server family. The SQL Server Express Edition shares the same code base as the other editions of SQL Server 2008 and is able to support small scale multiuser databases. The SQL Server 2008 Express Edition is a free download and it is often used as the built-in database for other Microsoft applications like SharePoint and the System Center family of products. Some of the important characteristics of the SQL Server 2008 Express Edition include

- Support for 32-bit & 64-bit processors
- Support for 1 CPU
- Support for up to 1GB of RAM
- Maximum database size of 4GB
- Support for 16 instances
- No SQL Server Management Studio Basic
- No support for Reporting Services
- No support for SQL Server Agent

SQL Server 2008 Express with Advanced Services

The SQL Server 2008 Express Edition with Advanced Services has the same features as the SQL Server 2008 Express Edition with the addition of the SQL Server Management Studio Basic and support for Reporting Services. The Reporting Services included with SQL Server Express with Advanced Services is limited to reporting on the local database. Like the regular SQL Server 2008 Express Edition, the SQL Server 2008 Express Edition with Advanced Services is a free download. Some of the features in the SQL Server 2008 Express Edition with Advanced Services include

- Support for 32-bit & 64-bit processors
- Support for 1 CPU
- Support for up to 1GB of RAM
- Maximum database size of 4GB

- Support for 16 instances
- Includes SQL Server Management Studio Basic
- Reporting Services
- Report Designer

SQL Server Compact Edition 3.5

The SQL Server Compact Edition is not like any of the other editions of SQL Server 2008, including the Express Edition. The Compact Edition is built on a different code base than the other editions of SQL Server. The SQL Server Compact edition is included with Visual Studio 2008 and is a small footprint in-process database designed to provide desktop applications with limited relational database capabilities. The SQL Server Compact Edition 3.5 is also available as a free download from http://www.microsoft.com/sql/editions/compact/downloads.mspx. Some of the important characteristics of the SQL Server Compact Edition include

- In-process database
- Single workstation connectivity
- Support for 32-bit processors only
- Maximum database size of 4GB
- No support for stored procedures

SQL Server 2008 Developer's Edition

The SQL Server 2008 Developer Edition provides the same feature set as the SQL Server 2008 Enterprise Edition. However, the Developer Edition is intended for development and testing purposes and is not licensed for production use. The Developer Edition is available as a part of the Microsoft Developer Network (MSDN) or it can be licensed separately for $50.00.

Installing SQL Server 2008

SQL Server 2008's installation is different than the installation process for any of the previous versions of SQL Server. SQL Server 2008's installation is started using the Autorun file on the DVD or by running the setup.exe program found in the DVD's root directory. The installation media contains the x86 32-bit, x64 64-bit, and IA-64 64-bit versions of SQL Server 2008. When you launch the SQL Server 2008 setup.exe

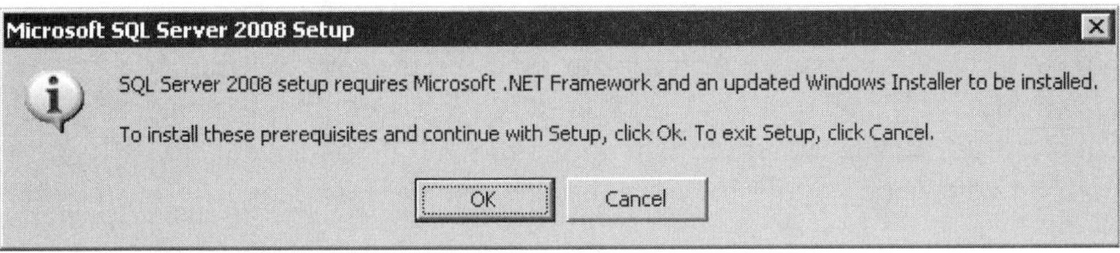

Figure A-1 *Installing the SQL Server 2008 prerequisites*

program the setup program first checks for the presence of the .NET Framework 3.5. If the .NET Framework 3.5 is not present on your system, you are prompted to download and install it as you can see in Figure A-1.

Clicking OK launches the .NET Framework 3.5 SP1 installation program, which you can see in Figure A-2.

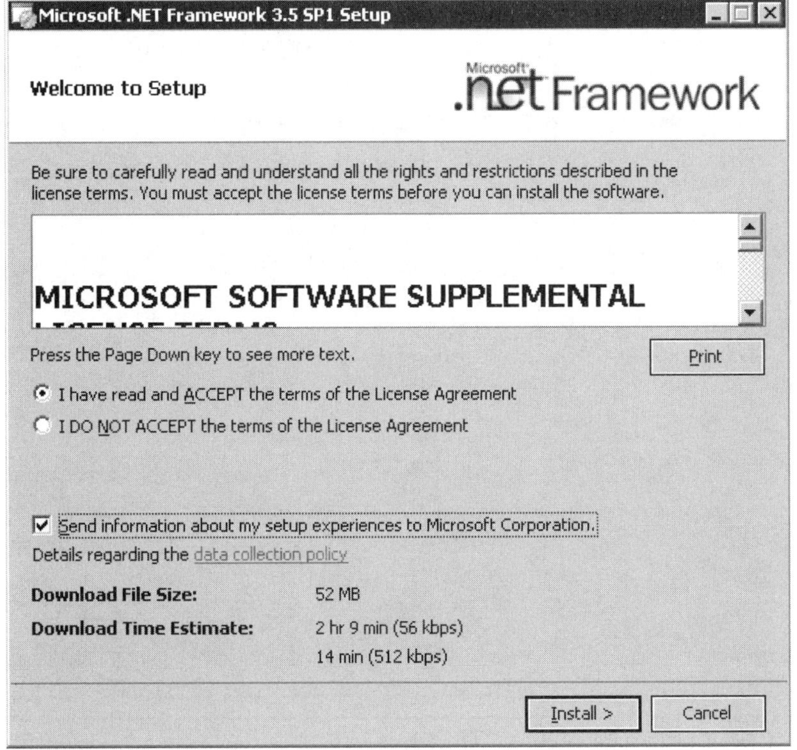

Figure A-2 *Installing .NET Framework 3.5 SP1*

The first screen of the .NET Framework 3.5 SP1 installation program greets you with the end-user license agreement for the .NET Framework. Selecting the I Have Read and ACCEPT the Terms of the License Agreement option and then clicking Install begins the download and installation of the .NET Framework 3.5 SP1. After the .NET Framework 3.5 SP1 has been installed you'll see a dialog like the one shown in Figure A-3.

Clicking Exit closes the .NET Framework dialog. If you're installing SQL Server 2008 on Windows Server 2003, then the next dialog that you'll see is the software update dialog for installing the latest version of the Windows Installer as is shown in Figure A-4.

Clicking Next displays the mandatory end-user license agreement dialog for the Windows Installer version 4.5 that you can see in Figure A-5.

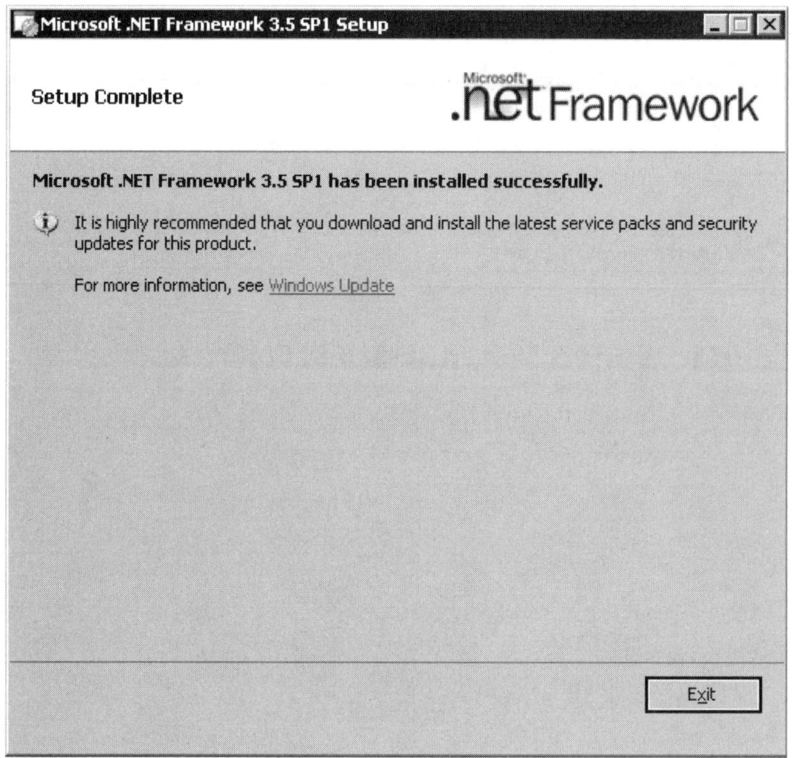

Figure A-3 *Completing the installation of the .NET Framework 3.5 SP1*

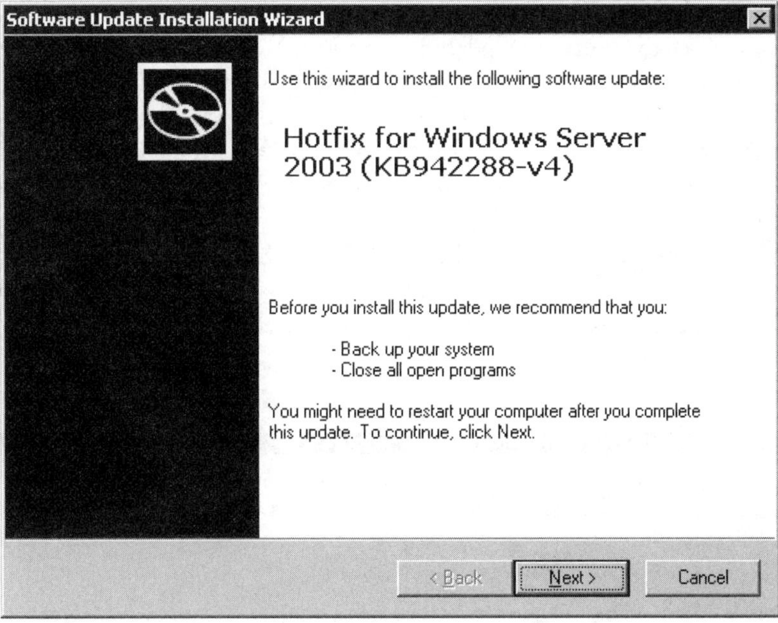

Figure A-4 *Installing the latest Windows Installer on Windows Server 2003*

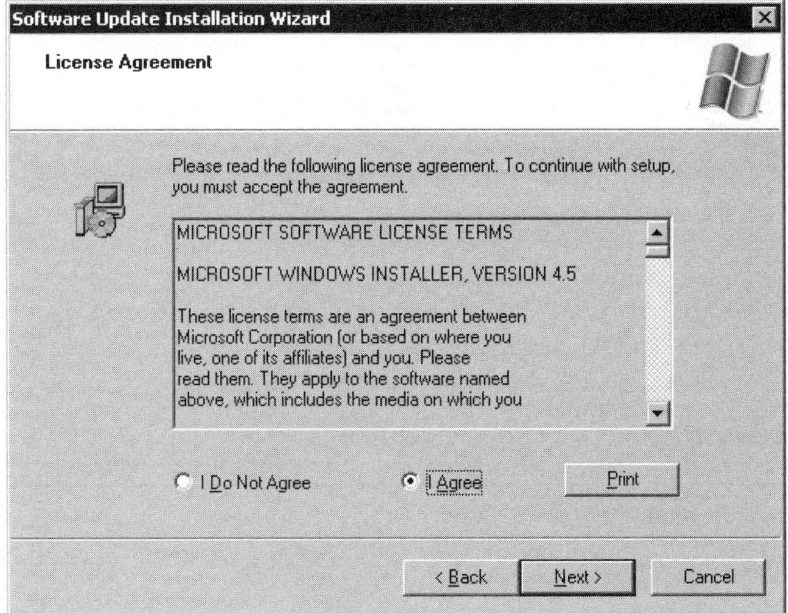

Figure A-5 *Accepting the license agreement for Windows Installer 4.5*

Clicking Next installs the new Windows Installer 4.5. After the system update has completed, you'll see the Software Update Installation Wizard dialog shown in Figure A-5. Note that the wizard normally prompts you to restart the system at this point, but that option is disabled here. As is typical with Windows Server updates, clicking Finish prompts you to reboot the system which you must do manually. After the reboot completes, the SQL Server installation resumes and displays the SQL Server Installation Center screen that you see in Figure A-6.

The Planning link displays a number of different SQL Server 2008 information sources, but in all likelihood if you're running an installation program you're past the planning stage. To install SQL Server 2008 you click the Installation link,

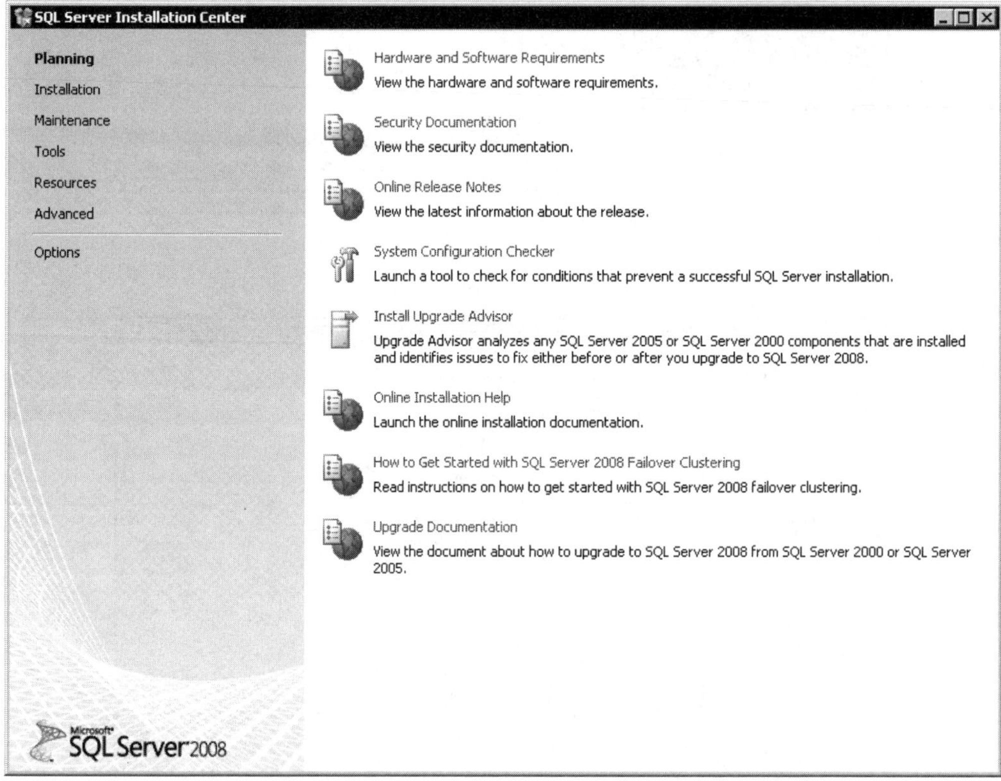

Figure A-6 *SQL Server 2008 Installation Center*

which displays the different SQL Server 2008 installation options that you see in Figure A-7.

The new SQL Server 2008 installation is now completely cluster-aware and has options to install SQL Server 2008 as a standalone server, as the first node in a new cluster, or as an additional node in an existing cluster. You can also upgrade an existing SQL Server 2000 or 2005 instance to SQL Server 2008. For more information about upgrading to SQL Server 2008, you can refer to the Upgrading from SQL Server 2005 to SQL Server 2008 section later in this chapter. To install a new instance of SQL Server 2008, click on the New SQL Server standalone installation or add features to an

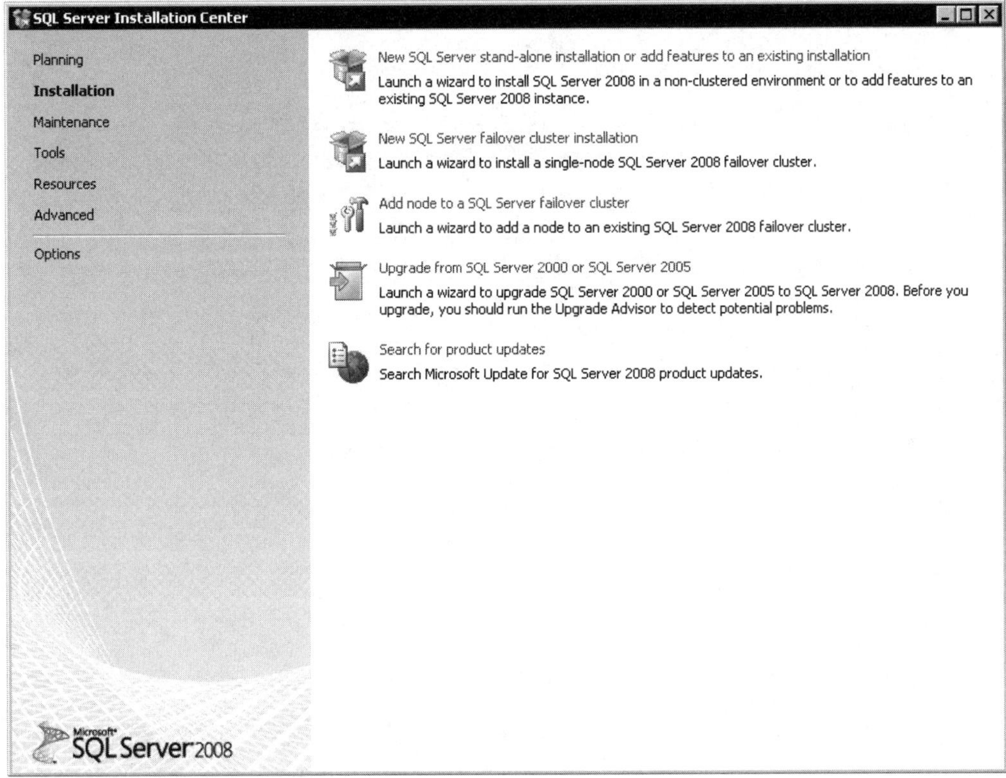

Figure A-7 *SQL Server 2008 installation options*

existing installation link. This will display the SQL Server 2008 Setup Support Rules dialog that you see in Figure A-8.

The Setup and Support Rules dialog automatically checks your system for problems that might prevent the successful installation of SQL Server 2008. In Figure A-8 you can see that the Setup Support Rules performs tests for six different system requirements, including tests for the minimum operating system level, if you're running the setup program as an administrator, and if the WMI service is running. Clicking OK displays the Setup Support Files dialog that you can see illustrated in Figure A-9.

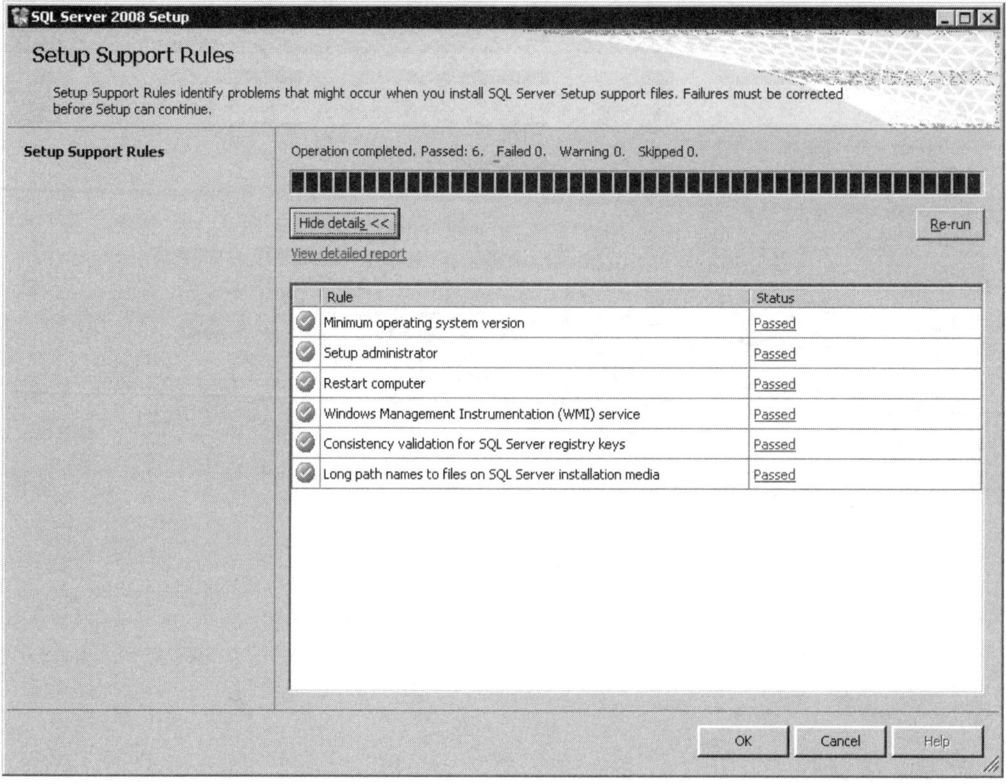

Figure A-8 *Setup and Support Rules dialog*

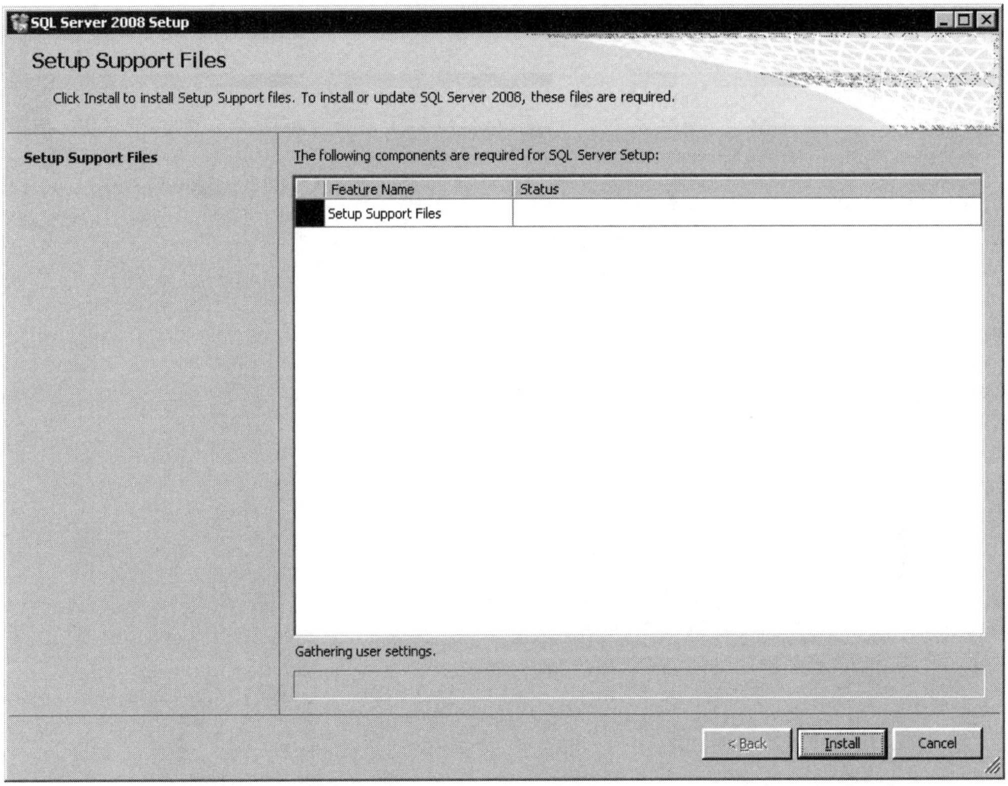

Figure A-9 *Setup Support Files dialog*

The Setup Support Files dialog installs the components that are required by SQL Server 2008 setup program. Clicking Install copies the required setup files to the system and displays the Setup Support Rules screen that you can see in Figure A-10.

The Setup Support Rules dialog performs a second set of tests to determine if there will be any problems running the setup program. Like the previous Setup Support Rules screen, a green check indicates that the condition is OK and that the installation can proceed. A red X indicates that there is a problem that needs to be corrected before the setup can proceed. Clicking on the link under the Status column will provide more

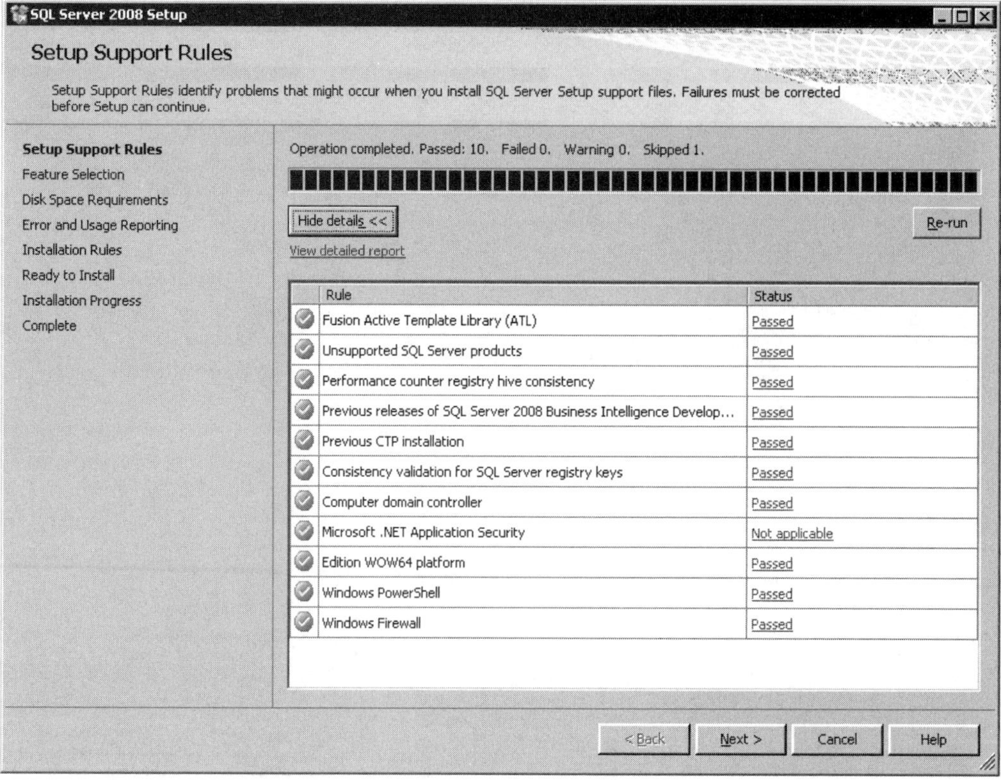

Figure A-10 *Setup Support Rules dialog*

information about any error conditions. If all of the conditions are passed and there are green check marks next to all the items as you can see in Figure A-10 then you can click Next. This will continue the installation and will display the the SQL Server 2008 Product Keys dialog shown in Figure A-11.

The next screen in the SQL Server 2008 setup process prompts you to enter your product key information. If you're installing one of the evaluation versions of SQL Server 2008, you would select the Specify a free edition radio button and then click

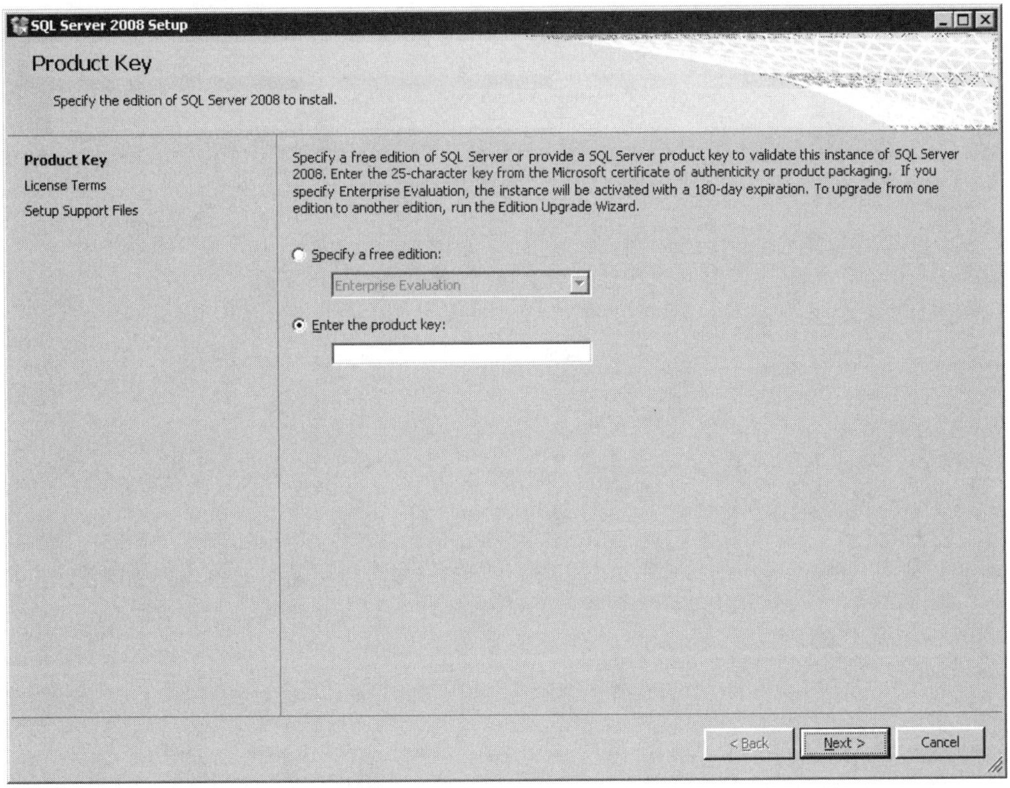

Figure A-11 *SQL Server 2008 Product Key dialog*

Next. Otherwise, if you are installing a licensed version of SQL Server 2008, you would select the Enter the product key radio button and then type in the product installation key and click Next. This will display the the End User License Agreement (EULA) in the License Terms dialog that you can see in Figure A-12.

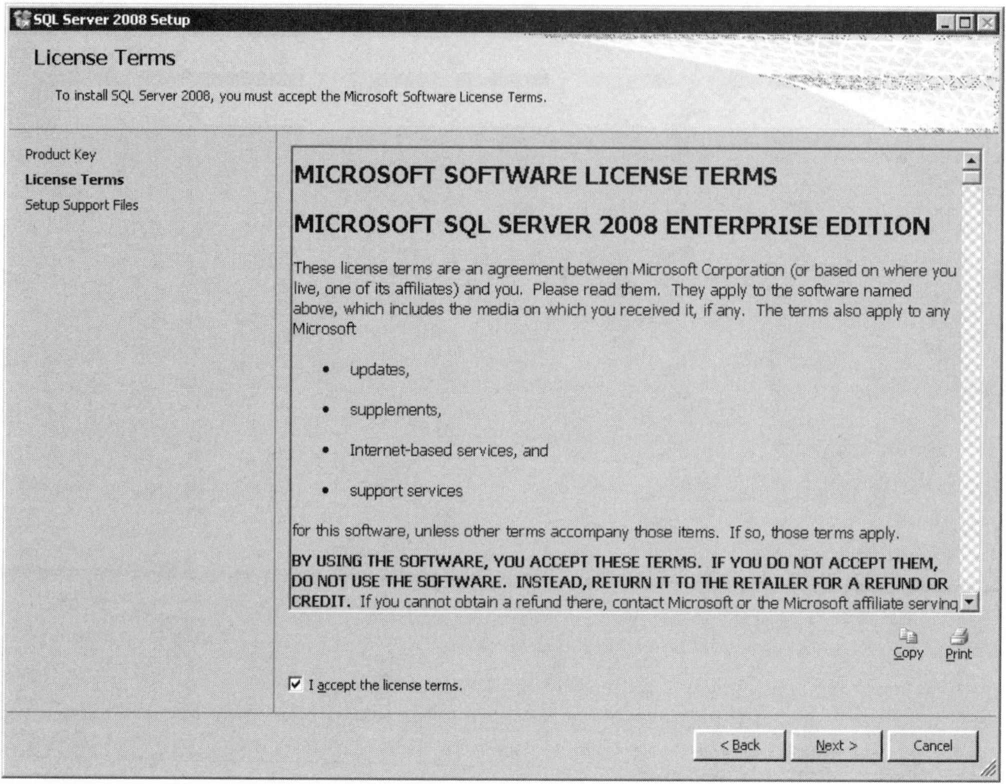

Figure A-12 *License Terms dialog*

After you accept the license agreement by first placing a check in the I accept the license terms box and then clicking Next, you will see the SQL Server 2008 Feature Selection dialog that's shown in Figure A-13.

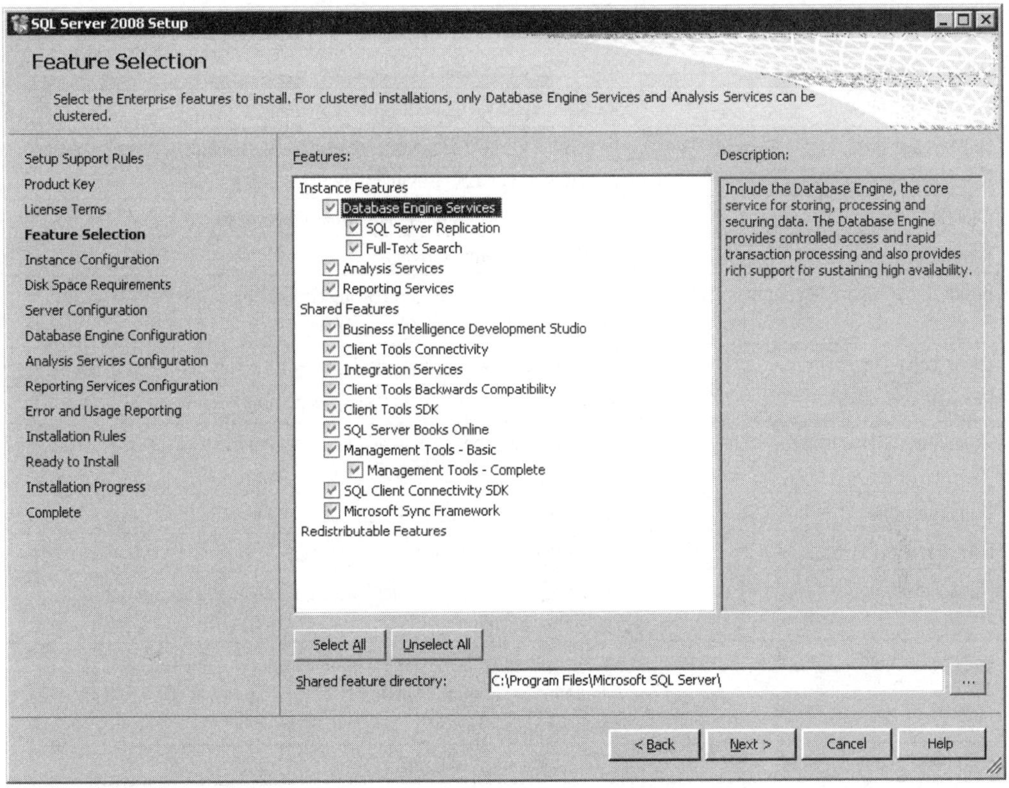

Figure A-13 *Feature Selection dialog*

The Feature Selection dialog enables you to select which SQL Server 2008 components you want to install. Table A-1 describes the available SQL Server 2008 features.

Feature	Description
Database Engine Services	Installs the core relation database engine
SQL Server Replication	Installs support for replicating database objects
Full-text Search	Installs the full-text search engine which allows linguistic aware searching for text words and phrases in columns
Analysis Services	Installs the analytical processing (OLAP) subsystem
Reporting Services	Installs the reporting subsystem
Business Intelligence Development Studio	Installs the IDE for developing BI objects like cubes, Integration Services packages, and Reporting Service reports
Client Tools Connectivity	Installs the middleware that enables network clients to connect to SQL Server
Integration Services	Installs the data transfer and transformation subsystem
Client Tools Backwards Compatibility	Install the components required to run existing DTS packages that were created with SQL Server 2000
Client Tools SDK	Installs the software development samples and tools
SQL Server Books Online	Installs the online product documentation
Management Tools – Basic	Installs SQL Server Management Studio, SQLCMD, and the SQL Server PowerShell provider
Management Tools – Complete	Installs SQL Server Management Studio support for Analysis Services, Integration Services, and Reporting Services, as well as SQL Profiler and the Database Tuning Advisor
SQL Client Connectivity SDK	Installs software development samples and tools
Microsoft Sync Framework	Installs the components to support synchronization with offline applications and mobile devices

Table A-1 *SQL Server 2008 Installable Features*

NOTE

To set up a typical administrative workstation, select just the Management Tools—Basic option.

For each feature, you can select the shared feature directory that will be used. By default, all of the shared features are installed into the C:\Program Files\Microsoft SQL Server.

NOTE

No sample databases or applications are installed. If you want to install the sample AdventureWorks or AdventureWorksDW databases then you must download them from http://www.codeplex.com/MSFTDBProdSamples/Release/ProjectReleases.aspx?ReleaseId=16040.

After you've selected the components that you want to install, click Next to display the Instance Configuration dialog that you see in Figure A-14.

If this is the first time you've run through the installation program, you have the option to either set up the default instance or set up a named instance. If you've already set up a default SQL Server instance, the setup program will detect that instance and offer you only the option to set up a named instance. Each named instance is essentially an additional copy of SQL Server installed on the same server. The Enterprise Edition and Standard Edition support up to 50 named instances on a given system. The other SQL Server 2008 editions support up to 16 named instances. Most implementations will only use the default instance. ISPs and web hosting providers are examples of businesses that most often make use of named instances. If you create a named instance, each name must be 16 characters or less. Instance names are not case sensitive, but the first character of the name must be a letter. They cannot have any embedded spaces

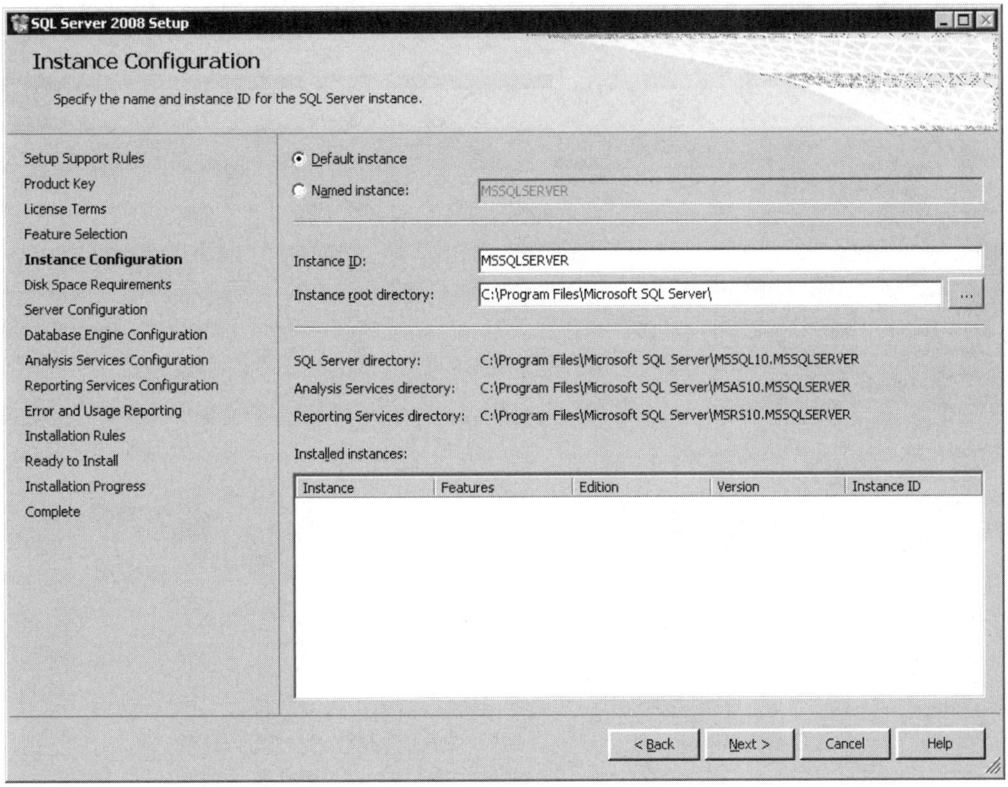

Figure A-14 *Instance Configuration dialog*

and must not contain the backslash (\), comma (,), colon (:), single quote ('), dash (-), ampersand (&), number sign (#), or at sign (@). Instance names also cannot contain the reserved words Default or MSSQLServer (which is the default SQL Server instance name). The full list of reserved words can be found in the setup program's online Help.

NOTE

*If you create a named instance, the SQL Server service name will be named as follows: MSSQL$*InstanceName *(where* InstanceName *is replaced with the instance name that you create).*

You can also specify the directory that you want to use to install the SQL Server instance. The default installation directory is C:\Program Files\Microsoft SQL Server. After you either accept the default instance or create a named instance, click Next to display the Disk Space Requirements dialog shown in Figure A-15.

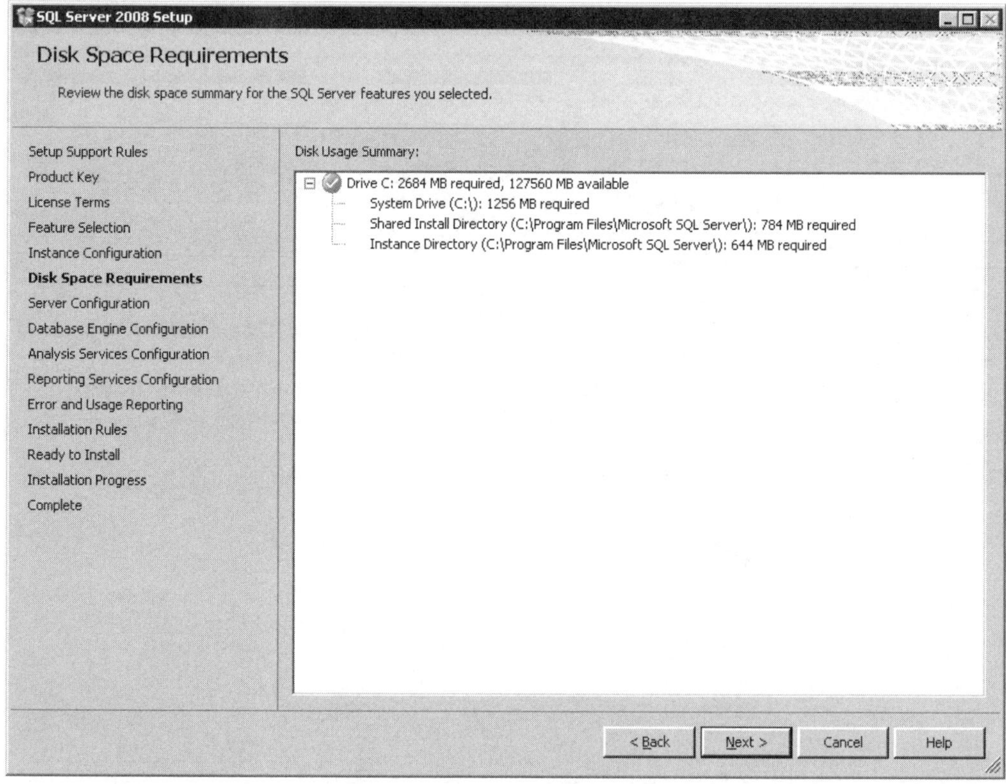

Figure A-15 *Disk Space Requirements dialog*

The Disk Space Requirements dialog displays the installation directories that you previously selected as well as the required and available storage space for each drive. If you need to change the target directories, you can use the Back button to page back to the Features Selection and Instance Configuration dialogs to change the target directories. If all of the disk requirements are acceptable, then you can click Next to display the Server Configuration dialog that's illustrated in Figure A-16.

The Server Configuration dialog allows you to specify the accounts that each of the different SQL Server services will run under. The values in the Server Configuration dialog specify the user accounts used by the SQL Server service, as well as the SQL Server Agent, Analysis Services, Integration Services, and Reporting Server. This is important because it sets the permissions level that each of these services runs under. Microsoft recommends using a domain account to run each of the services. You can use the administrative account, but because of its high privilege level, it's not a recommended. You can also select the Local System account; however, this account is very powerful,

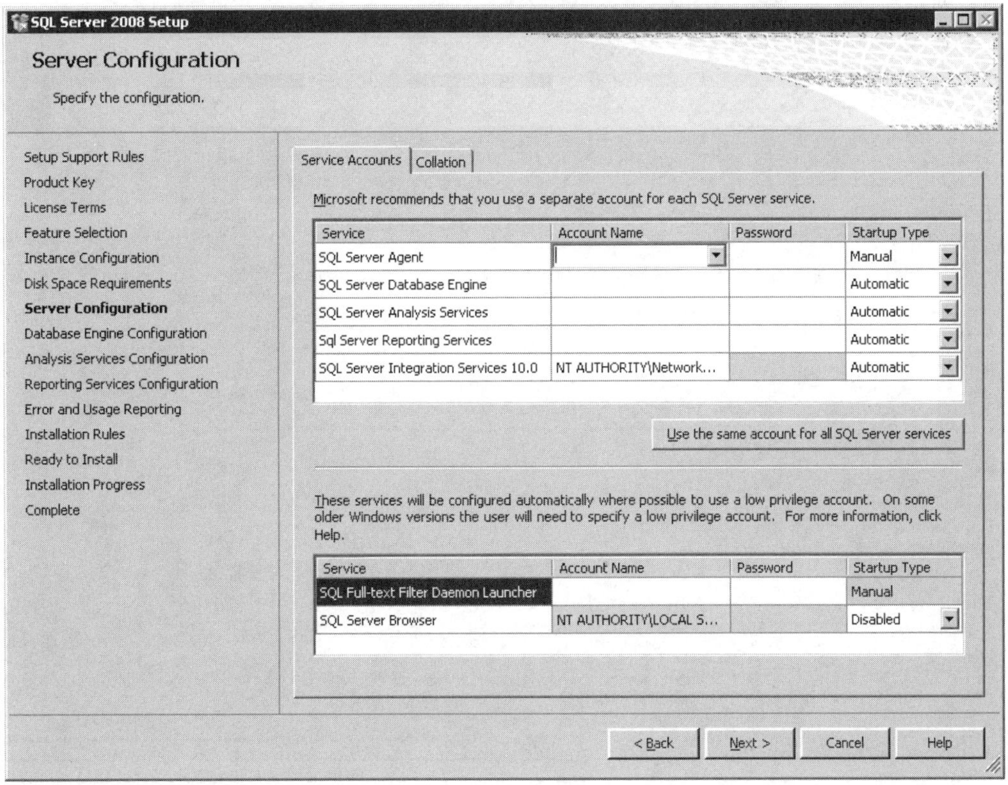

Figure A-16 *Server Configuration dialog*

having administrative-like permissions, and is limited in its ability to access network resources. In addition, Microsoft also recommends using a separate account for each service. Typically, you would want to create a domain user account for each SQL Server service to run under and then select these accounts for the corresponding services. This gives you the ability to control the permissions that the various services possess at a more granular level.

In addition to specifying the authentication for the various SQL Server 2008 services, you can also click on the Collation tab and change the collation order used by this SQL Server instance. Most organizations will want to use SQL Server's default collation. After supplying the authentication information for the SQL Server services, clicking Next displays the Database Engine Configuration dialog that you see in Figure A-17.

The Database Engine Configuration dialog defines the type of user authentication that SQL Server 2008 will use. The default value is Windows Authentication,

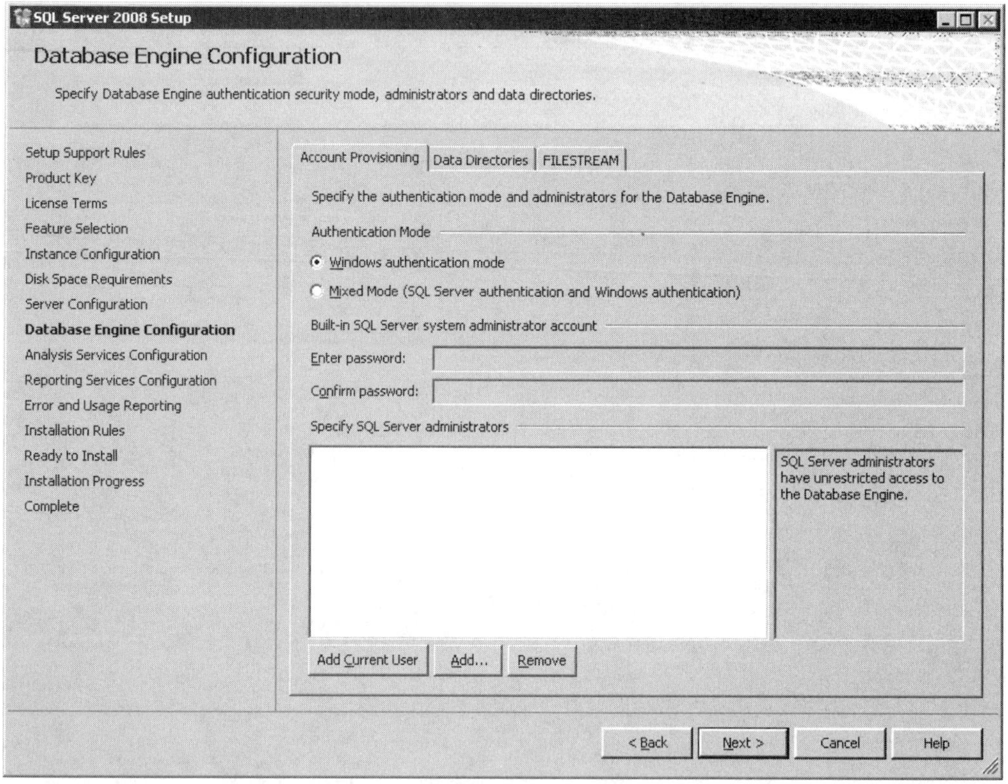

Figure A-17 *Database Engine Configuration dialog*

meaning that the Windows user accounts will be used to authenticate to SQL Server. Typically this is what you want, because it provides easier management in that only one set of login accounts needs to be managed and maintained by the host operating system. It is also more secure because with Windows authentication the application does not need to pass the password across the network. You can also choose Mixed Mode Authentication, which means that both Windows logins and SQL Server logins can be accepted. In the case of SQL Server logins, you must manually add these logins to SQL Server; they are maintained independently from the Windows login. If you're using Windows authentication you typically would want to click the Add Current User button to add the current user as a SQL Server administrator. If you select Mixed Mode authentication, you then need to select a password for the SQL Server System Administrator (sa) login. For security reasons, you must select a non-blank password. You should strongly consider making this a strong password, which is at least eight characters in length and contains characters, numbers, and special characters.

In addition to the SQL Server authentication mode, you can also use the Data Directories and the FILESTREAM tabs to configure SQL Server's data storage options. The Data Directories tab allows you to change the default directories used to store database files, log files, the temp DB database and log, as well as where disk backups are stored. By default, users, databases and logs are stored in C:\Program Files\Microsoft SQL Server\MSSQL10.MSSQLSERVER\MSSQL\Data. The default directory for backups is C:\Program Files\Microsoft SQL Server\MSSQL10 .MSSQLSERVER\MSSQL\Backup. The FILESTREAM tab is used to enable FILESTREAM access for the server. In order to enable FILESTREAM access you need to check the Enable FILESTREAM for Transact-SQL access checkbox. You also have the option to enable FILESTREAM access for Win32 clients. If you do so, you are prompted to also create a file share. The default name for the file share is MSSQLSERVER. If you don't enable FILESTREAM access during setup, you can change this later by updating the system configuration with the sp_configure command.

If you selected to install Analysis Services in the earlier Feature Selection screen, clicking Next displays the Analysis Service Configuration dialog that you see in Figure A-18.

Like the Database Engine Configuration screen, the Analysis Services Configuration screen allows you to select the administrative account as well as set up the default directories that will be used to store Analysis Services databases. The Account Provisioning tab allow you to select the Analysis Services administrative account. If you want the current user to be the Analysis Services administrator, click the Add Current User button. You can also click the Add button and select the Windows account that you want to act as Analysis Services Administrator.

To change the default directory that Analysis Services uses, click on the Data Directories tab. The Data Directories tab allows you to change the default directories

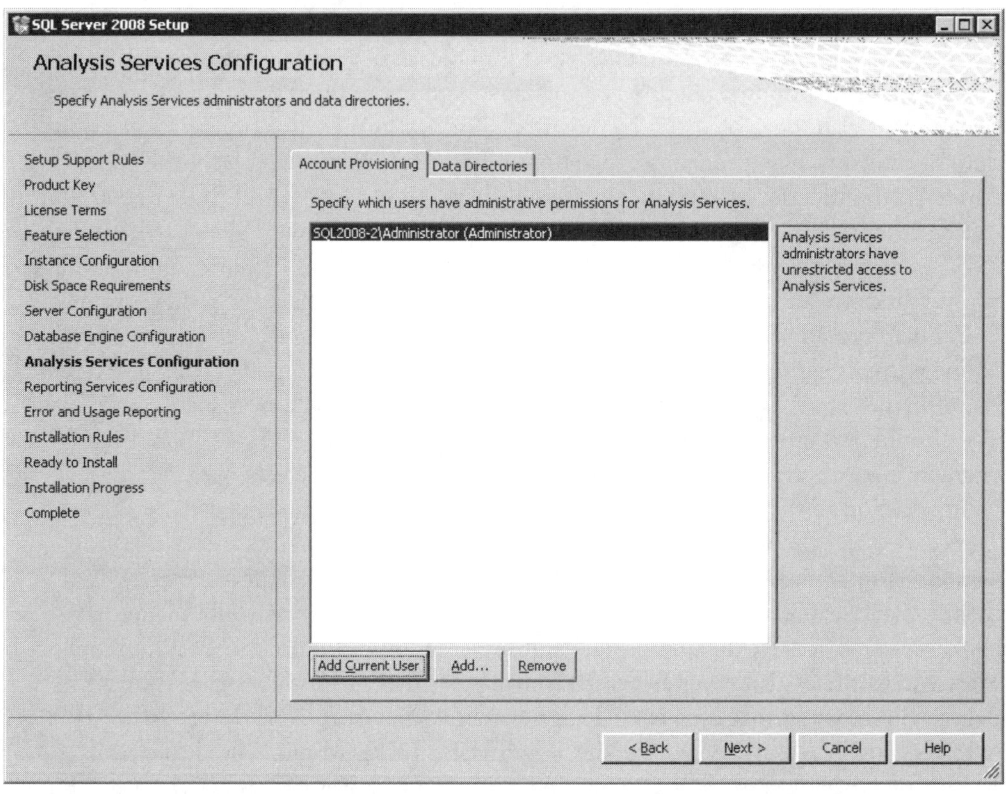

Figure A-18 *Analysis Services Configuration dialog*

that are used to store Analysis services data and log files, as well as the Analysis Services temp and backup directories. By default Analysis Services uses the C:\Program Files\Microsoft SQL Server\MSAS10.MSSQLSERVER\OLAP\Data directory for data files. For log file storage, the default directory is C:\Program Files\Microsoft SQL Server\MSAS10.MSSQLSERVER\OLAP\Log. The default directory for Analysis Services temp storage is C:\Program Files\Microsoft SQL Server\MSAS10.MSSQLSERVER\OLAP\Temp. The default directory for Analysis Services backups is C:\Program Files\Microsoft SQL Server\MSAS10.MSSQLSERVER\OLAP\Backup.

If you selected to install Reporting Services, clicking Next displays the Reporting Services Configuration dialog that you see in Figure A-19.

The Reporting Services Configuration dialog enables you to specify the Reporting Services configuration that you want to use. You can choose either to Install the native mode default configuration, Install the SharePoint integrated mode default configuration,

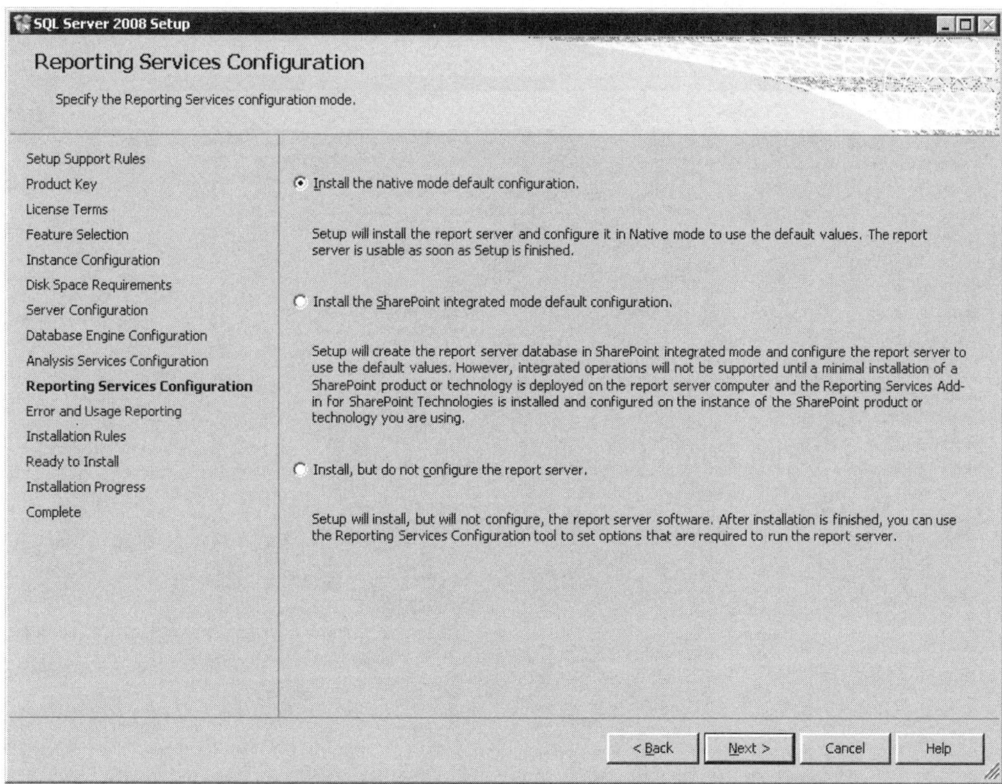

Figure A-19 *Reporting Services Configuration dialog*

or Install, but do not configure the report server. Installing the native mode default configuration will create the Reporting Services database in the current SQL Server instance and Reporting Service will be usable at the end of the installation. Selecting the SharePoint integrated mode will also create the Reporting Services database. In integrated mode, Reporting Services is managed using SharePoint rather than the built-in Reporting Services Manger. Integrated mode is not active until SharePoint is installed. The final option, Install, but do not configure the report server, copies the Reporting services programs to the server but doesn't create the database or perform any of the other required configuration steps. If you select this option, then you must manually configure Reporting Services after the SQL Server installation.

After selecting the Reporting Services configuration, clicking Next displays the Error and Usage Reporting screen that you can see in Figure A-20.

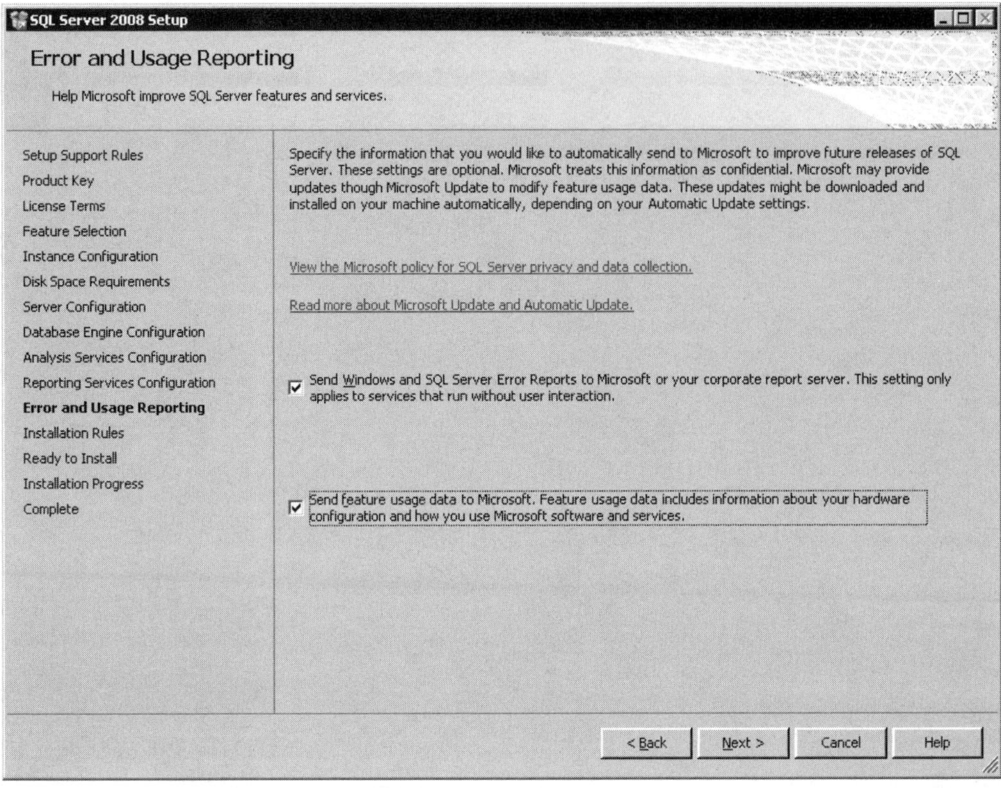

Figure A-20 *Error and Usage Reporting screen*

SQL Server 2008's Error and Usage Reporting screen enables you to optionally report errors in the SQL Server database service and other subsystem service errors to Microsoft. Likewise, the usage reports show Microsoft that you use the product. Microsoft does not collect any personal information from these reports. Microsoft just uses this information to better understand how SQL Server is used, as well as to identify and eliminate problems that may occur within SQL Server. SQL Server 2008's error reports send the following information to Microsoft:

- The status of the service when the error occurred
- The operating system version
- The basic hardware configuration

- SQL Server's Digital Product ID (which is used to identify your license)
- The server's IP address
- Information about the process that caused the error

Participating in SQL Server 2008's error and usage reporting is totally optional. After you address the Error and Usage Reporting dialog, clicking Next displays the Installation Rules dialog that is shown in Figure A-21.

The Installation Rules dialog performs a final check for any conditions that might block the installation process. If any error condition is found it will be shown in the Installation Rules dialog with a red X. If all of the items have green check marks, as you

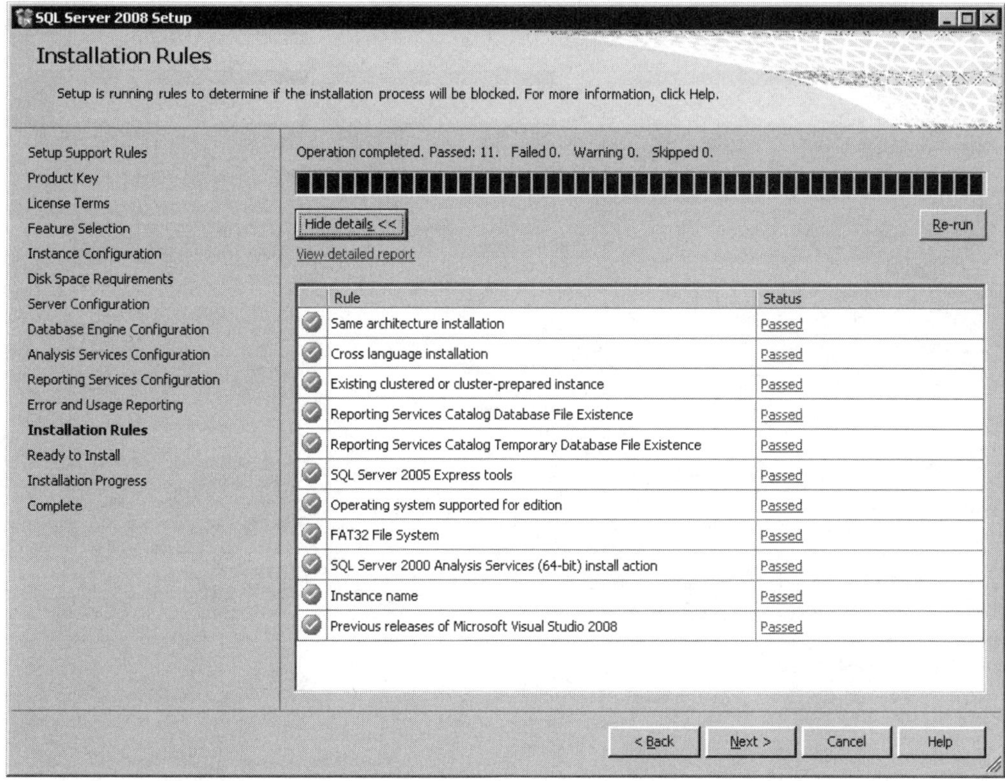

Figure A-21 *Installation Rules dialog*

can see in Figure A-21, then the installation is ready to proceed. Clicking Next displays the Ready to Install dialog shown in Figure A-22.

The Ready To Install dialog enables you to confirm your choices. If you need to change anything, you can use the Back button to page back through the previous installation screens. Clicking the Install button on the Ready To Install dialog begins the installation process for SQL Server 2008. The installation itself will take several

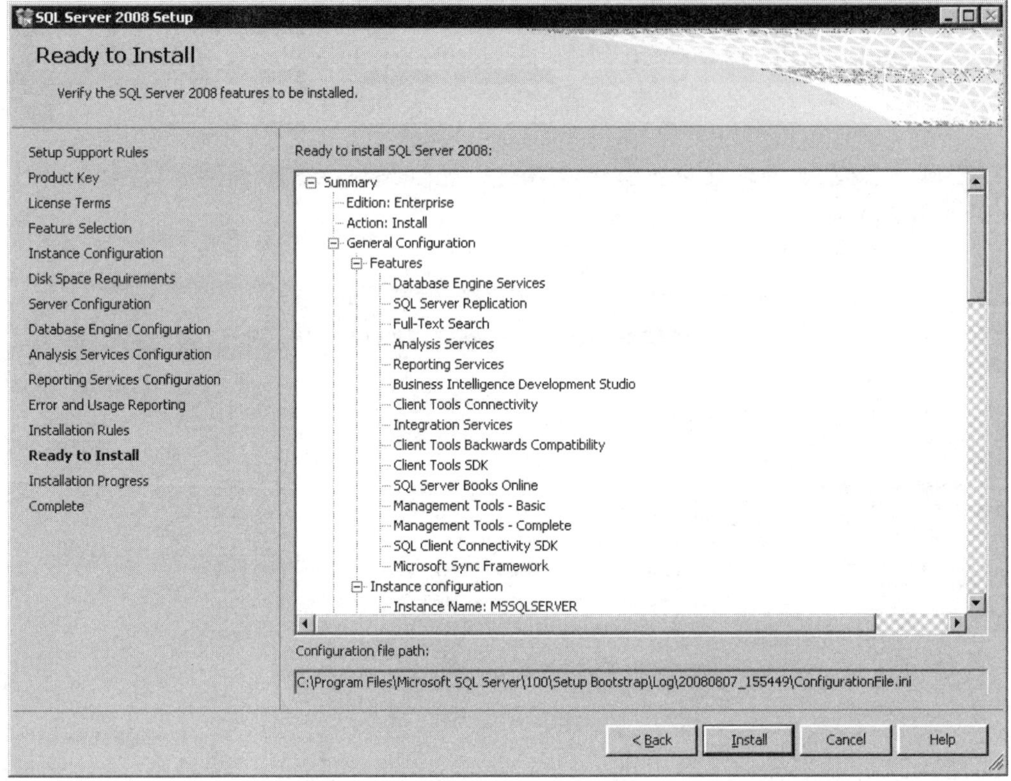

Figure A-22 *Ready to Install dialog*

minutes, depending on the hardware that you're using and the installation media. As the installation program runs, the current status is shown in the Installation Progress window. You can see the Installation Progress screen shown in Figure A-23.

When the SQL Server 2008 installation is complete you'll see the Complete dialog shown in Figure A-24.

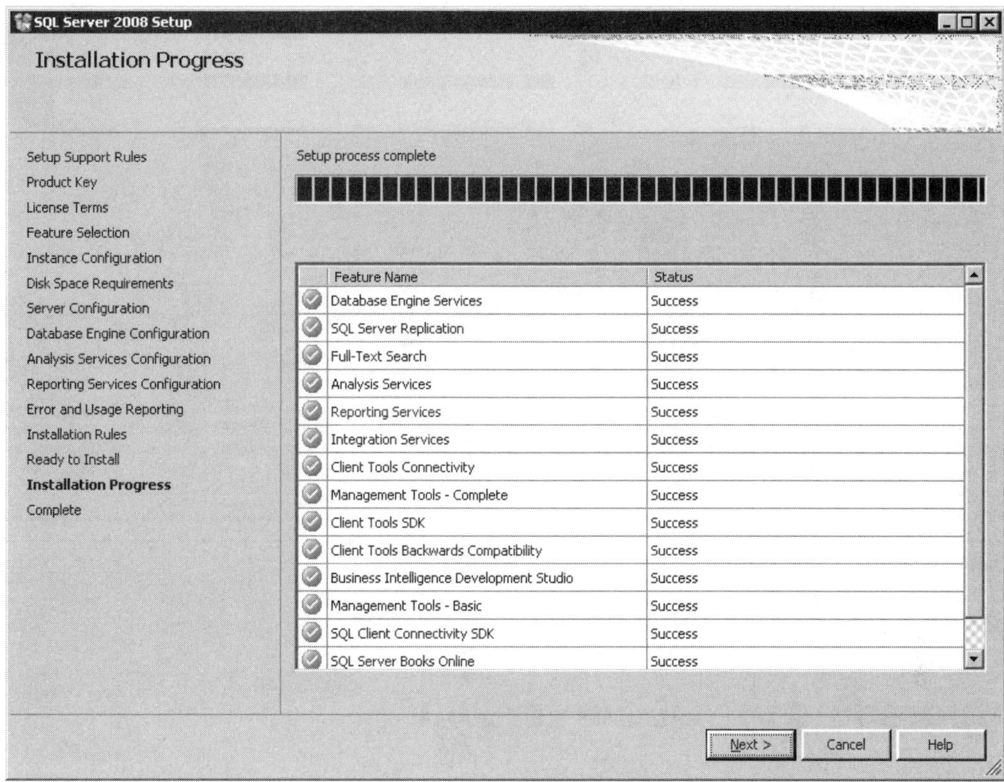

Figure A-23 *Installation Progress screen*

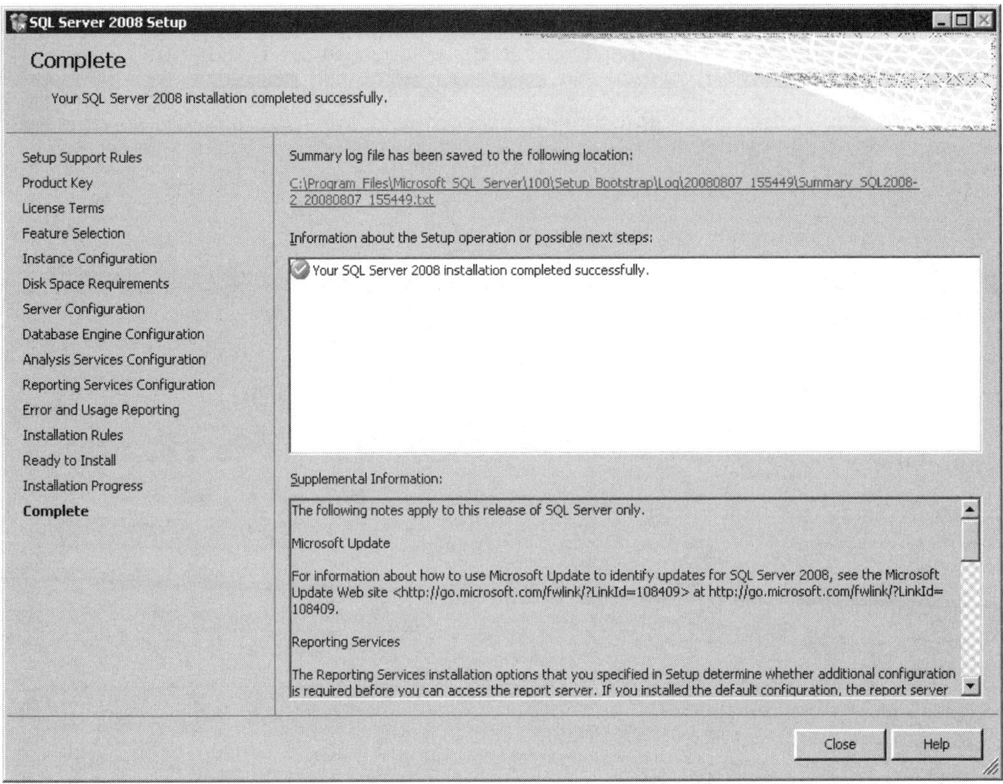

Figure A-24 *Complete dialog*

Upgrading to SQL Server 2008

In addition to creating new installations, the SQL Server 2008 setup program can also be used to upgrade existing SQL Server 2000 and SQL Server 2005 installations. However, it cannot be use to upgrade versions of SQL Server previous to this.

Upgrading from SQL Server 2000 or SQL Server 2005

The setup program supports direct upgrades to SQL Server 2008 from SQL Server 2000 and SQL Server 2005. SQL Server's essential on-disk structures are the same, and the setup program can successfully perform an in-place migration for both SQL Server 2000 and SQL Server 2005 installations to SQL Server 2008.

To initiate the upgrade to SQL Server 2008 you can execute the Autorun program on the SQL Server 2008 installation media or you can launch the setup.exe program found in the installation media's root directory. As with the clean installation process described in the previous section, the setup program first checks for the presence of the .NET Framework 3.5 SP1. If it isn't found, then the setup program will download and install the .NET Framework 3.5 SP1. These steps are exactly the same as you saw earlier in Figures A-1 through A-3.

After installing the .NET Framework 3.5 SP1, the installation process next updates the system with the Windows Installer 4.5. This process is exactly the same as you saw earlier in Figures A-4 and A-5. After upgrading to the Windows Installer 4.5, you are prompted to restart the system and rerun the SQL Server 2008 setup program. The SQL Server portion of the upgrade process begins when the setup program displays the SQL Server 2008 Installation Center, as you can see in Figure A-25.

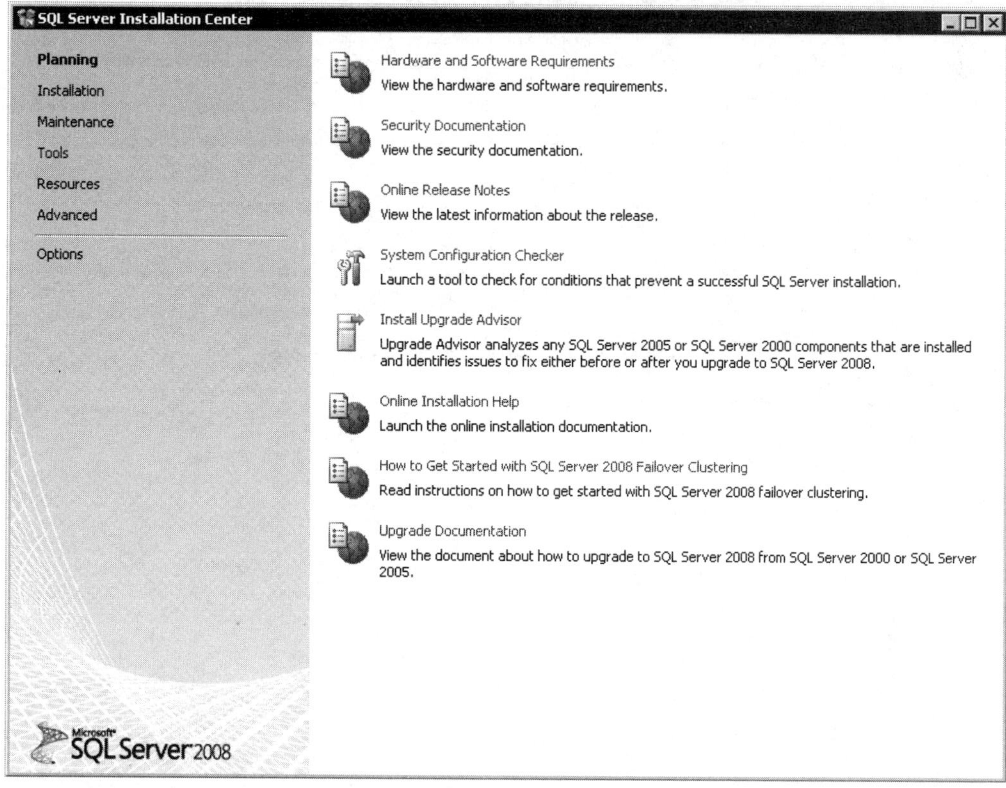

Figure A-25 *SQL Server 2008 Installation Center*

Before performing the upgrade, it's a good idea to install and run the Upgrade Advisor. Selecting the Install Upgrade Advisor option from the Planning tab will install the Upgrade Advisor on your system. After completing the installation you can run the Upgrade Advisor, which will check your SQL Server system configuration and code. The Upgrade Advisor will warn you about changes or depreciated features that may affect your system upgrade. You can optionally generate a report from the Upgrade Advisor that you can use to systematically address any potential upgrade issues. When you're ready to perform the actual upgrade, you can click on the Installation link and then select the Upgrade from the SQL Server 2000 or SQL Server 2005 option that you can see in Figure A-26.

Selecting the Upgrade from SQL Server 2000 or SQL Server 2005 option launches the SQL Server 2008 installation program. As with a clean installation, the first thing the SQL Server 2008 setup program does is run the Setup Support Rules to check

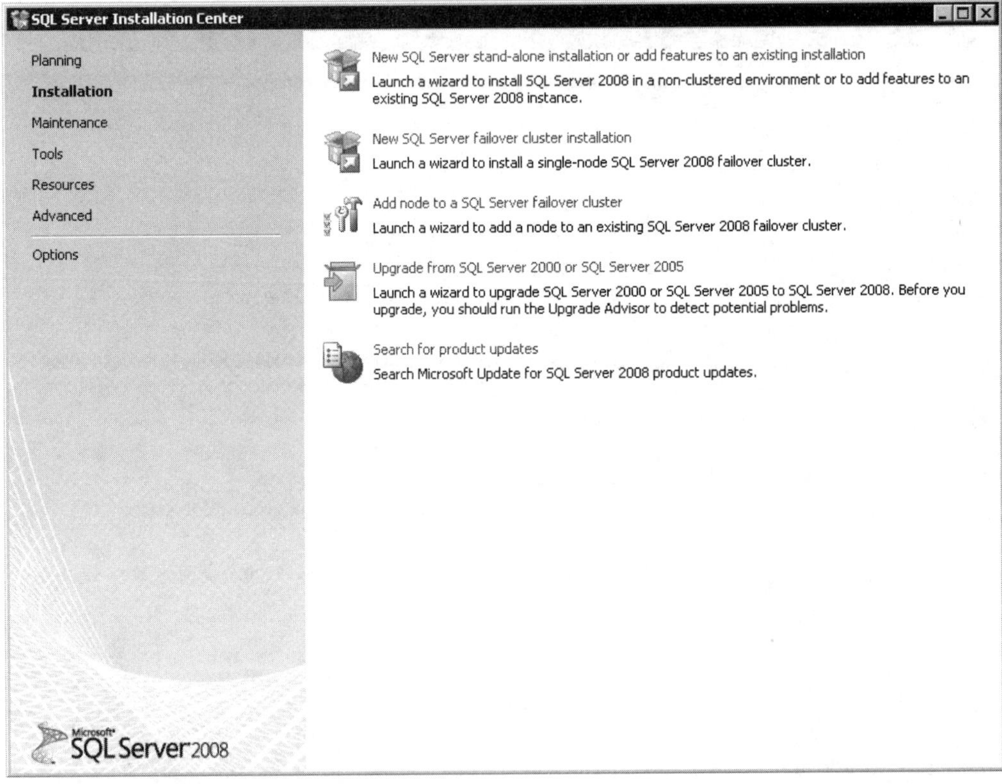

Figure A-26 *Upgrade from SQL Server 2000 or SQL Server 2005*

if there are any system issues that would interfere with the upgrade. This is the same screen that was shown earlier in Figure A-8.

Next, the setup program displays the Product Key dialog, allowing you to either choose to install the Evaluation Edition or to enter your SQL Server 2008 product key. This is the same dialog that was shown earlier in Figure A-11.

After entering the product key, the next dialog in the upgrade process displays the License Terms. This is the same dialog that was shown earlier in Figure A-12.

To proceed with the upgrade, you need to check the I Accept the License Terms box and then click Next. This will display the Setup Support Files dialog. This dialog is the same as the one that was presented earlier in Figure A-9. Clicking Install will copy the files needed to upgrade to SQL Server 2008 to your SQL Server 2000 or SQL Server 2005 system. Next the Setup Support Rules dialog checks for any problem that might have occurred from installing the setup support files. This is the same dialog that was shown earlier in Figure A-10. Clicking Next displays the Select Instance dialog that you can see in Figure A-27.

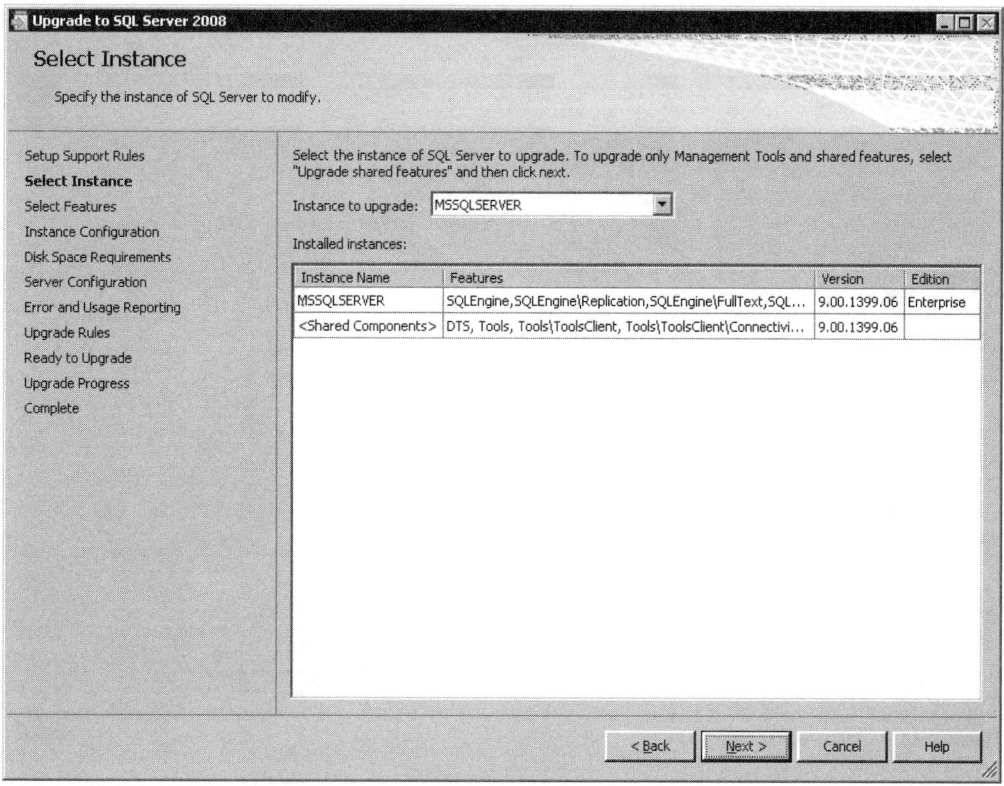

Figure A-27 *Select Instance dialog*

The Select Instance dialog allows you to choose the SQL Server instance that you want to upgrade. SQL Server supports up to 50 instances on the same system and each named instance is essentially a different installation of the SQL Server code. (You need to upgrade each instance separately.) As you can see in Figure A-26, the default instance is named MSSQLSERVER. Clicking Next displays the Select Features dialog shown in Figure A-28.

The Feature Selection dialog shows you the installed features that will be upgraded. All of the installed options are checked by default. You can't choose to just update some features. When performing an upgrade to SQL Server 2008 you must update all of the installed features in the selected instance at the same time. Clicking Next displays the Instance Configuration screen like the one shown in Figure A-29.

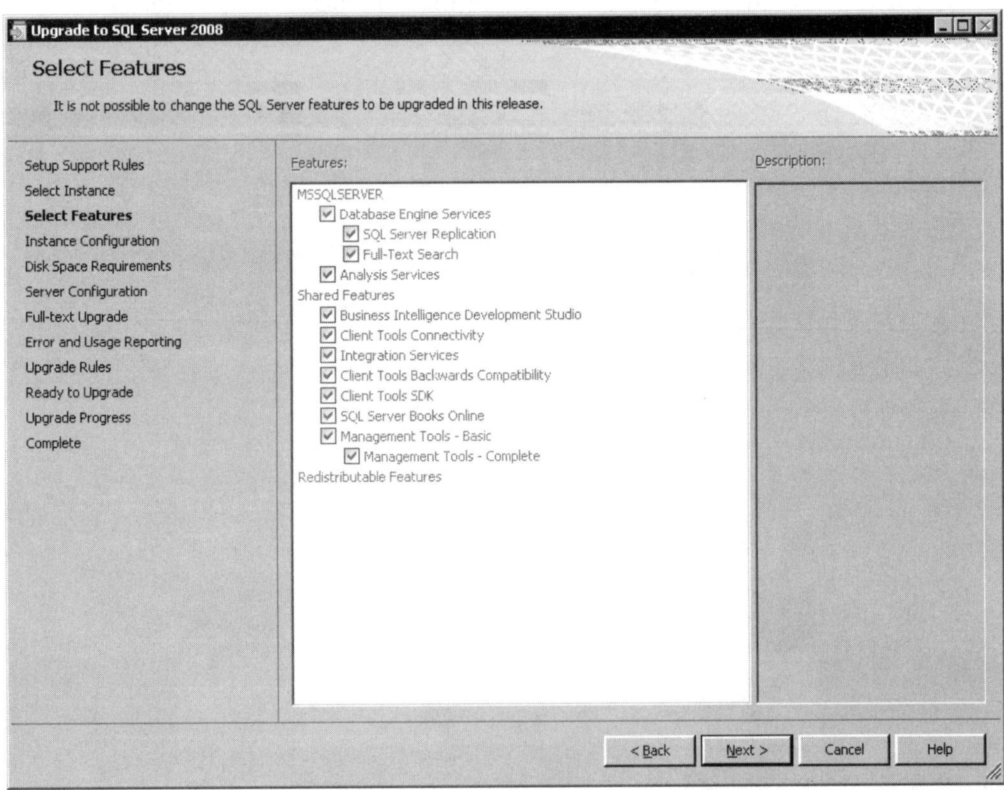

Figure A-28 *Select Features dialog*

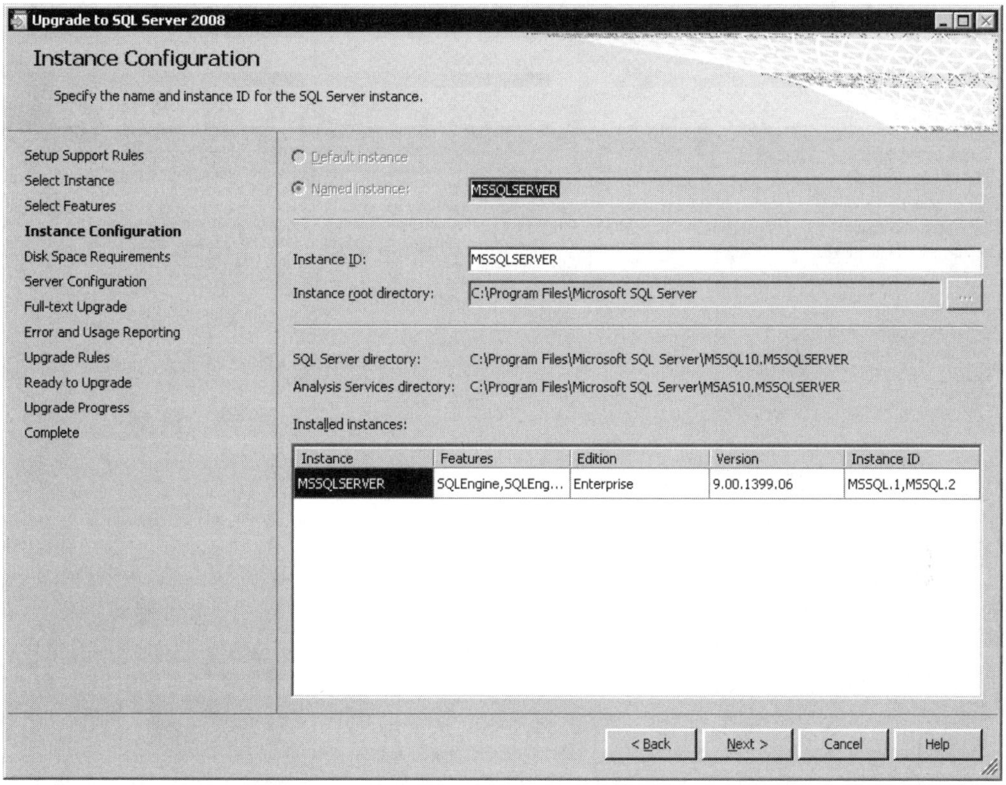

Figure A-29 *Instance Configuration screen*

The upgrade process will detect the installed SQL Server instances, and all of the installed instances will be listed in the Installed instance box at the bottom of the screen. You can choose to keep the installed instance name or you can opt to change it. In most cases, you will want the upgrade process to use the same SQL Server instance name. In Figure A-29 you can see that the upgrade process will update the default MSSQLSERVER instance. Clicking Next displays the Disk Space Requirements dialog illustrated in Figure A-30.

The Disk Space Requirements screen shows the disk space that will be required by the upgrade process, as well as the available disk space for the volume. As you can see in Figure A-30, it also displays the required disk storage for each installation directory. If there is adequate space to proceed with the installation, a green checkmark will be

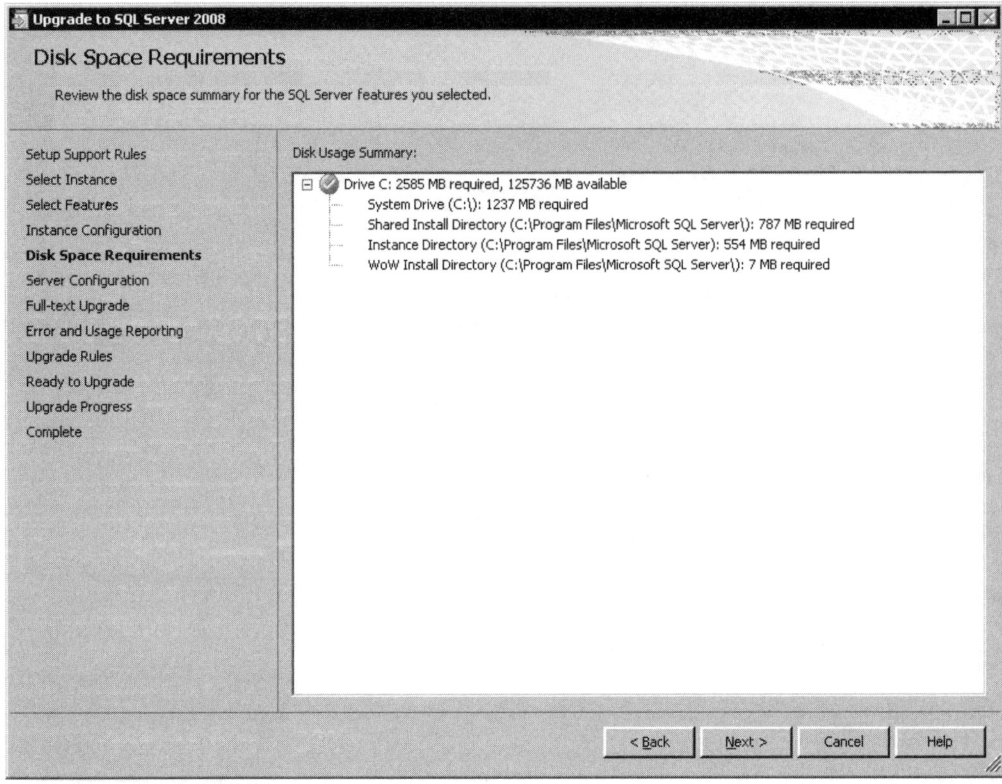

Figure A-30 *Disk Space Requirements dialog*

displayed at the top of the screen. If there is not enough disk space to perform the upgrade, a red X will be displayed. Clicking Next displays the Server Configuration screen that you can see in Figure A-31.

The Server Configuration dialog enables you to change the default startup type and authentication information for SQL Server Integration Services, SQL Full-text Filter Daemon Launcher, and SQL Server Browser services. You can set the authentication to a domain user account or you can accept the default values and click Next to display the next upgrade dialog.

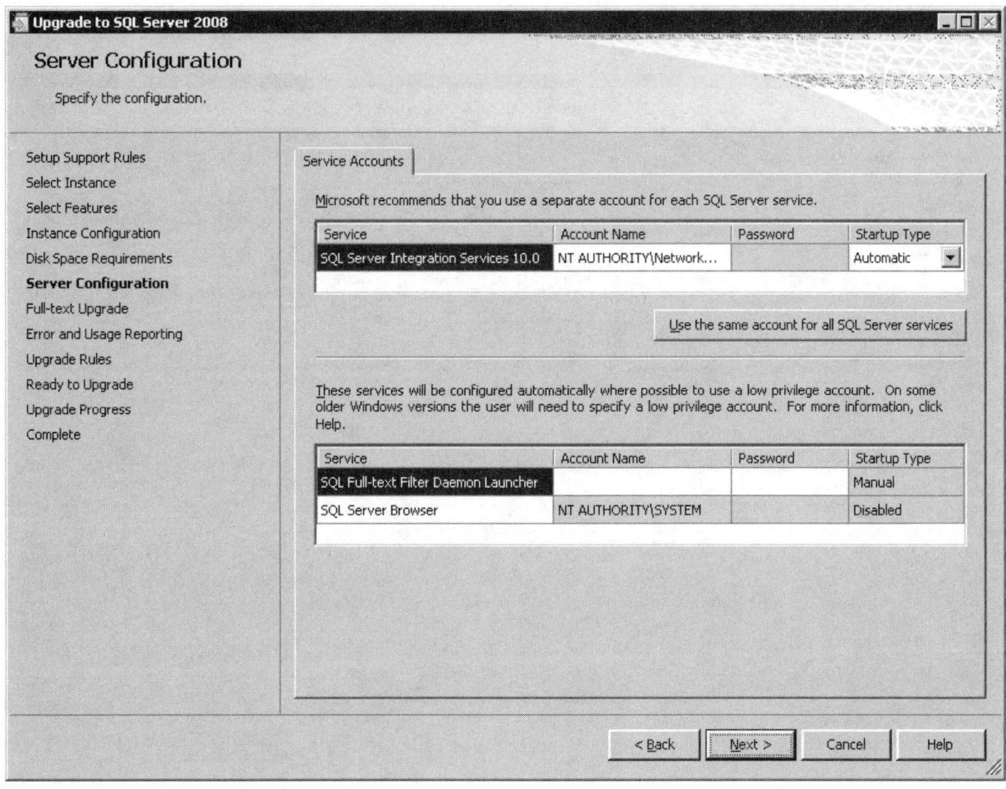

Figure A-31 *Server Configuration screen*

If you installed the full-text search feature on your previous SQL Server instance, then you'll see the Full-text upgrade dialog shown in Figure A-32.

You use the Full-text Upgrade screen to specify how you want the upgrade process to deal with any existing full-text search catalogs. You can choose to import the existing catalogs without any changes, or you can choose to rebuild or reset the full-text catalogs. Importing is the default option and it leaves the full-text catalogs unchanged but that means that they also cannot take advantage of the some of the enhanced SQL Server 2008 full-text search functionality. Rebuilding will rebuild the catalogs, adding the new

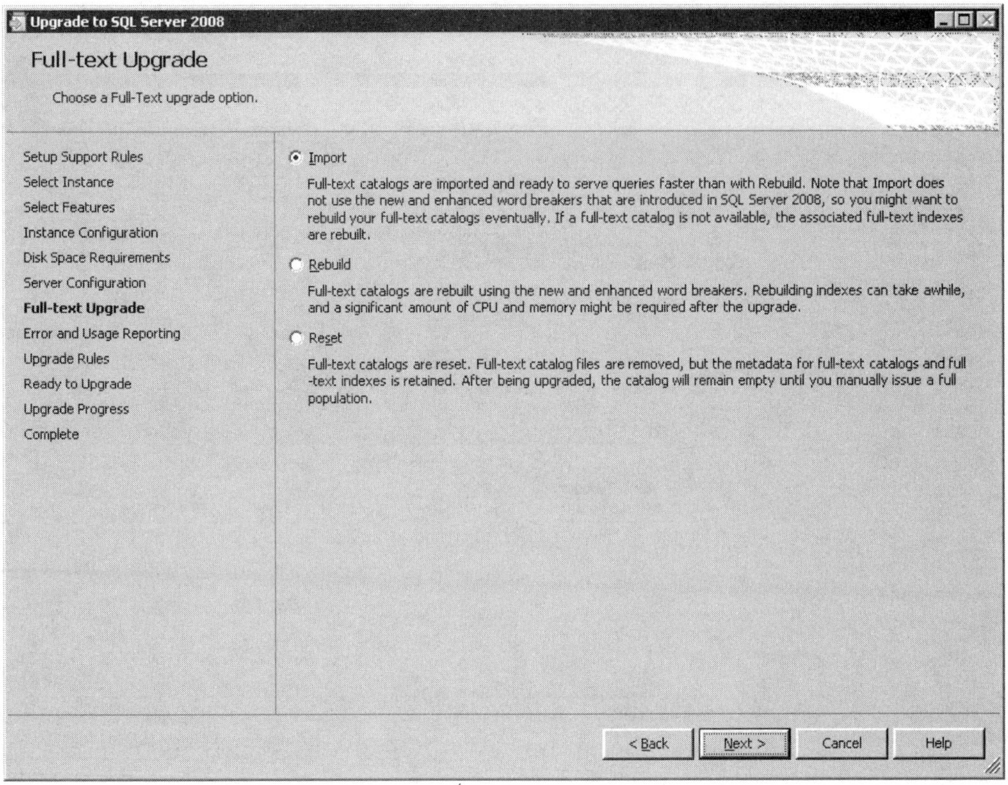

Upgrade to SQL Server 2008

Full-text Upgrade

Choose a Full-Text upgrade option.

Setup Support Rules
Select Instance
Select Features
Instance Configuration
Disk Space Requirements
Server Configuration
Full-text Upgrade
Error and Usage Reporting
Upgrade Rules
Ready to Upgrade
Upgrade Progress
Complete

Import

Full-text catalogs are imported and ready to serve queries faster than with Rebuild. Note that Import does not use the new and enhanced word breakers that are introduced in SQL Server 2008, so you might want to rebuild your full-text catalogs eventually. If a full-text catalog is not available, the associated full-text indexes are rebuilt.

Rebuild

Full-text catalogs are rebuilt using the new and enhanced word breakers. Rebuilding indexes can take awhile, and a significant amount of CPU and memory might be required after the upgrade.

Reset

Full-text catalogs are reset. Full-text catalog files are removed, but the metadata for full-text catalogs and full -text indexes is retained. After being upgraded, the catalog will remain empty until you manually issue a full population.

< Back | Next > | Cancel | Help

Figure A-32 *Full-text Upgrade screen*

functionality, but using this option can considerably lengthen the upgrade process. The reset option clears the existing full-text catalog data but does not rebuild it during the upgrade. If you select the reset option you can rebuild the catalog data manually after the installation. If you choose the default Import option you can optionally rebuild the full-text catalogs at some point after the upgrade has completed. Clicking Next displays the Error and Usage Reporting dialog.

The Error and Usage Reporting dialog shown during the upgrade process is essentially the same as the dialog used in the clean installation shown earlier in Figure A-20.

It allows you to optionally send SQL Server error reports and usage information to Microsoft. Clicking Next displays the Upgrade Rules dialog shown in Figure A-33.

The Upgrade Rules dialog performs a final check for any conditions that might cause the upgrade process to fail. If any error conditions are found, they will be shown in the Rule listing, prefaced with a red X. If all of the rules have green checkmarks, then you can proceed with the upgrade. Clicking Next displays the Ready to Upgrade dialog shown in Figure A-34.

The Ready To Upgrade dialog enables you to see a summary of the upgrade actions that will be performed. If you need to change anything, you can use the Back button

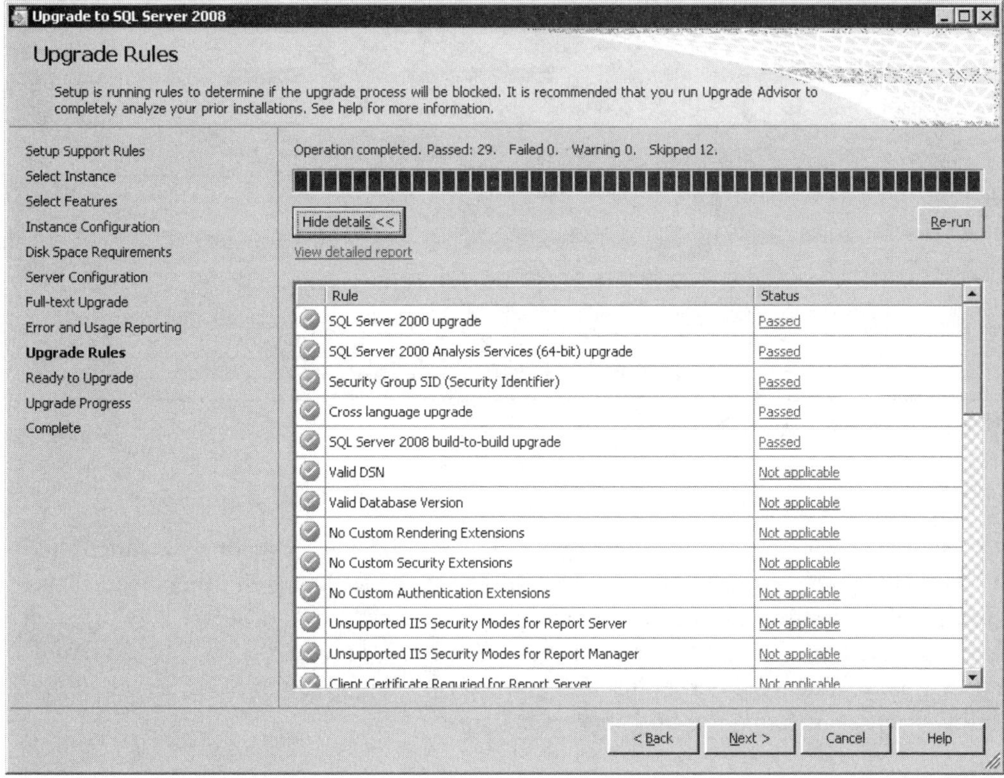

Figure A-33 *Upgrade Rules dialog*

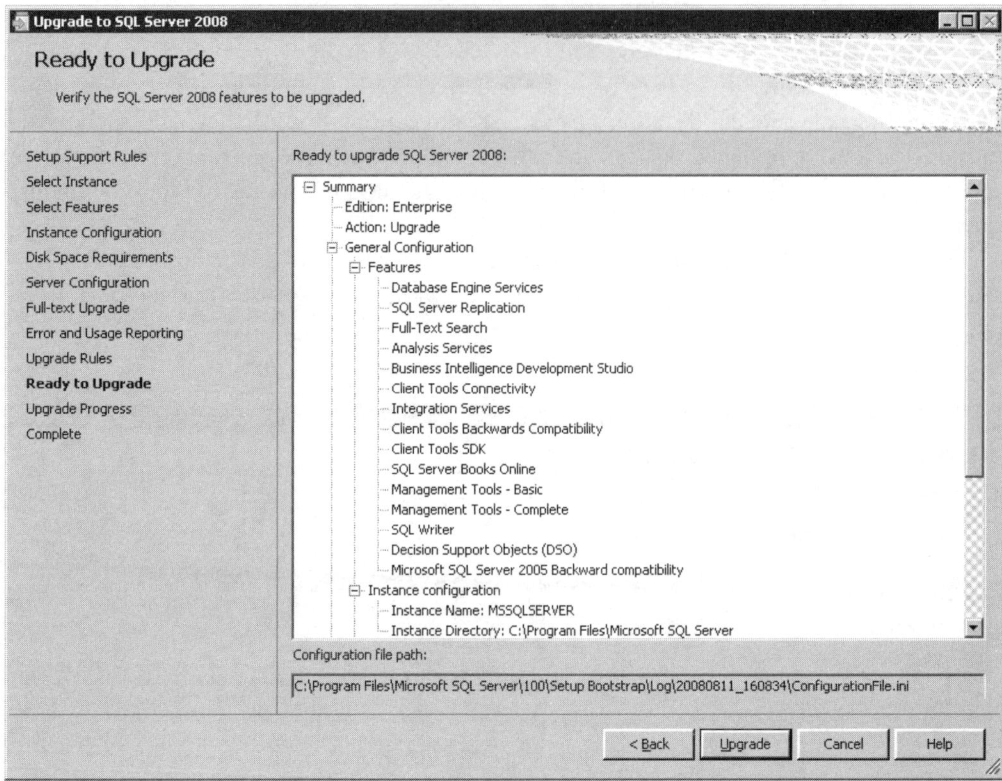

Figure A-34 *Ready to Upgrade dialog*

to page back through the previous upgrade dialogs. Clicking Upgrade will launch the SQL Server 2008 upgrade process. The Upgrade Progress dialog will then be displayed showing the current status of the upgrade process. After the SQL Server 2008 upgrade has completed, the Complete dialog that you can see in Figure A-35 will be displayed. At that point your SQL Server instance will have been upgrade to SQL Server 2008 and you can begin using the SQL Server instance.

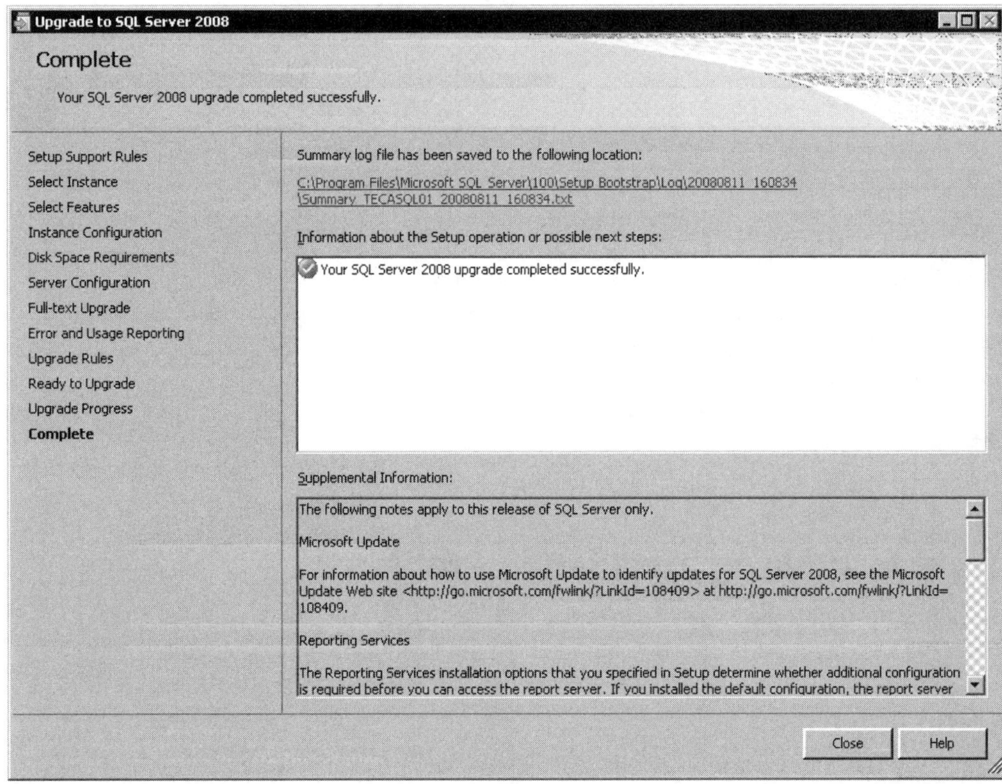

Figure A-35 *Complete dialog*

Verifying the Installation

You can verify the installation of SQL Server 2008 by checking to see if the necessary services are running. You can see these services using the Start | Administrative Tools | Services menu option.

Service	Description
SQL Server (MSSQLSERVER)	The SQL Server relational database engine
SQL Server Agent (MSSQLSERVER)	The SQL Server job scheduling agent
SQL Server Analysis Services (MSSQLSERVER)	SQL Server Analysis Services
SQL Server Integration Services 10.0	SQL Server Integration Services
SQL Server Reporting Services (MSSQLSERVER)	SQL Server Reporting Services
SQL Server Browser	The SQL Server Browser Service

Table A-2 *SQL Server 2008 Services*

Services

Table A-2 lists the services used by SQL Server 2008.

Troubleshooting Installation Problems

To help you troubleshoot installation problems, SQL Server 2008 provides a set of setup log files. These files are text based and can be viewed using Notepad.

Setup Log Files

Table A-3 lists the log files used by SQL Server 2008.

Log File	Directory	Description
Summary.txt	<drive>:\Program Files\Microsoft SQL Server\100\Setup Bootstrap\LOG\	This file contains the SQL Server 2008 setup log. Each setup will generate a new time stamped folder
Detail_GlobalRules.txt	<drive>:\Program Files\Microsoft SQL Server\100\Setup Bootstrap\LOG\<time_stamp>	Output from global rules check
Detail_ComponentUpdate.txt	<drive>:\Program Files\Microsoft SQL Server\100\Setup Bootstrap\LOG\<time_stamp>	Output from component check
Detail.txt	<drive>:\Program Files\Microsoft SQL Server\100\Setup Bootstrap\LOG\<time_stamp>	Output from global rules check

Table A-3 *SQL Server 2008 Setup Log Files*

Appendix B

Quick Facts

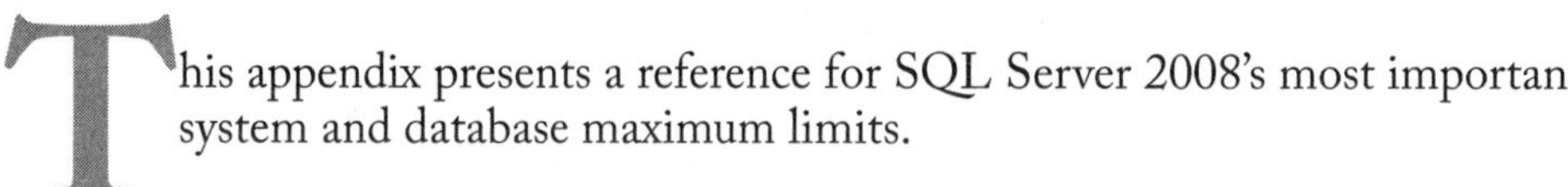

This appendix presents a reference for SQL Server 2008's most important system and database maximum limits.

System Maximum Limits

System

Category	Capacity
Maximum addressable memory	Operating system maximum limit
SQL Server 2008 Enterprise Edition	Windows Server 2003
SQL Server 2008 Standard Edition	Standard Edition SP2 x86 – 4GB
SQL Server 2008 Web Edition	Enterprise Edition SP2 x84 – 64GB
	Datacenter Edition SP2 x86 – 128GB
	Enterprise Edition SP2 x64 – 2TB
	Datacenter Edition SP2 x64 – 2TB
	Enterprise Edition SP2 IA64 – 2TB
	Datacenter Edition SP2 IA64 – TB
	Windows Server 2008
	Standard Edition x86 – 4GB
	Enterprise Edition x86 – 64GB
	Datacenter Edition x86 – 64GB
	Standard Edition x64 – 32GB
	Enterprise Edition x64 – 2TB
	Datacenter Edition x64 – 2TB
	For Itanium-based Systems IA62 – 2TB
Maximum addressable memory	Limited editions
SQL Server 2008 Workgroup Edition	4GB
SQL Server 2008 Express Edition	1GB
Maximum number of processors	(SQL Server licenses processors by socket)
SQL Server 2008 Enterprise Edition	Operating system maximum (64)
SQL Server 2008 Standard Edition	4
SQL Server 2008 Web Edition	4
SQL Server 2008 Workgroup Edition	2
SQL Server 2008 Express Edition	1
Maximum nodes for failover clustering	
SQL Server 2008 Enterprise Edition	OS Maximum;
	8 - Windows Server 2003
	16 – Windows Server 2008
SQL Server 2008 Standard Edition	2

Category	Capacity
SQL Server instances per server	50 16 for the Workgroup Edition
Locks per instance	Limited only by memory (64-bit) 2,147,483,647 (32-bit)

Database Maximum Limits

Database

Category	Capacity
Databases per server instance	32,767
Database size	524,272 TB
Files per database	32,767
File groups per database	32,727
File size (data)	16TB
File size (log)	2TB
Objects in a database	2,147,483,647
Identifier length	128

Tables

Category	Capacity
Tables per database	Limited by the number of objects in a database
Rows per table	Limited by available storage
Clustered indexes per table	1
Non-clustered indexes per table	999
Foreign key references per table	253
Triggers per table	Limited by the number of objects in a database
Partition per table or index	1,000

Columns

Category	Capacity
Columns per index	16
Columns per primary key	16
Columns per foreign key	16

Category	Capacity
Columns per non wide table	1024
Columns per wide table	30,000
Bytes per index key	900
Bytes per primary key	900
Bytes per foreign key	900
Bytes per row	8060
Bytes per character or binary column	8000
Bytes per image, text, ntext, varchar(max), varbinary(max), xml column	2GB (2^31-1)

T-SQL Maximum Limits

Category	Capacity
Batch size	65,536 * Network Packet Size
Tables per SELECT statement	256
Bytes in source text of a stored procedure	Lesser of batch size or 250 MB
Parameters per stored procedure	2100
Parameters per user-defined function	2100
Nested subqueries	32
Nested trigger levels	32
Columns per SELECT statement	4096
Columns per INSERT statement	4096
Number of distinct expressions in the GROUP BY clause	32
Number of GROUPING SETS	4096

Replication Limits

Category	Capacity
Articles per Merge publication	256
Articles per Snapshot, Transactional publication	32,767
Columns per table for Merge publication	246
Columns per table for Snapshot or Transactional publication	1,000
Columns in an Snapshot or Transactional Oracle publication	995

Index

B

C

D

M

N

O

R

S

T

U

V

W

X